Data Science Building Blocks

Analytics Starter Kit

Jyothsna Sravanthi
Malaya Rout
Radhakrishnan Guhan

notionpress.com
INDIA • SINGAPORE • MALAYSIA

Notion Press

Old No. 38, New No. 6
McNichols Road, Chetpet
Chennai - 600 031

First Published by Notion Press 2020

ISBN

Domestic: 978-1-64828-728-2
International: 978-1-64892-924-3

Contents

Foreword

This book on Data Analytics is a unique one which combines both technical and practical aspects and deliberates on how to practice data analytics in any organization.

The authors bring their passion and wide experience as practicing data scientists. They provide a working view on solving problems using data science. As such, this book describes about the data analysis procedures and realization tools including Exploratory Data Analysis, Statistical Modeling of Data, Linear and Logistic Regressions, Decision Trees, et cetera. Due to clear drafting of the concepts, this book confers confidence that will expose anyone to the art of data science while reading and practising. Having used R Programming as the data analytics tool, the book acts as a remarkable resource for understanding the R packages and the facts of data analysis as well. The study of data science is more appropriate when doing practical things while learning rather than simply learning through classroom lectures. This book handled the concept of "Learn by Doing" very well. Certainly, this book on Data Analytics would be a unique and finest resource for the data science aspirants and for the developers to practice data analytics strategies using statistical models. I am sure that the book will fill the knowledge gaps generally experienced in theoretical illustrations and make the readers to experience the world of informatics in practical dimension. This book certainly helps the students to start to work on capstone projects and for the faculty to pursue research in a new dimension.

– Dr. V. Ramachandran,

Former Vice Chancellor, Anna University Tiruchirappalli & Founder Director,
National Institute of Technology Nagaland

Note to Readers

Let us start by talking about what this book is not. If you are looking for formal definitions of linear regression, clustering and other modeling techniques, then this book is not for you. There are hundreds of books that already solve that purpose. We have put our best efforts into providing you with something practical and different from academic books. You could very well consider this a reference book while you work on your project or assignment.

Data Science Building Blocks is useful for students and professionals who are starting their data science journey. Outputs, such as summaries and plots, are found throughout this book. They are produced using the R programming language. We have deliberately kept full R codes away and only provided the function names because we would like you to explore them for yourself. Usually, there are multiple ways of dealing with the same analytics problem statement. *Data Science Building Blocks* provides just one of those methods for each business problem we have chosen.

Conventions Used in this Book

1. Italics
   a. We have used italics for the name of a dataset or the name of a column of a dataset.
   b. Exceptions are
      i. When the name of a column contains a dot. We have used English phrases to denote such a variable.
      ii. When a sentence starts with the name of a column whose first character is in lower case.
2. Numbering a figure or a table
   a. If we needed to place a figure/table between figures/tables numbered 3.7 and 3.8, we have numbered it 3.7.5.
3. Above or below
   a. Each reference to a figure or a table is accompanied by a mention of whether you should look above or below for the figure/table.
4. Visualizations are in the form of either tables or figures. All of them are generated using the R programming language.

Additional Note to Readers

We have revised *Data Science Building Blocks* by adding a new chapter to it (Machine Learning Using Python – Chapter 10). This is where we have provided snippets of Python codes and captured their corresponding outputs. The comment lines in each snippet give us valuable information about the code. We have not provided a full description of the Python codes and outputs separately because we believe that the underlying concepts of Machine Learning remain the same. You can learn them using either R or Python. Concepts are explained using the R outputs in the first nine chapters of the book. So, go ahead and enjoy the journey.

Acknowledgement

We would like to express our immense gratitude to all who have contributed in realizing this project. Family and friends have been the greatest support. We are grateful to Notionpress for doing a wonderful job in shaping this book in its current form. Thanks to all the reviewers who have gone through the contents of the book many times over and have given us timely feedback.

Chapter 1

Exploratory Data Analysis

We will discuss the following items in this chapter:

- The summary of a dataset
- The conversion from a numeric to a categorical variable
- The structure of a dataset
- The head of a dataset
- The subset of a dataset
- The tabulation of a single categorical variable
- The addition of a derived column to a dataset
- Univariate analysis – histogram, box plot, bar plot
- Bivariate Analysis – scatter plot, multiple boxplots, cross-tabulation
- Observation versus insight
- Correlation matrix, scatter plot matrix, heat map, pie chart

In the world of data science, Exploratory Data Analysis (EDA) is the process of understanding the data available at hand. EDA throws insight into the data and paves the way for any predictive modeling work. Sometimes all we need to solve a business problem is an insight derived from an EDA.

1.1 Getting the Summary of a Dataset

Package: ISLR

Dataset: Auto

A data frame with 392 observations on the following 9 variables.

mpg	Miles per gallon
cylinders	Number of cylinders between 4 and 8
displacement	Engine displacement (cu. inches)
horsepower	Engine horsepower

weight	Vehicle weight (lbs.)
acceleration	Time to accelerate from 0 to 60 mph (sec.)
year	Model year (modulo 100)
origin	Origin of car (1. American, 2. European, 3. Japanese)
name	Vehicle name

R Function Used for Generating the Output

- *summary()*

```
      mpg          cylinders      displacement     horsepower        weight      acceleration        year
 Min.   : 9.00   Min.   :3.000   Min.   : 68.0   Min.   : 46.0   Min.   :1613   Min.   : 8.00   Min.   :70.00
 1st Qu.:17.00   1st Qu.:4.000   1st Qu.:105.0   1st Qu.: 75.0   1st Qu.:2225   1st Qu.:13.78   1st Qu.:73.00
 Median :22.75   Median :4.000   Median :151.0   Median : 93.5   Median :2804   Median :15.50   Median :76.00
 Mean   :23.45   Mean   :5.472   Mean   :194.4   Mean   :104.5   Mean   :2978   Mean   :15.54   Mean   :75.98
 3rd Qu.:29.00   3rd Qu.:8.000   3rd Qu.:275.8   3rd Qu.:126.0   3rd Qu.:3615   3rd Qu.:17.02   3rd Qu.:79.00
 Max.   :46.60   Max.   :8.000   Max.   :455.0   Max.   :230.0   Max.   :5140   Max.   :24.80   Max.   :82.00

     origin                     name    
 Min.   :1.000   amc matador       :  5  
 1st Qu.:1.000   ford pinto        :  5  
 Median :1.000   toyota corolla    :  5  
 Mean   :1.577   amc gremlin       :  4  
 3rd Qu.:2.000   amc hornet        :  4  
 Max.   :3.000   chevrolet chevette:  4  
                 (Other)           :365  
```

Table 1.1 Summary of *Auto*

The way to read the summary output is as follows: For numeric variables, it gives the minimum, the maximum, the first quartile, the median (second quartile), the third quartile and the mean. The first quartile is that number below which 25% of the entries lie in a series of numbers when sorted in ascending order. 75% of the entries lie below the third quartile. This representation tells us how the numbers are distributed in that variable. In contrast, a categorical variable is represented by a frequency of occurrence for each class of the variable. Classes with higher frequencies are displayed.

Refer to the summary output above for the *Auto* dataset. Do you find something not right? Yes, the *origin*. How do you interpret an average value of *origin*? By default, the data type of *origin* is considered to be numeric by the tool because the variable has discrete values in numeric form. From the description of the dataset, we clearly see that *origin* should be a categorical and not a numeric variable. So we explicitly convert *origin* into a categorical variable or a factor, as shown in the summary below.

R Function Used for Generating the Output

- *summary()*

```
     mpg          cylinders      displacement     horsepower        weight      acceleration        year       origin
Min.   : 9.00   Min.   :3.000   Min.   : 68.0   Min.   : 46.0   Min.   :1613   Min.   : 8.00   Min.   :70.00   1:245
1st Qu.:17.00   1st Qu.:4.000   1st Qu.:105.0   1st Qu.: 75.0   1st Qu.:2225   1st Qu.:13.78   1st Qu.:73.00   2: 68
Median :22.75   Median :4.000   Median :151.0   Median : 93.5   Median :2804   Median :15.50   Median :76.00   3: 79
Mean   :23.45   Mean   :5.472   Mean   :194.4   Mean   :104.5   Mean   :2978   Mean   :15.54   Mean   :75.98
3rd Qu.:29.00   3rd Qu.:8.000   3rd Qu.:275.8   3rd Qu.:126.0   3rd Qu.:3615   3rd Qu.:17.02   3rd Qu.:79.00
Max.   :46.60   Max.   :8.000   Max.   :455.0   Max.   :230.0   Max.   :5140   Max.   :24.80   Max.   :82.00

                 name
amc matador      :  5
ford pinto       :  5
toyota corolla   :  5
amc gremlin      :  4
amc hornet       :  4
chevrolet chevette:  4
```

Table 1.2 Summary of *Auto* with *Origin* transformed

It is a good time now to take a look at the structure of the dataset, as mentioned below. It includes information such as the data type of the dataset, the data type of each variable, the total number of observations and the total number of variables. It also includes a few sample values of each variable. *Origin* is already converted to a categorical (factor) variable. So we are good to go.

R Function Used for Generating the Output

- *str()*

```
'data.frame':	392 obs. of  9 variables:
 $ mpg         : num  18 15 18 16 17 15 14 14 14 15 ...
 $ cylinders   : num  8 8 8 8 8 8 8 8 8 8 ...
 $ displacement: num  307 350 318 304 302 429 454 440 455 390 ...
 $ horsepower  : num  130 165 150 150 140 198 220 215 225 190 ...
 $ weight      : num  3504 3693 3436 3433 3449 ...
 $ acceleration: num  12 11.5 11 12 10.5 10 9 8.5 10 8.5 ...
 $ year        : num  70 70 70 70 70 70 70 70 70 70 ...
 $ origin      : Factor w/ 3 levels "1","2","3": 1 1 1 1 1 1 1 1 1 1 ...
 $ name        : Factor w/ 304 levels "amc ambassador brougham",..: 49 36 231 14 161 141 54 223 241 2 ...
```

Table 1.3 Structure of *Auto*

1.2 Checking a Few Data Rows

R Function Used for Generating the Output

- *Head()*

The top six rows of the dataset are displayed here. We subset a dataset (rows and columns) based on certain conditions. It solves the purpose of focusing our attention on a certain part of the dataset while ignoring others. We may also subset to see a sample set of rows and columns.

mpg	cylinders	displacement	horsepower	weight	acceleration	year	origin	name
18	8	307	130	3504	12.0	70	1	chevrolet chevelle malibu
15	8	350	165	3693	11.5	70	1	buick skylark 320
18	8	318	150	3436	11.0	70	1	plymouth satellite
16	8	304	150	3433	12.0	70	1	amc rebel sst
17	8	302	140	3449	10.5	70	1	ford torino
15	8	429	198	4341	10.0	70	1	ford galaxie 500

Table 1.4 Head of *Auto*

Row numbers 4 to 25 only for two variables are shown below.

R Function Used for Generating the Output

- *subset()*

	mpg	origin
4	16	1
5	17	1
6	15	1
7	14	1
8	14	1
9	14	1
10	15	1
11	15	1
12	14	1
13	15	1
14	14	1
15	24	3
16	22	1
17	18	1
18	21	1
19	27	3
20	26	2
21	25	2
22	24	2
23	25	2
24	26	2
25	21	1

Table 1.5

Let us introduce you to another dataset.

R Function Used for Generating the Output

- *str()*

```
'data.frame':   150 obs. of  5 variables:
 $ Sepal.Length: num  5.1 4.9 4.7 4.6 5 5.4 4.6 5 4.4 4.9 ...
 $ Sepal.Width : num  3.5 3 3.2 3.1 3.6 3.9 3.4 3.4 2.9 3.1 ...
 $ Petal.Length: num  1.4 1.4 1.3 1.5 1.4 1.7 1.4 1.5 1.4 1.5 ...
 $ Petal.Width : num  0.2 0.2 0.2 0.2 0.2 0.4 0.3 0.2 0.2 0.1 ...
 $ Species     : Factor w/ 3 levels "setosa","versicolor",..: 1 1 1 1 1 1 1 1 1 1 ...
```

Table 1.6 Structure of *iris* dataset

Sepal.Length Length of the sepal

Sepal.Width Width of the sepal

Petal.Length Length of the petal

Petal.Width Width of the petal

Species Species name of the flower

Below is a snapshot of the tabulation output for *Species* column in the *iris* dataset, which gives the frequency distribution of each unique value of *Species*.

R Function Used for Generating the Output

- *table()*

```
    setosa versicolor  virginica
        50         50         50
```

Table 1.7 Table of Species

1.3 Conversion of Variables from Numeric to Categorical

```
8 4 6 3 5
```

Table 1.8 Unique values of *cylinders*

The table shown above is a list of unique values of cylinders in the *Auto* dataset. As seen below, it is numeric.

Let's check *cylinders* as numeric and *cylinders* as a factor. What information is lost when *cylinders* is converted from numeric to categorical? The ordering information. The fact that three *cylinders* are lesser than five *cylinders* is lost. That's why we have to be careful in converting numeric to categorical.

R Functions Used for Generating the Output

- *as.factor()*
- *str()*

```
'data.frame':   392 obs. of  9 variables:
 $ mpg         : num  18 15 18 16 17 15 14 14 14 15 ...
 $ cylinders   : num  8 8 8 8 8 8 8 8 8 8 ...
 $ displacement: num  307 350 318 304 302 429 454 440 455 390 ...
 $ horsepower  : num  130 165 150 150 140 198 220 215 225 190 ...
 $ weight      : num  3504 3693 3436 3433 3449 ...
 $ acceleration: num  12 11.5 11 12 10.5 10 9 8.5 10 8.5 ...
 $ year        : num  70 70 70 70 70 70 70 70 70 70 ...
 $ origin      : Factor w/ 3 levels "1","2","3": 1 1 1 1 1 1 1 1 1 1 ...
 $ name        : Factor w/ 304 levels "amc ambassador brougham",..: 49 36 231 14 161 141 54 223 241 2 ...
```

Table 1.9 Numeric *cylinders*

In the structure below, we see that *cylinders* is already converted to a factor. Is it wrong to do that? Not exactly, but we will lose information. We can still go ahead with *cylinders* as a factor variable and complete the whole analysis. If you are still curious, try out both the approaches and let us know how it went.

R Functions Used for Generating the Output

- *as.factor()*
- *str()*

```
'data.frame':   392 obs. of  9 variables:
 $ mpg         : num  18 15 18 16 17 15 14 14 14 15 ...
 $ cylinders   : Factor w/ 5 levels "3","4","5","6",..: 5 5 5 5 5 5 5 5 5 5 ...
 $ displacement: num  307 350 318 304 302 429 454 440 455 390 ...
 $ horsepower  : num  130 165 150 150 140 198 220 215 225 190 ...
 $ weight      : num  3504 3693 3436 3433 3449 ...
 $ acceleration: num  12 11.5 11 12 10.5 10 9 8.5 10 8.5 ...
 $ year        : num  70 70 70 70 70 70 70 70 70 70 ...
 $ origin      : Factor w/ 3 levels "1","2","3": 1 1 1 1 1 1 1 1 1 1 ...
 $ name        : Factor w/ 304 levels "amc ambassador brougham",..: 49 36 231 14 161 141 54 223 241 2 ...
```

Table 1.10 Categorical *cylinders*

R Functions Used for Generating the Output

- *cbind()*
- *colnames()*

Add a derived column to a data frame. This is the original data frame.

	Sepal.Length	Sepal.Width	Petal.Length	Petal.Width	Species
1	5.1	3.5	1.4	0.2	setosa
2	4.9	3.0	1.4	0.2	setosa
3	4.7	3.2	1.3	0.2	setosa
4	4.6	3.1	1.5	0.2	setosa
5	5.0	3.6	1.4	0.2	setosa
6	5.4	3.9	1.7	0.4	setosa

Table 1.11 Head of original *iris* dataset

An additional column is added with values equivalent to twice the petal width.

	Sepal.Length	Sepal.Width	Petal.Length	Petal.Width	Species	2 * (iris1$Petal.Width)
1	5.1	3.5	1.4	0.2	setosa	0.4
2	4.9	3.0	1.4	0.2	setosa	0.4
3	4.7	3.2	1.3	0.2	setosa	0.4
4	4.6	3.1	1.5	0.2	setosa	0.4
5	5.0	3.6	1.4	0.2	setosa	0.4
6	5.4	3.9	1.7	0.4	setosa	0.8

Table 1.12 *iris* with a new column

Rename the new column to twice_petal_width.

	Sepal.Length	Sepal.Width	Petal.Length	Petal.Width	Species	twice_petal_width
1	5.1	3.5	1.4	0.2	setosa	0.4
2	4.9	3.0	1.4	0.2	setosa	0.4
3	4.7	3.2	1.3	0.2	setosa	0.4
4	4.6	3.1	1.5	0.2	setosa	0.4
5	5.0	3.6	1.4	0.2	setosa	0.4
6	5.4	3.9	1.7	0.4	setosa	0.8

Table 1.13 New column with the changed name

1.4 Univariate Analysis – Histogram, Box Plot, Bar Plot

When we analyze the distribution of a single variable, it is known as univariate analysis. With two variables, it is called bivariate analysis.

R Function Used for Generating the Output

- *hist()*

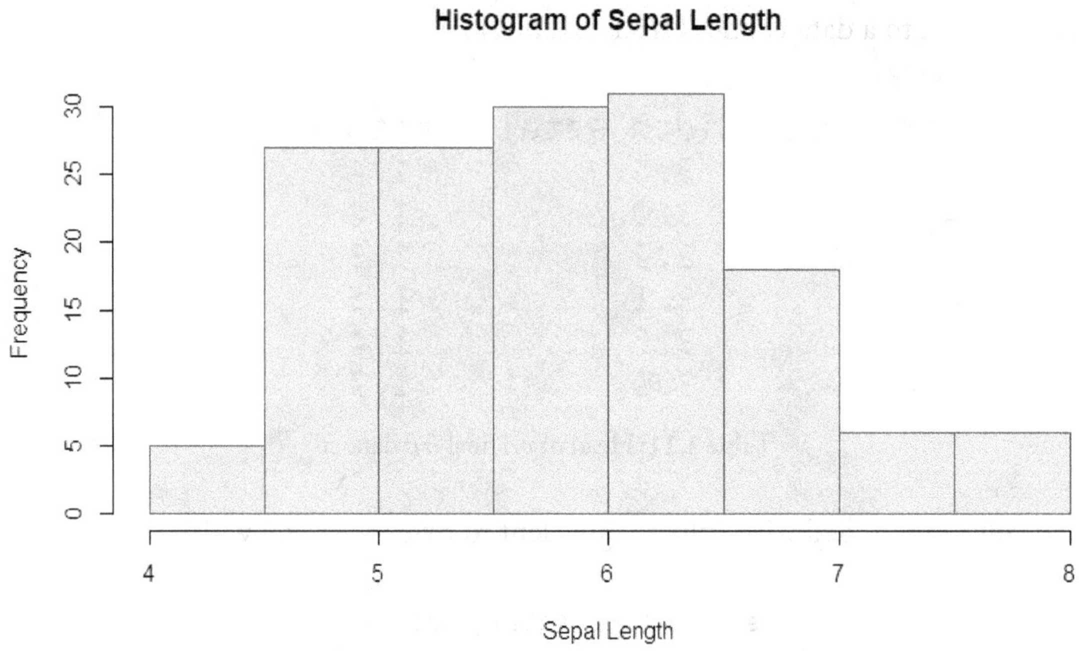

Figure 1.1 Histogram of sepal length

It is evident from the above histogram in figure 1.1 that most of the flowers have a sepal length between 5.5 cm and 6.5 cm. Very few flowers have a sepal length between 4 cm and 4.5 cm or between 7 cm and 8 cm.

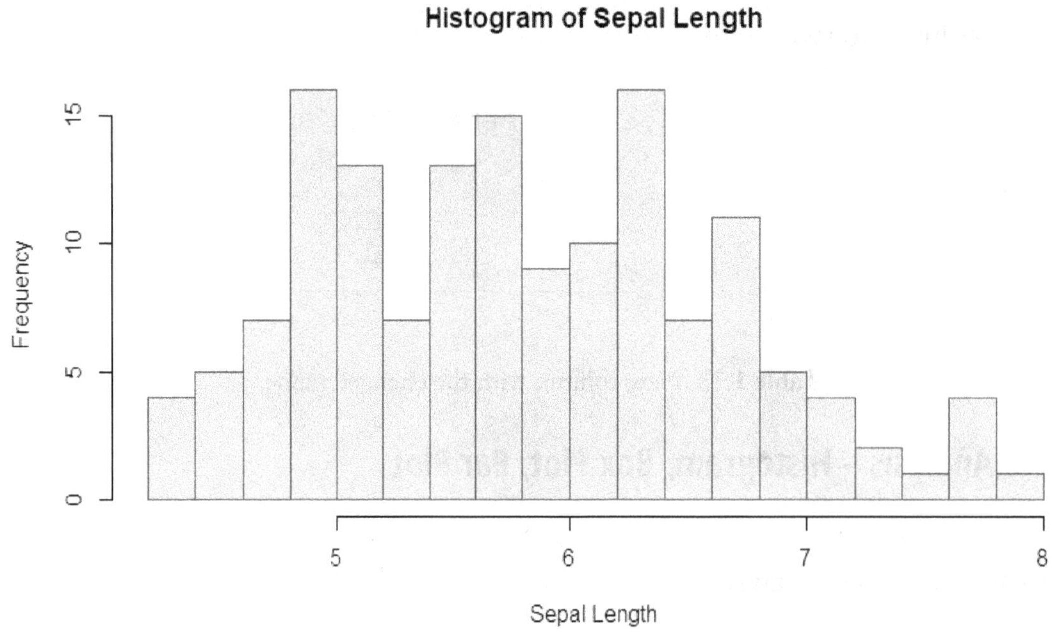

Figure 1.2 Histogram of sepal length finer

The histogram above (figure 1.2) has a finer sepal length bucket when compared to the first histogram in figure 1.1. This is similar to drilling down into more details of each bucket. The histogram in figure 1.1 has a bin size of 0.5 cm and that in figure 1.2 has a bin size of 0.2 cm. Because the latter is finer, we come to know the distribution behavior for every small segment. We will be able to zero in on abnormal frequencies easily if any.

R Function Used for Generating the Output

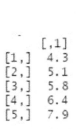

- *boxplot()*

```
      [,1]
[1,]   4.3
[2,]   5.1
[3,]   5.8
[4,]   6.4
[5,]   7.9
```

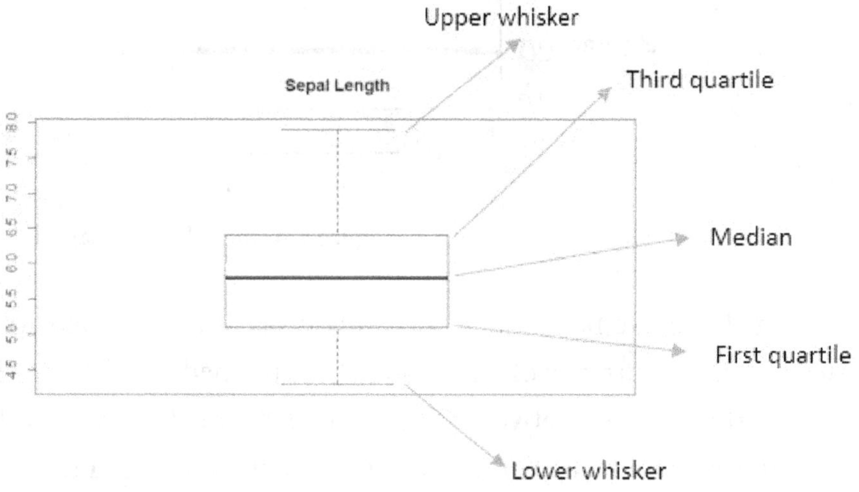

Figure 1.3 Box plot of sepal length

Lower whisker = 4.3 cm

First quartile = 5.1 cm

Median = 5.8 cm

Third quartile = 6.4 cm

Upper whisker = 7.9 cm

Figure 1.3 gives a box plot of sepal length. There are no outliers in the sepal length set of numbers. Outliers lie below the lower whisker and above the upper whisker.

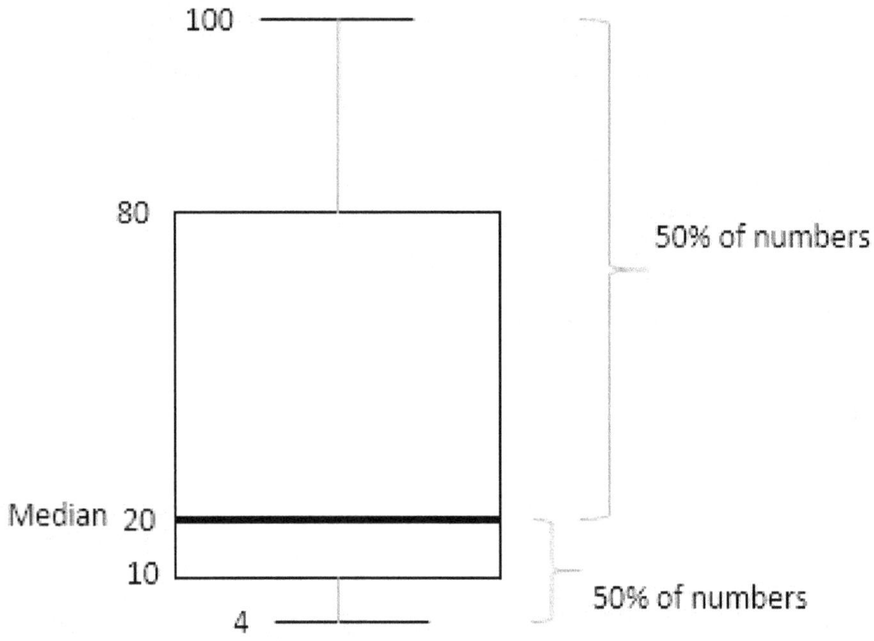

Figure 1.4 Box plot for example

Looking at the above box plot, what can you say about the density of occurrence of numbers below the median and occurrence of numbers above the median? 50% of the numbers lie between 4 cm and 20 cm. Another 50% lie between 20 cm and 100 cm. This means that the numbers are more closely packed between the median and lower whisker than between the median and upper whisker.

We have seen a box plot and a histogram. How are they different? What information does a box plot provide that the histogram does not? A box plot highlights the first quartile, median and third quartile. It shows the minimum and maximum values that are not outliers. It displays the outliers clearly below the lower whisker and above the upper whisker. The biggest advantage of a box plot over the histogram is while comparing a group of distributions. A box plot is plotted per distribution and placed side by side. This makes it very convenient for comparing multiple distributions at the same time.

The numbers below give us the mean petal length grouping by species. In general terms, we can say that *virginica* has longer petals than *versicolor,* which has longer petals than *setosa.*

R Function Used for Generating the Output

- *tapply()*

```
setosa versicolor  virginica
 1.462      4.260      5.552
```

Table 1.14 Use of *tapply* on species

Figure 1.5 below shows a bar plot. There are 50 flowers, each of *virginica*, *versicolor* and *setosa*. What's the difference between a histogram and a bar plot while they look similar and both have a frequency in the y-axis, as seen in the figure below? The x-axis of a histogram contains a continuous variable such as age, height, sales, revenue, etc., segregated into continuous buckets.

In contrast, the x-axis of a bar plot contains a categorical variable, such as a species of flower or a region (east/west/north/south). It is absolutely fine that a bar plot has gaps between two bars. Moreover, the y-axis of a bar plot need not have frequency every time. There can be any other numeric variables such as revenue in rupees, sales in numbers, rainfall in cm, etc.

Notice a thing here, though. A bar plot with frequency on the y-axis can be treated as a univariate tool; whereas a bar plot with a numeric variable other than frequency (such as temperature) is a bivariate tool.

R Function Used for Generating the Output

- *barplot()*

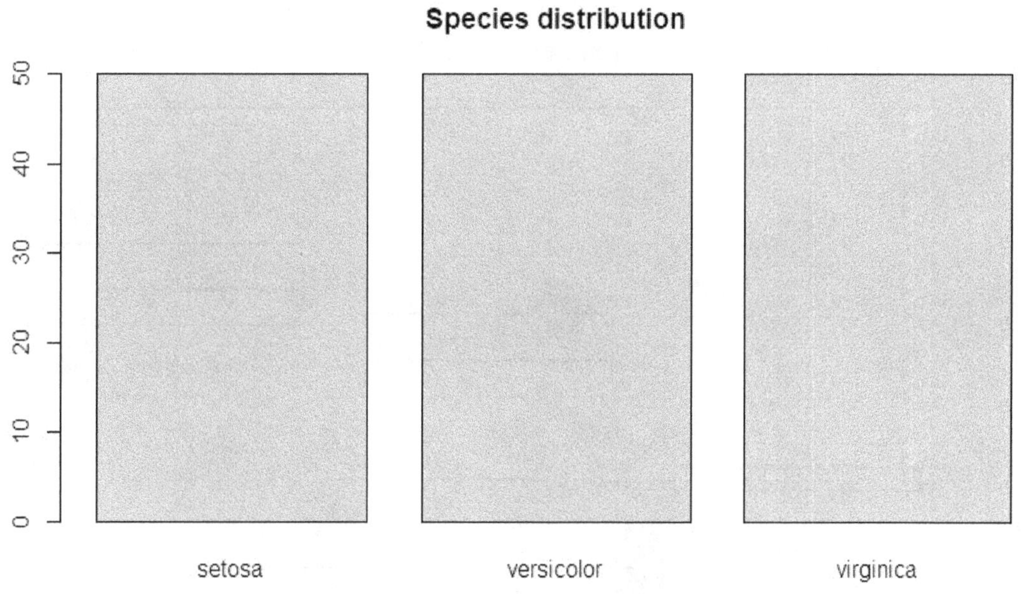

Figure 1.5 Bar plot on species

1.5 Bivariate Analysis – Scatter Plot, Multiple Boxplots, Cross-Tabulation

The bivariate analysis involves the study of the empirical relationship between two variables. The study tells us whether the relationship is positive or negative, linear or non-linear and impacting or non-impacting.

First variable:	numeric
Second variable:	numeric
Plot:	scatter plot
First variable:	categorical
Second variable:	numeric
Plot:	box plot (multiple)
First variable:	categorical
Second variable:	categorical
Plot:	cross-tabulation

R Function Used for Generating the Output

- *boxplot()*

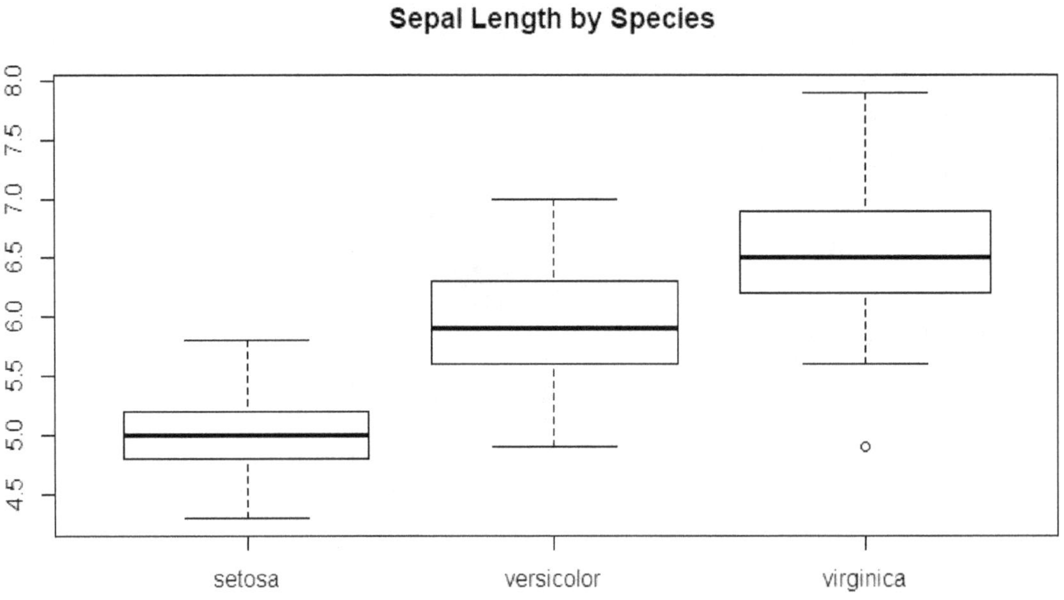

Figure 1.6 Box plot of sepal length by species

Figure 1.6 above shows a comparison of box plots for sepal length for the three species. Speaking in general, *virginica* → *versicolor* → *setosa* are in the decreasing order of sepal lengths. Note the outlier in *virginica* below the lower whisker.

R Function Used for Generating the Output

- *plot()*

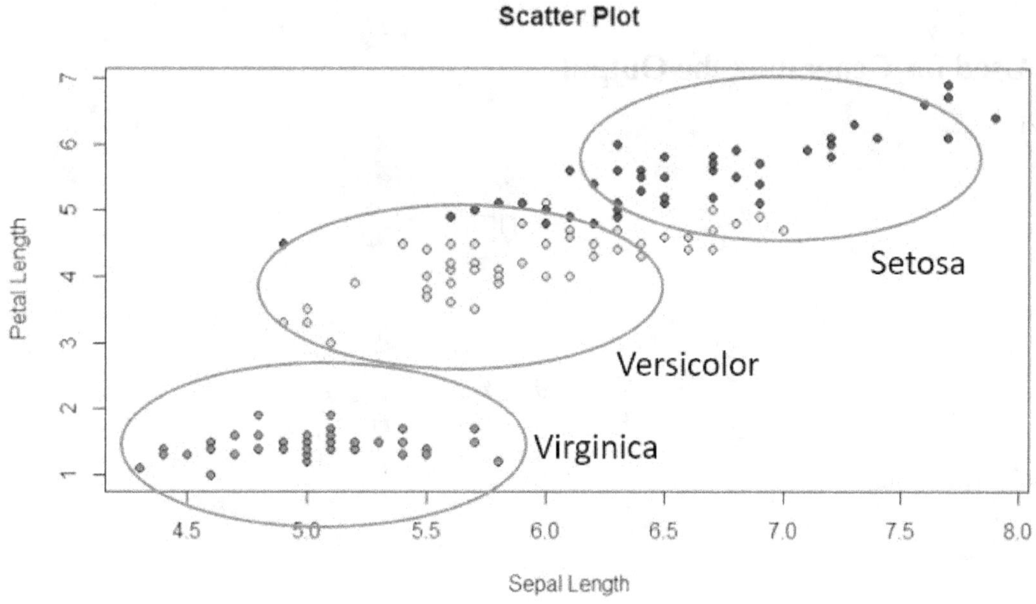

Figure 1.7 Scatter plot of sepal length versus petal length

A scatter plot shows the relationship between two continuous numeric variables. The plot in figure 1.7 above indicates that as the sepal length increases, the petal length also increases. In other words, there exists a positive linear relationship between sepal length and petal length. Data points with varying shades and encircled denote flowers of the three different species.

R Function Used for Generating the Output

- *str()*

Cross-tabulation

```
'data.frame':    392 obs. of  9 variables:
 $ mpg          : num  18 15 18 16 17 15 14 14 14 15 ...
 $ cylinders    : Factor w/ 5 levels "3","4","5","6",..: 5 5 5 5 5 5
 $ displacement: num  307 350 318 304 302 429 454 440 455 390 ...
 $ horsepower  : num  130 165 150 150 140 198 220 215 225 190 ...
 $ weight       : num  3504 3693 3436 3433 3449 ...
 $ acceleration: num  12 11.5 11 12 10.5 10 9 8.5 10 8.5 ...
 $ year         : num  70 70 70 70 70 70 70 70 70 70 ...
 $ origin       : Factor w/ 3 levels "1","2","3": 1 1 1 1 1 1 1 1 1
 $ name         : Factor w/ 304 levels "amc ambassador brougham",..:
```

Table 1.15 Structure of *Auto* and cross-tabulation

Let's try out something here. In the *Auto* dataset, convert *cylinders* into a categorical variable. We already have *origin* as a categorical variable. If we want to understand the relationship between *cylinders* and *origin*, we have to create a cross-tabulation, as shown below.

R Function Used for Generating the Output

- *table()*

Origin

Cylinders	1	2	3
3	0	0	4
4	69	61	69
5	0	3	0
6	73	4	6
8	103	0	0

Table 1.16 Cross-tabulation of *cylinders* versus *origin*

1.6 Observation Versus Insight

What is the output or takeaway from an EDA exercise? An observation? An insight? What's the difference between the two? Anything you see explicitly in a plot is an observation. The implicit idea or interpretation of observation is called an insight. A spike in sales in December seen from a graph is an observation. If you say the following things about the spike, then that becomes an insight:

- The spike is because of the holiday season
- The spike happens every December
- Next year, the spike will be even taller
- Hence, stock up enough numbers of your product before December next year

1.7 Actionable Insight Versus Non-Actionable Insight

The insight on the spike in sales mentioned in the previous section is actionable because the manager can make a decision to stock up more quantity of the product before next December. Let's assume a business has various transaction types, namely A, B and C. Transactions of type A give the highest number of sales. For the current analysis, if a modification of the transaction type is not in scope, then this becomes a non-actionable insight. The information is consumed. It explains. However, no action can be taken on the insight. You can further qualify actionable insights with different levels of complexity of implementation, priority, expected duration necessary and business impact.

1.8 Correlation Matrix

R Function Used for Generating the Output

- *cor()*

	Sepal.Length	Sepal.Width	Petal.Length	Petal.Width
Sepal.Length	1.0000000	-0.1175698	0.8717538	0.8179411
Sepal.Width	-0.1175698	1.0000000	-0.4284401	-0.3661259
Petal.Length	0.8717538	-0.4284401	1.0000000	0.9628654
Petal.Width	0.8179411	-0.3661259	0.9628654	1.0000000

Table 1.17 Correlation among numeric variables

The above Table 1.17 shows a correlation matrix. Only numeric variables can participate here. Correlation between two numeric variables tells us how both of them move together. Correlation does not imply causation. The correlation coefficient ranges between – 1 and 1. Petal length and petal width are highly positively correlated (approximately 0.96). Petal length and sepal width are mildly negatively correlated (approximately – 0.42). Correlation between A and B is the same as the correlation between B and A.

1.9 Scatter Plot Matrix

R Function Used for Generating the Output

- *pairs()*

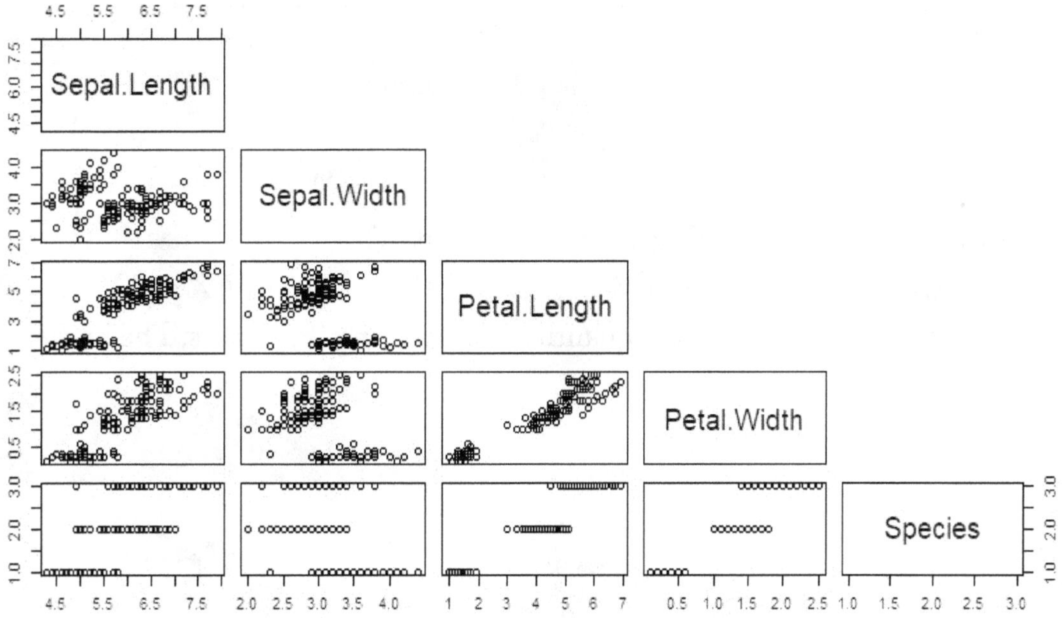

Figure 1.8 Scatter plot matrix

Earlier, we have seen what a scatter plot is. In order to accommodate scatter plots between two variables at a time from a bunch of variables, a scatter plot matrix is created. This is a quick way of analyzing correlations visually (high/low versus linear/non-linear versus positive/negative). For example, we are able to inspect visually that the sepal length and petal width are more or less positively and linearly related to each other. Note that the encircled box in figure 1.8 has sepal length on the x-axis and petal width on the y-axis.

1.10 Heat Map

categorical variable 1

categorical variable 2

	A	B	C	D	E	F
M	1	50	0	0	0	0
N	5	0	0	0	0	0
O	0	16	0	0	0	0
P	0	19	0	0	0	0
Q	0	28	3	0	0	0
R	0	7	2	0	0	0
S	3	0	0	0	8	0
T	2	0	0	0	30	0
U	1	0	31	34	0	0
V	0	0	0	0	0	0
W	0	0	0	0	0	0
X	0	0	0	0	0	0
Y	0	0	0	0	0	0

Figure 1.9 Heat map

How many dimensions does the above heat map have? Two? Three?

- Variable 1 having six unique values A, B, C, D, E and F.
- Variable 2 having 13 unique values M, N, O, P, Q, R, S, T, U, V, W, X and Y.
- The color of the cell is based on the quantity of something it contains. The higher the number, the greener the cell is.

1.11 Pie Chart

MS Excel Used for Generating the Output

Region	Sales (thousand rupees)	Sales contribution
P	30	9%
Q	40	12%
R	50	15%
S	25	7%
T	190	57%

Table 1.18 Data for a pie chart

Check the information given in Table 1.18 above and that given in the pie chart in figure 1.10 below. What's the difference? The pie chart visually represents the contribution of each region to the overall sales of the company.

MS Excel Used for Generating the Output

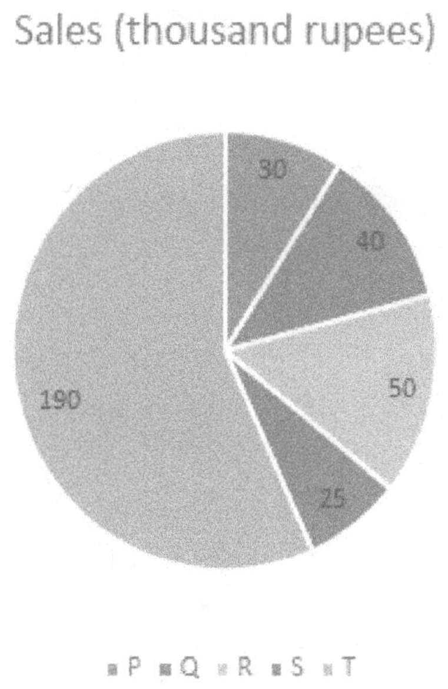

Figure 1.10 Pie chart

Chapter 2

Concepts of Statistical Modeling

We will discuss the following items in this chapter:

- What is a model?
- Dependent and independent variables
- Supervised and unsupervised learning
- Train and test data
- Classification and regression
- Correlation and regression
- Train and test diagnostics

In the context of data science, a model is a relationship between the dependent variable and one or many independent variables.

Consider the following data:

x	1	2	3	4	5	6
y	1	4	9	16	25	36

Intuitively, you could represent the value of y as a square of the value of x.

$$y = square(x)$$

The function that is applied to transform the value of x to obtain the value of y is a square function.

$$y = f(x)$$

$$f(x) = square(x)$$

We have taken the help of Python programming at particular places in the book. This has helped us explain the concept better. In general, we believe that the concepts of data science are language-agnostic.

If we were to define it as a function in Python:

def square(x):

*return x*x*

x = input('Enter value of x: ')

y = square(int(x))

print(y)

The output would prompt the user to input a value, and it would return its square.

Enter the value of x: 4

16

```
def square(x):
    return x*x


x = input('Enter value of x: ')
y = square(int(x))
print(y)
```

```
Enter value of x: 4
16
```

The relationship can be represented in the form of an equation (as in linear regression explained below) or in the form of a sequential set of rules (as in decision trees explained in chapter five of this book).

$$Y = 2X + 3$$

Here, X is the independent variable that impacts Y, which is the dependent variable. The term model and equation can be used interchangeably. This is a model that can be used to predict the value of Y for future values of X. Once a model is built, it can be used for prediction as many times as required. However, it is always advisable to rebuild the model when a sufficient volume of data is available. This prevents the model from getting stale.

There are two ways in which a model can be potentially enhanced. First, you can simply retrain the model with the latest data collected from a more recent time window. Second, keep the time window the same and rebuild the model by including or excluding a few more independent variables. Moreover, we might have to move the window and include/exclude variables at the same time and enhance the model.

Let us explain various terminologies that a data scientist frequently comes across during his day to day work.

- Dependent and independent variables:
  A dependent variable is a variable that is impacted by a set of independent variables. Independent variables influence, while the dependent variable gets influenced. Usually, we come across scenarios where there are only one dependent variable and many independent variables. However, we can design an analytics solution where more than one dependent variable is necessary. Such problems are called multivariate problems. Independent variables are also called inputs or features or predictors or X variables or attributes. The dependent variable is also called output or outcome variable or Y variable.

- Supervised and unsupervised learning:
  In supervised learning, we build a model using a set of independent variables and an outcome variable. We build the model using historical labeled data. The meaning of labeled data is a dataset that has the Y variable available and known for each row. Prediction is done internally using the model and the input variables. Then the predicted Y is compared with the actual Y to find how the model has performed. Examples of supervised learning are linear regression, logistic regression and decision trees. In unsupervised learning, we don't have the idea of dependent and independent variables. The whole set of variables is taken and analyzed for any patterns, groupings, insights or rules. An example of unsupervised learning is clustering. A quick task for you – find out more examples of unsupervised learning.

- Train and test data:
  The dataset, which is used to build the model, is called the train data. A portion of the dataset is kept aside for testing the model, which is called the test data. A train/test split could be 90/10, 80/20, 70/30, 60/40. Can it just be the reverse? Is there a problem if we take the train/test split to be 30/70? Yes, there is a risk. Assume that the model is not trained on all classes of a categorical variable, and a new class is encountered during test prediction. The prediction will fail because the trained model does not know how to react to the new class. The thumb rule goes here: Train on more and test on less. Are we missing something? Find out in what context a validation set is used.

- Classification and regression:
  In classification scenarios, the dependent variable is categorical having two (called binary output) or more classes (called multinomial output). The classes could be nominal or ordinal. We predict and classify for observation the class it belongs to. In multinomial classification problems, there are more than two classes for the dependent variable. Prediction usually gives a probability of the row falling into each class. The class indicated with the highest probability should be the class it belongs to. In regression scenarios, the dependent variable is continuous in nature. Note that the independent variables could be either categorical or continuous. That does not determine whether we are dealing with a classification analytics

problem or a regression analytics problem. Also, note that both classification and regression come under the subject of supervised learning.

- Correlation and regression:
  Correlation does not say whether a change in one variable causes a change in the other variable. It simply shows how the two variables move together. In contrast, regression results in finding out which variable causes a change in the outcome variable and by how much.

- Train and test diagnostics:
  The exercise of building a model is also known as training the model. There are defined statistical evaluations (called diagnostics) to be carried out in conjunction after building the model. Only when all the statistical evaluations are successful, we can confidently deliver it for production deployment. The evaluation strategies are driven by whether we are dealing with a classification or regression analytics problem.

Chapter 3

Linear Regression

We will discuss the following items in this chapter:

- Mathematical understanding of Linear Regression
- Understanding the Salaries dataset
- Displaying column names of a dataset
- Data exploration
- Model building
- Understanding the model output summary
- Model diagnostics
  - MAPE
  - Residual scatter plot
  - Normality of residuals
  - Homoscedasticity
  - Absence of multicollinearity
  - Linearity between dependent and independent variables
  - Cook's distance
  - Outliers
- Stepwise Linear Regression

For the given two data points (x1, y1) and (x2, y2) in a plane, we can determine the distance between the two points using the formula: $\sqrt{(x_2-x_1)^2+(y_2-y_1)^2}$.

Consider the points P(4,8) and Q(6,10).

The value of distance would be:

$$\sqrt{(6-4)^2+(10-8)^2} = \sqrt{8} = 2\sqrt{2} .$$

If we were to draw a straight line connecting the above points P and Q, the slope of the line would be: y_2-y_1 / x_2-x_1 .

That is $10-8 / 6-4 = 1$. The slope of this line is positive.

Now that we have the slope, we could determine the intercept with the equation $y=mx+c$. For point P(4,8) we would have: $8=1*4+c$. We would arrive at $c=4$.

Slope, m is 1 and Intercept, c is 4. So the equation of the line is $y=1.x+4$ or $y=x+4$.

If we were to introduce newer values of x, based on the equation, we would be able to calculate the value of y. The difference between the estimated value (Yi) or the value calculated as per the equation we have arrived at and the observed value of yi at that given value of xi is called a residual $(y_i - Y_i)$.

The principle of least squares sets to minimize the sum of squares of residuals for all estimated and observed values of y in a given dataset. $\sum_{i=1}^{n}(y_i - Y_i)^2$ should be minimum.

Consider the following data points:

x	1	7	10	15	20	24
y	12	17	19	21	27	32

Let us attempt to fit a straight line to this dataset.

Let $Y=aX+b$ be the equation of this straight line. Applying the principle of least squares, the values of slope (*a*) and intercept (*b*) can be determined with the following normal equations of a straight line.

$$\sum y = n.b + a.\sum x$$

$$\sum xy = b.\sum x + a.\sum x^2$$

A line derived with these above equations is called the line of best fit for this given data set.

Applying this method to our dataset:

x	y	x^2	Xy
1	12	1	12
7	17	49	119
10	19	100	190
15	21	225	315
20	27	400	540
24	32	576	768
$\sum x$ = 77	$\sum y$ = 128	$\sum x^2$ = 1351	$\sum xy$ = 1944

Substituting the values in normal equations for the straight line given above, we can see that:

$$128=6b+77a$$

$$1944=77b+1351a$$

Solving for a and b, using simultaneous equations, we get $a=0.8305$ and $b=10.6752$.

Hence, the line of best fit is: $Y=0.8305X+10.6752$.

Insert these data points in an MS Excel sheet as below.

	A	B
1	x	y
2	1	12
3	7	17
4	10	19
5	15	21
6	20	27
7	24	32
8		

Now, insert a line chart for values of x and y. Add a trend line to these data points. Set the type of trendline as linear. In the formatting options, choose to display the equation of the trendline along with the value of R^2. You will learn more about R^2 later in this chapter. You'll notice that the equation displayed is the same as the one we derived mathematically using the principle of least squares.

This example illustrates that the linear trendline function, inbuilt in excel, works on the same principle of least squares.

Try adjusting the line by using the Set Intercept feature. You will notice that it affects the R^2 value (value closer to one indicates better fit) and that the line is no longer the best fit.

Let us try solving the line of best fit through a Python program.

```
import pandas as pd
import numpy as np
from sklearn.linear_model import LinearRegression
from sklearn.metrics import mean_squared_error
import matplotlib.pyplot as plt
p = [1,7,10,15,20,24]
q = [12,17,19,21,27,32]
pq_df = pd.DataFrame({'p':p,'q':q})
pq_df
pq_df.plot('p','q',kind = 'scatter')
```

```
model1 = LinearRegression()
p1 = pq_df.p[0:6,np.newaxis]
q1 = pq_df.q[0:6,np.newaxis]
model1.fit(p1,q1)
q_pred = model1.predict(p1)
plt.scatter(p1,q1,s = 10, color = 'g')
plt.plot(p1,q_pred,color = 'r')
plt.show()
print('R-squared for training set: %4f' %model1.score(p1,q1))
mse1 = mean_squared_error(q1,q_pred)
print(mse1)
print(model1.intercept_)
print(model1.coef_)
```

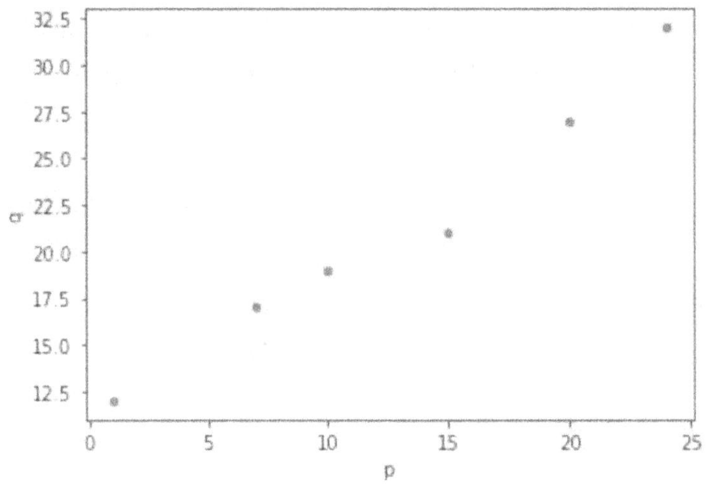

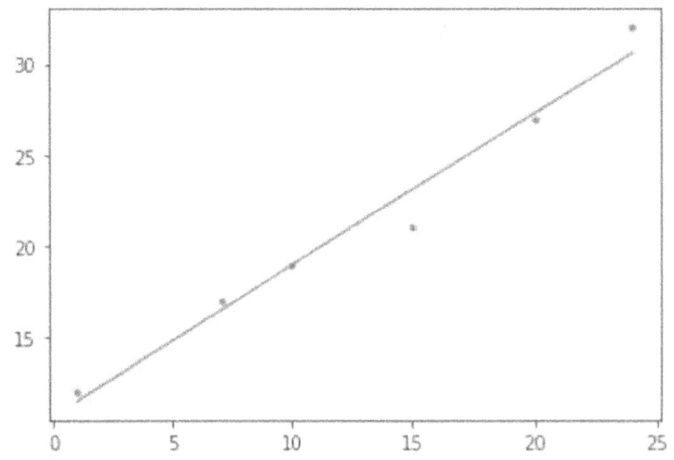

```
print('R-squared for training set: %4f' %model1.score(p1,q1))

mse1 = mean_squared_error(q1,q_pred)
print(mse1)

print(model1.intercept_)
print(model1.coef_)
```

```
R-squared for training set: 0.972503
1.1792987291379584
[10.67524116]
[[0.83050069]]
```

The values of slope and intercept calculated by the LinearRegression function are the same as what we calculated mathematically. The Python program above further illustrates that the *LinearRegression* function in the *sklearn* package also works on the same principle of least squares.

Next, take a look at the *Salaries* dataset in R.

Package: car

Dataset: Salaries

A data frame with 397 observations on the following 6 variables

rank	A factor with levels AssocProf, AsstProf and Prof
discipline	A factor with levels A ("theoretical" departments) or B ("applied" departments)
yrs.since.phd	Years since Ph.D
yrs.service	Years of service
sex	A factor with levels Female Male
salary	Nine-month salary, in dollars

View the column names of the dataset, as shown in Table 3.1 below.

R Function Used for Generating the Output

- *colnames()*

```
"rank"          "discipline"    "yrs.since.phd" "yrs.service"   "sex"           "salary"
```

Table 3.1 Column names of *Salaries* dataset

The column names are displayed above, and we can see that the dataset has six columns.

The following is the structure of the dataset.

R Function Used for Generating the Output

- *str()*

```
'data.frame':   397 obs. of  6 variables:
 $ rank         : Factor w/ 3 levels "AsstProf","AssocProf",..: 3 3 1 3 3 2 3 3 3 3
 $ discipline   : Factor w/ 2 levels "A","B": 2 2 2 2 2 2 2 2 2 2 ...
 $ yrs.since.phd: int  19 20 4 45 40 6 30 45 21 18 ...
 $ yrs.service  : int  18 16 3 39 41 6 23 45 20 18 ...
 $ sex          : Factor w/ 2 levels "Female","Male": 2 2 2 2 2 2 2 2 2 1 ...
 $ salary       : int  139750 173200 79750 115000 141500 97000 175000 147765 119250
```

Table 3.2 Structure of *Salaries* dataset

The structure gives us a list of columns with data types and sample values. We see three categorical and three numeric variables in Table 3.2 above. Understand the dataset better by looking at the summary, as shown in Table 3.3 below.

R Function Used for Generating the Output

- *summary()*

```
       rank     discipline yrs.since.phd    yrs.service        sex          salary
 AsstProf : 67   A:181      Min.   : 1.00   Min.   : 0.00   Female: 39   Min.   : 57800
 AssocProf: 64   B:216      1st Qu.:12.00   1st Qu.: 7.00   Male  :358   1st Qu.: 91000
 Prof     :266              Median :21.00   Median :16.00                Median :107300
                            Mean   :22.31   Mean   :17.61                Mean   :113706
                            3rd Qu.:32.00   3rd Qu.:27.00                3rd Qu.:134185
                            Max.   :56.00   Max.   :60.00                Max.   :231545
```

Table 3.3 Summary of *Salaries* dataset

What could be an analytics problem of interest to us? Predict the *salary* based on specific other parameters. Let's begin by doing a couple of bivariate analyses. It is essential to know here that the choice of the dependent variable is based on our definition of the problem statement. In this case, *salary* is the outcome variable as we are going to predict it. Ultimately, we should be able to come up with an appropriate model that helps us predict *salary*. Check whether the following steps make sense to you.

- Define the business problem
- Convert the business problem into an analytics problem statement
- Identify dependent and independent variables
- Carry out exploratory data analysis to understand the data and relationships better
- Capture insights
- Build the model
- Run model diagnostics and keep rebuilding model until all diagnostics are within acceptable ranges

Data Exploration

R Function Used for Generating the Output

- *plot()*

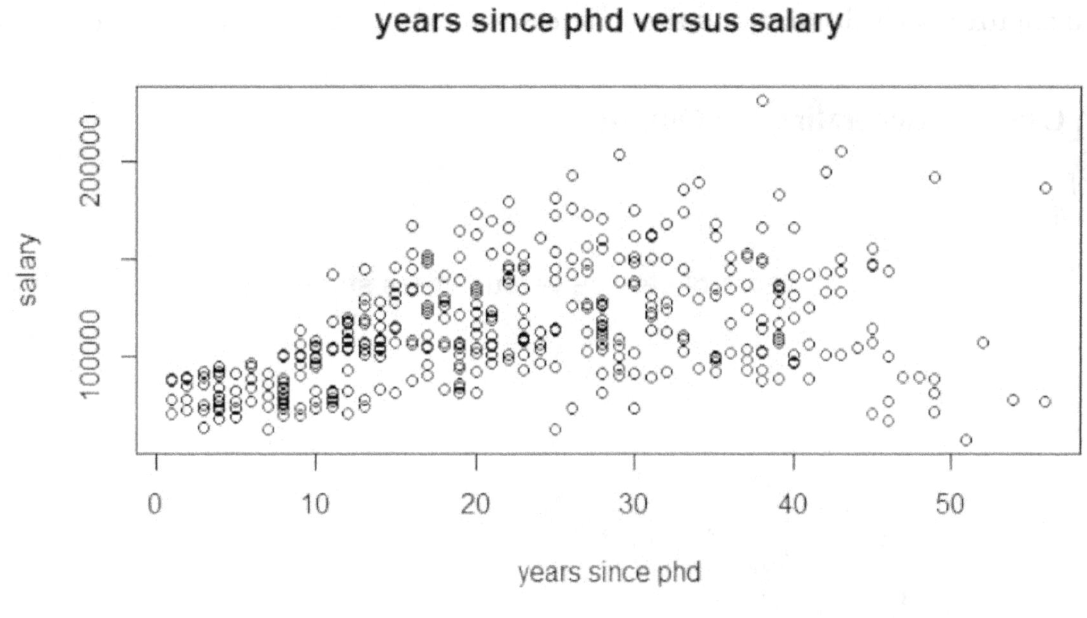

Figure 3.1 Scatter plot of years since Ph.D. versus *salary*

From figure 3.1 above, we see that as the years since Ph.D. increase, the *salary* also increases. They have a moderate positive linear relationship. There could be variables other than years since Ph.D. that impact the *salary* too.

R Function Used for Generating the Output

- *plot()*

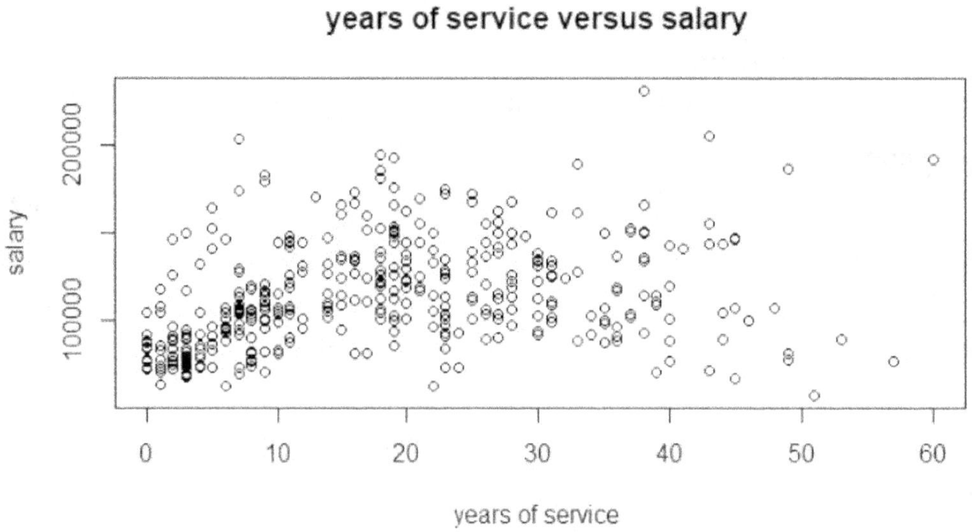

Figure 3.2 Scatter plot of years of service versus *salary*

The scatter plot of years of service versus *salary* in figure 3.2 shows that *salary* increases with years of service up to approximately 30 years and then decreases slowly with increasing years of service.

R Function Used for Generating the Output

- *plot()*

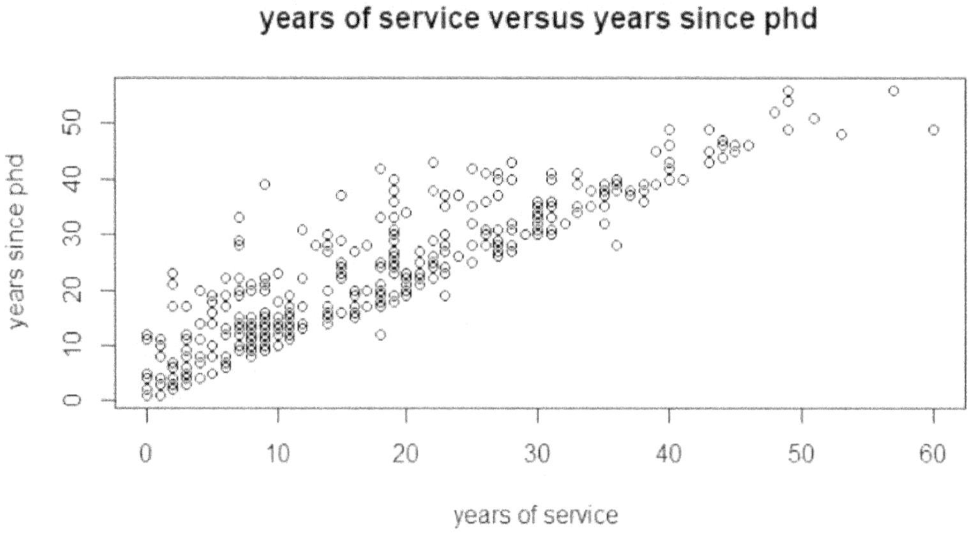

Figure 3.3 Scatter plot of years of service versus years since Ph.D.

Let's keep the dependent variable aside for a moment and focus on the two independent variables – years of service and years since Ph.D. The scatter plot in figure 3.3 shows a very positive and linear relationship between the two variables. It is expected that the correlation coefficient will be very high.

The correlation coefficient is 0.9096491, and indeed, it is high.

R Function Used for Generating the Output

- *boxplot()*

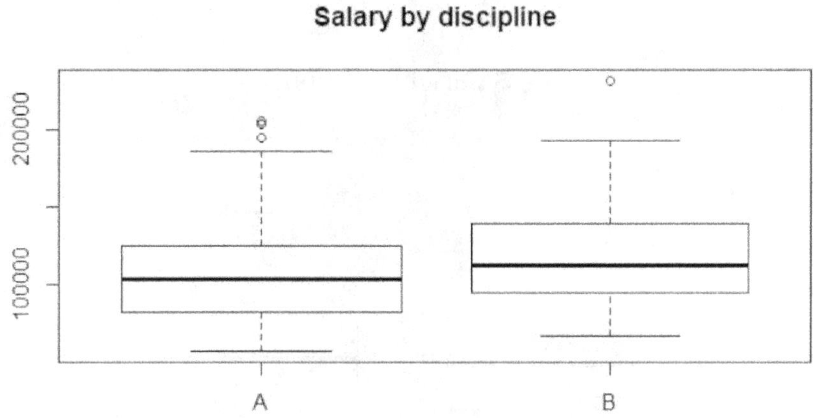

Figure 3.4 Box plot of *salary* by *discipline*

Figure 3.4 above shows the salary distribution by disciplines 'A' and 'B'. With a little visual inspection, it can generally be said that discipline 'B' gives a higher salary than discipline 'A', even though there are many individual professors in discipline 'A' who get a higher salary than certain professors in discipline 'B'.

R Function Used for Generating the Output

- *boxplot()*

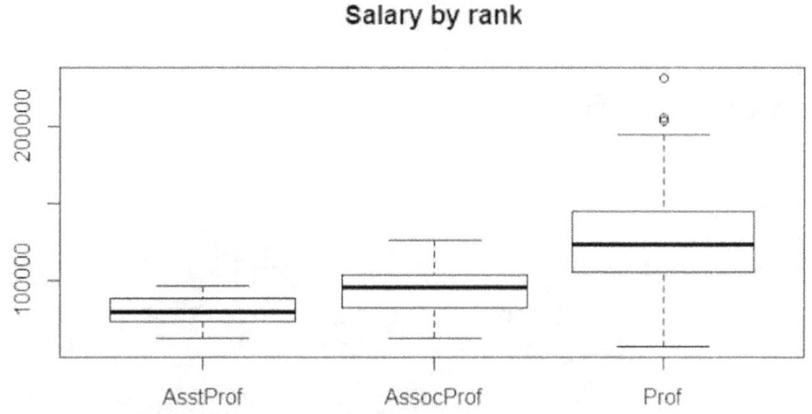

Figure 3.5 Box plot of *salary* by *rank*

What does the plot in figure 3.5 above tell you? In general, professors draw a higher salary than associate professors who, in turn, get a higher salary than assistant professors. If nothing else, this is intuitive. If that is the case, then is it fair to expect that all professors get a higher salary than any assistant professor? It does not look like that in the plots. This is because *rank* alone is not the only determining factor. There are other influencers such as *discipline*, gender, years of service, etc. All influencers should be considered simultaneously to be able to determine a salary.

R Function Used for Generating the Output

- *boxplot()*

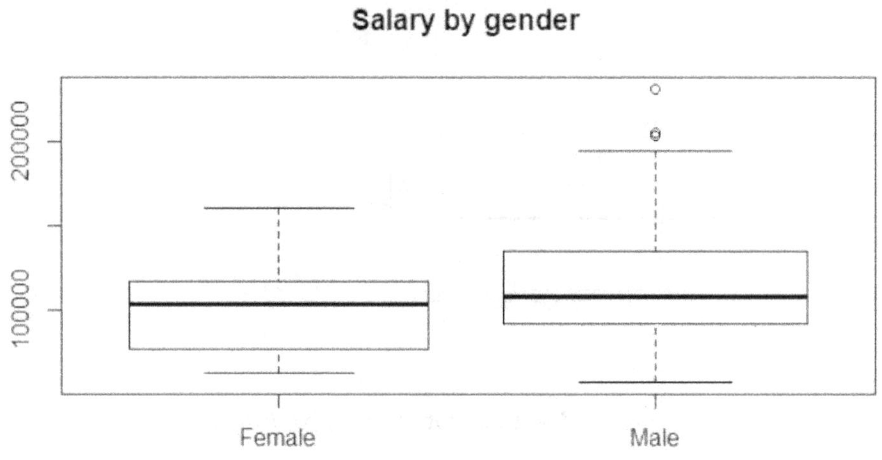

Figure 3.6 Box plot of *salary* by gender

The same discussion can be done for salary by gender in figure 3.6 above. It seems that males get a higher salary than females if we consider gender alone. Can we say that there is a bias in favor of males for deciding the salary? As explained earlier, please don't conclude too soon. Table 3.4 below tells us that nearly 93% of professors are male. That would explain the higher salary better. However, if you are really worried about gender discrimination, then the next step of analysis should be on why there are so few female professors.

R Function Used for Generating the Output

- *Table()*

	Female	Male
AsstProf	11	56
AssocProf	10	54
Prof	18	248

Table 3.4 Cross-tabulation of *rank* with gender

R Function Used for Generating the Output

- *boxplot()*

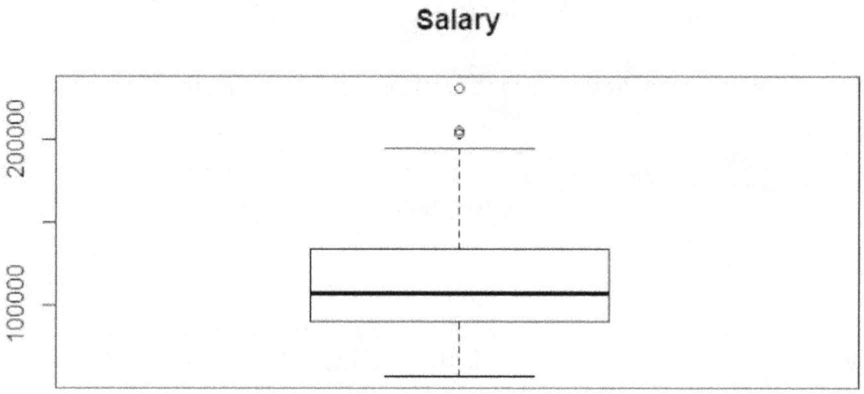

Figure 3.7 Box plot of *salary*

This is simply an innocent distribution of *salary* by itself in figure 3.7 above. Little did we suspect that there are so many stories hidden behind it.

What has our exploratory data analysis given us till now?

- Years since Ph.D. and years of service are sufficiently correlated to *salary* each.
- Years since Ph.D. and years of service are highly correlated with each other. We should pick only one of them to avoid multicollinearity among independent variables for modeling purposes.
- Discipline might influence *salary* to a certain extent.
- Rank seems to have a good impact on the *salary*.
- The number of professors is heavily skewed toward *Male*.

Modeling

R Function Used for Generating the Output

- *nrow()*

Number of rows in Salaries = 397

Number of rows in Train = 277 (70%)

Number of rows in Test = 120 (30%)

R Functions Used for Generating the Output

- *lm()*
- *summary()*

```
Call:
lm(formula = salary ~ yrs.service, data = Train)

1  Residuals:
     Min      1Q  Median      3Q     Max
-78574 -19745   -4432   15026   80860

2  Coefficients:                                    3
              Estimate Std. Error t value Pr(>|t|)
(Intercept)    97751.1     2733.5  35.760  < 2e-16 ***
yrs.service      757.3      123.5   6.133 2.99e-09 ***
---
Signif. codes:  0 '***' 0.001 '**' 0.01 '*' 0.05 '.' 0.1 ' ' 1

Residual standard error: 27430 on 275 degrees of freedom
Multiple R-squared:  0.1203,    Adjusted R-squared:  0.1171
F-statistic: 37.61 on 1 and 275 DF,  p-value: 2.994e-09     6
                  4
                                  5
```

Table 3.5 Linear Regression output

There are a few important things to focus on here, as denoted by the six circles.

1. Residuals:

R Function Used for Generating the Output

- *plot()*

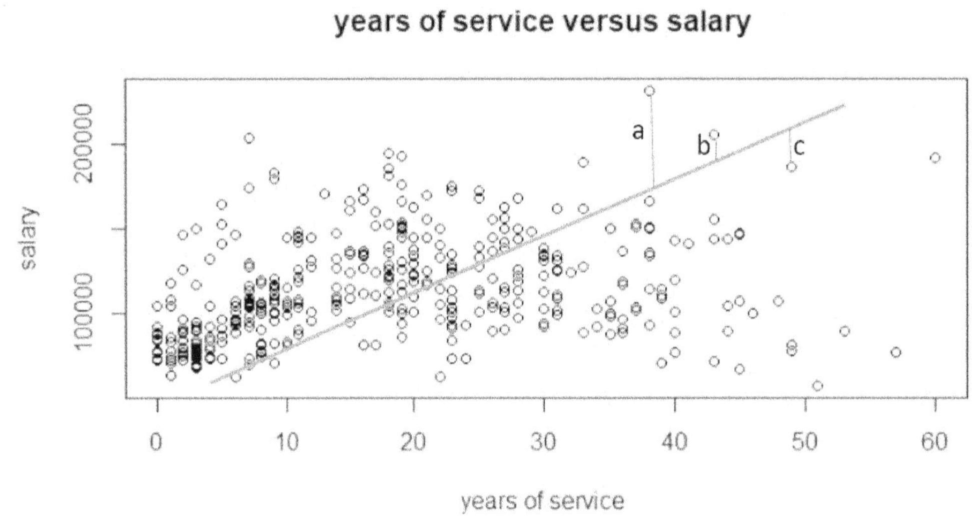

Figure 3.7.5 Arriving at the best fit line

See the distances a, b and c in figure 3.7.5 above; 'a' is a residual because that is the distance between the point on the prediction line and the position of the actual point. This is also called the prediction error. We can plot years of service versus salary, as shown in figure 3.7.5, on a two-dimensional surface because we have taken only one independent variable to explain this. We will have to rely on three-dimensional representation if we want to add one more independent variable and so on.

Sum of squared residuals = (a square) + (b square) + (c square) + ...

The regression line is chosen such that the sum of squared residuals is the minimum. That is called the best fit line. This is also known as the Least Squares Method (LSM).

2. Coefficients:
   Let's continue with the same example. The best fit line will have an equation y = mx + k, where m is the coefficient of the independent variable, and k is the intercept. The coefficient is also known as the slope of the line. It tells us the extent of the impact of a particular independent variable on the dependent variable.

3. p-value against each variable:
   A small p-value indicates that the relationship between the independent and dependent variables is not by chance. Note the significance codes represented by stars for each coefficient. One, two or three stars would mean that it is a highly significant variable.

4. R-Squared:
   R-squared value tells us how well the regression line is fitting the data points. It's a measure of the linear relationship between the dependent and independent variables. The R-squared value we got is 0.12, which means that years of service alone explain only 12% of the variability in salary. R-squared values lie between 0 and 1. R-squared values closer to one are preferred. Hence, at first glance, we don't seem to have a very good model.

5. F statistic p-value:
   This is left for the readers to explore and find out for themselves.

6. Adjusted R-Squared:
   R-squared values will go on increasing with the addition of more and more independent variables. Hence, adjusted R-squared is a better measure because it adjusts to the number of independent variables that are considered. It penalizes the model for adding new variables that have no impact.

R Functions Used for Generating the Output

- *lm()*
- *summary()*

```
Call:
lm(formula = salary ~ rank, data = Train)

Residuals:
   Min     1Q Median     3Q    Max 
-66922 -15167  -1867  11651  68278 

Coefficients:
              Estimate Std. Error t value Pr(>|t|)    
(Intercept)      80652       3125  25.808  < 2e-16 ***
rankAssocProf    12696       4536   2.799  0.00548 ** 
rankProf         44070       3552  12.406  < 2e-16 ***
---
Signif. codes:  0 '***' 0.001 '**' 0.01 '*' 0.05 '.' 0.1 ' ' 1

Residual standard error: 22540 on 274 degrees of freedom
Multiple R-squared:  0.4084,	Adjusted R-squared:  0.4041 
F-statistic: 94.56 on 2 and 274 DF,  p-value: < 2.2e-16
```

Table 3.6 Linear Regression output with rank

With *rank* alone as the influencing variable, the adjusted R-squared increased to 0.4, as shown in Table 3.6. This means that *rank* explains variations in *salary* in a better way than years of service does.

R Functions Used for Generating the Output

- *lm()*
- *summary()*

```
Call:
lm(formula = salary ~ rank + discipline, data = Train)

Residuals:
   Min     1Q Median     3Q    Max 
-64365 -13006    159   9576  68667 

Coefficients:
              Estimate Std. Error t value Pr(>|t|)    
(Intercept)      71968       3339  21.557  < 2e-16 ***
rankAssocProf    13012       4300   3.026  0.00272 ** 
rankProf         45389       3376  13.445  < 2e-16 ***
disciplineB      14568       2581   5.644 4.17e-08 ***
---
Signif. codes:  0 '***' 0.001 '**' 0.01 '*' 0.05 '.' 0.1 ' ' 1

Residual standard error: 21360 on 273 degrees of freedom
Multiple R-squared:  0.4702,	Adjusted R-squared:  0.4644 
F-statistic: 80.76 on 3 and 273 DF,  p-value: < 2.2e-16
```

Table 3.7 Linear Regression output with rank and discipline

Rank and *discipline* together seem to do well with an adjusted R-squared of 0.46, as shown in Table 3.7.

Interaction Terms

R Functions Used for Generating the Output

- *lm()*
- *summary()*

```
Call:
lm(formula = salary ~ rank + discipline + yrs.since.phd * yrs.service,
    data = Train)

Residuals:
   Min     1Q Median     3Q    Max
-58482 -11371   -147   8450  76205

Coefficients:
                            Estimate Std. Error t value Pr(>|t|)
(Intercept)                 68027.35    3912.90  17.385  < 2e-16 ***
rankAssocProf                7831.23    5423.95   1.444   0.1499
rankProf                    37315.47    6554.23   5.693 3.24e-08 ***
disciplineB                 14691.63    2616.04   5.616 4.85e-08 ***
yrs.since.phd                 711.56     344.92   2.063   0.0401 *
yrs.service                   228.50     443.50   0.515   0.6068
yrs.since.phd:yrs.service     -17.88      10.23  -1.748   0.0817 .
---
Signif. codes:  0 '***' 0.001 '**' 0.01 '*' 0.05 '.' 0.1 ' ' 1

Residual standard error: 21260 on 270 degrees of freedom
Multiple R-squared:  0.4813,    Adjusted R-squared:  0.4697
F-statistic: 41.75 on 6 and 270 DF,  p-value: < 2.2e-16
```

Table 3.8 Linear Regression output with *rank*, *discipline*, years since Ph.D. and years of service

When the effect of an independent variable on a dependent variable changes, depending on the values of other independent variables, we say that there is an interaction effect. If we use the interaction in our model, we can explain variability in the dependent variable better. In Table 3.8 shown above, we have included the interaction between years since Ph.D. and years of service. The R-squared value has increased to 0.48.

Let's take some time to understand the following behavior in R. The way a categorical variable having n classes is handled in R is by creating n-1 new columns and populating them with zeros and ones (1 for occurrence and 0 for non-occurrence). For example, *rank* is a categorical variable having three classes. So we get two new variables related to *rank* named *rankAssocProf* and *rankProf*.

The column corresponding to *rankAssistantProf* need not be created as *rankAssocProf = 0 and rankProf = 0 will indicate* an occurrence of *rankAssistantProf.*

Salary ~ rank + discipline

Let's go back to the scenario where we used *rank* and *discipline* together for building the model for predicting *salary.*

The model has the following set of properties giving additional information. We will mostly need to use coefficients, residuals and fitted values that contain the estimated coefficients, errors and predicted values, respectively. Refer to Table 3.9 below.

Here, we would like you to clearly understand what predicted values mean in the context of building and evaluating a model. In the previous chapter, we discussed the train dataset and test dataset. We said that the train dataset is used for building the model, while the test dataset is used for finding the performance of the model. The way we test that is by taking all independent variables (dependent variable is not taken) and passing them to our newly built model. We will then get predictions of the test data. These predictions are then compared with the actual observed Y values for purposes of finding accuracy.

Note that we talk about predictions on the train data too. This happens internally, and we don't need to explicitly call the model to make predictions for us. Again, we compare predicted values with the actual observed values and find the accuracy. So there is a train accuracy and a test accuracy. This means that any diagnostics we carry out for any of the supervised learning techniques will have a train performance behavior and a test performance behavior. The test performance and train performance must be close to each other to evaluate the model to be good.

R Functions Used for Generating the Output

- *lm()*
- *names()*

Components Available in the Model Entity

```
"coefficients"  "residuals"  "effects"      "rank"       "fitted.values"
"assign"        "qr"         "df.residual"  "contrasts"  "xlevels"
"call"          "terms"      "model"
```

Table 3.9 Components of the model

Let's take a look at a few samples of coefficients (Table 3.10), residuals (Table 3.11) and predicted values (Table 3.12).

R Functions Used for Generating the Output

- *lm()*
- *model$coefficients*

Coefficients

```
(Intercept) rankAssocProf      rankProf   disciplineB
   71967.56      13012.43      45388.69      14567.87
```

Table 3.10 Coefficients from linear Regression

R Functions Used for Generating the Output

- *Lm()*
- *model$residuals*

Residuals

```
        123         103         219          23         185         190         318         145 
-20094.2446  21378.8836  10102.1397 -23452.2446 -30924.1164  21825.8836 -64365.1164 -19228.1164 
        213          67         242         341         108         154         293         256 
 -3524.1164 -30924.1164   5518.7554 -25693.1164  -2379.9886   4446.1397  66443.7554  -1979.9886 
         78         136         137         261         203         268         202         281 
 61075.8836  18643.7554  -9094.2446   3620.0114  28475.8836 -13006.2446 -12224.1164  19143.7554 
```

Table 3.11 Residuals from linear Regression

R Functions Used for Generating the Output

- *lm()*
- *model$fitted.values*

Fitted (Predicted) Values

```
      123       103       219        23       185       190       318       145       213 
117356.24 131924.12  99547.86 117356.24 131924.12 131924.12 131924.12 131924.12 131924.12 
       67       242       341       108       154       293       256        78       136 
131924.12 117356.24 131924.12  84979.99  99547.86 117356.24  84979.99 131924.12 117356.24 
      137       261       203       268       202       281       157        64       286 
117356.24  84979.99 131924.12 117356.24 131924.12 117356.24  99547.86  99547.86  84979.99 
```

Table 3.12 Fitted (predicted) values from linear Regression

Diagnostics

1. ***MAPE***

Mean absolute percentage error (MAPE) is an important metric for determining how erroneous the model is.

train_MAPE = mean (abs (train_residuals/train_salary)) = 0.1382. This is MAPE for the train dataset.

The steps for calculating MAPE for the test dataset are:

- Predict on the test dataset
- Calculate the residuals
- Calculate the percentage error
- Take absolute values of the percentage errors
- Take the mean of absolute values

R Functions Used for Generating the Output

- *lm()*
- *predict()*
- *cbind()*

rank	discipline	yrs.since.phd	yrs.service	sex	salary	results
Prof	B	19	18	Male	139750	131924.12
Prof	B	20	16	Male	173200	131924.12
AsstProf	B	4	3	Male	79750	86535.43
AssocProf	B	6	6	Male	97000	99547.86
Prof	B	21	20	Male	119250	131924.12
Prof	B	12	3	Male	117150	131924.12

Table 3.13 Predictions on train data

R Function Used for Generating the Output

- *cbind()*

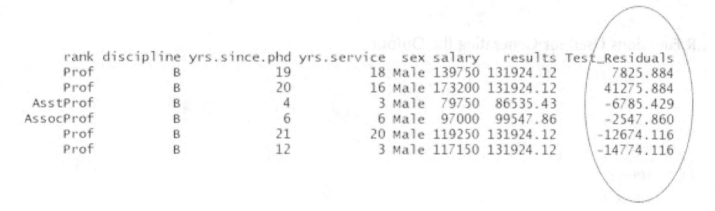

	rank	discipline	yrs.since.phd	yrs.service	sex	salary	results	Test_Residuals
	Prof	B	19	18	Male	139750	131924.12	7825.884
	Prof	B	20	16	Male	173200	131924.12	41275.884
	AsstProf	B	4	3	Male	79750	86535.43	-6785.429
	AssocProf	B	6	6	Male	97000	99547.86	-2547.860
	Prof	B	21	20	Male	119250	131924.12	-12674.116
	Prof	B	12	3	Male	117150	131924.12	-14774.116

Table 3.14 Predictions on test data

test_MAPE = mean (abs (test_residuals/test_salary)) = 0.1432. This is MAPE for the test dataset.

Since train and test MAPE are close enough, we can say that we are on the right track.

2. ***Residual Scatter Plot***

R Functions Used for Generating the Output

- *plot()*
- *abline()*

The residuals should be randomly distributed without any visible patterns.

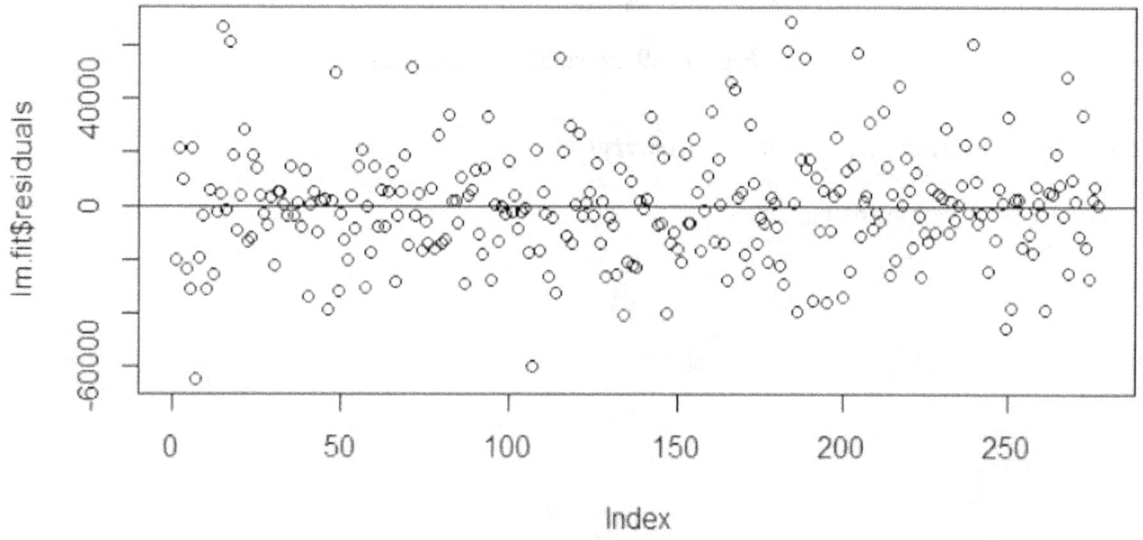

Figure 3.8 Residual scatter plot

3. ***Normality of Residuals***

Studentized residuals should be normally distributed. It is left to the readers to explore and find out the calculation of studentized residuals.

R Functions Used for Generating the Output

- *studres()*
- *hist()*
- *mean()*
- *sd()*
- *dnorm()*
- *curve()*

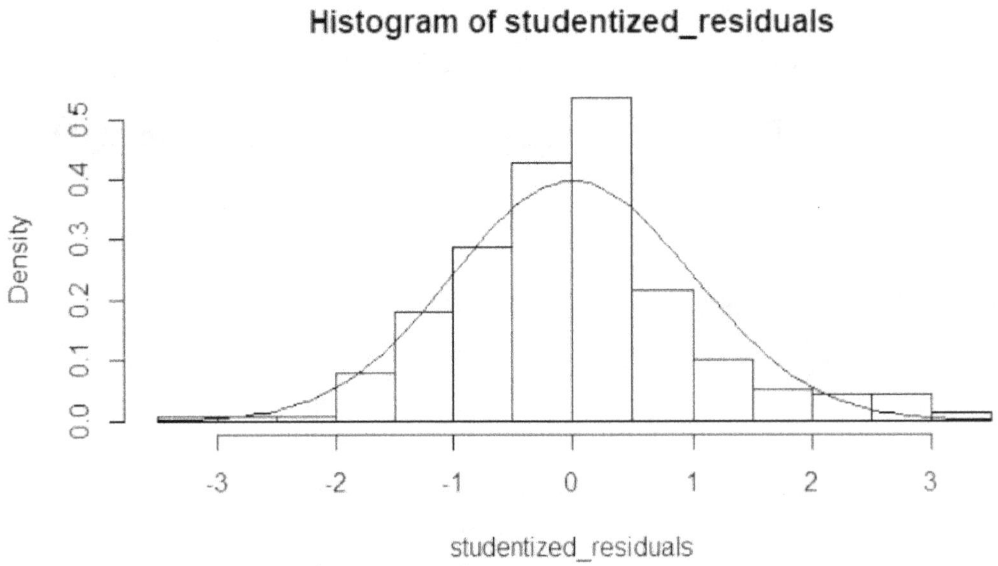

Figure 3.9 Normality of residuals

4. ***Constant Error Variance (Homoscedasticity)***

Residuals should have constant variances.

R Functions Used for Generating the Output

- *ncvTest()*
- *spreadLevelPlot()*

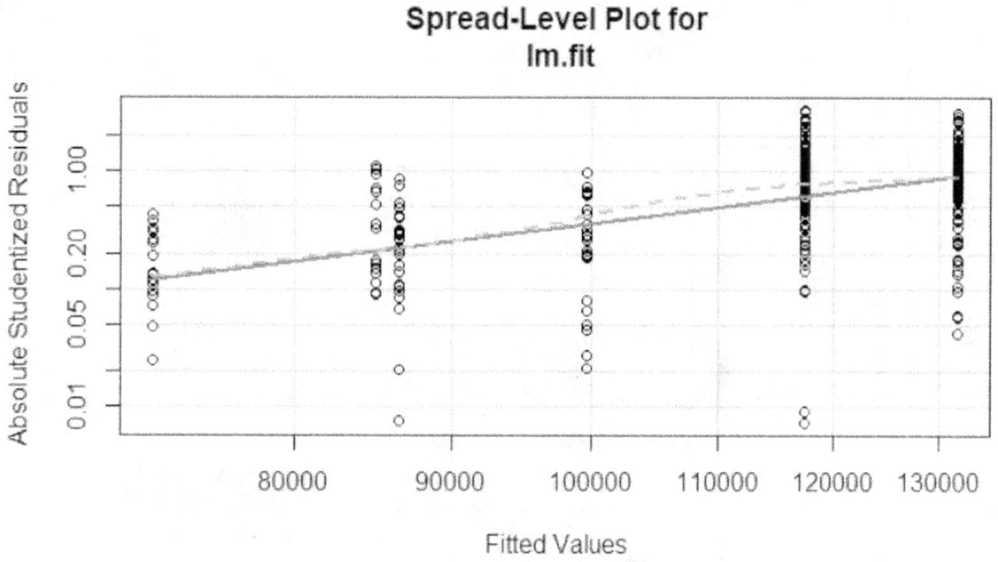

Figure 3.10 Homoscedasticity

5. ***Absence of Multicollinearity***

Multicollinearity can be identified by computing a score called the variance inflation factor (VIF), which measures how much the variance of a regression coefficient is inflated due to multicollinearity in the model. VIF values of less than five are considered to be good.

R Function Used for Generating the Output

- *Vif()*

```
               GVIF Df GVIF^(1/(2*Df))
rank       1.006149  2        1.001534
discipline 1.006149  1        1.003070
```

Table 3.15 Multicollinearity

6. ***Linearity Between Dependent and Independent Variables***

The relationship between the dependent variable and each independent variable should be linear for the model to perform well. For example, *salary* versus years since Ph.D. and *salary* versus years of service are seen to have more or less a linear relationship.

R Function Used for Generating the Output

- *pairs()*

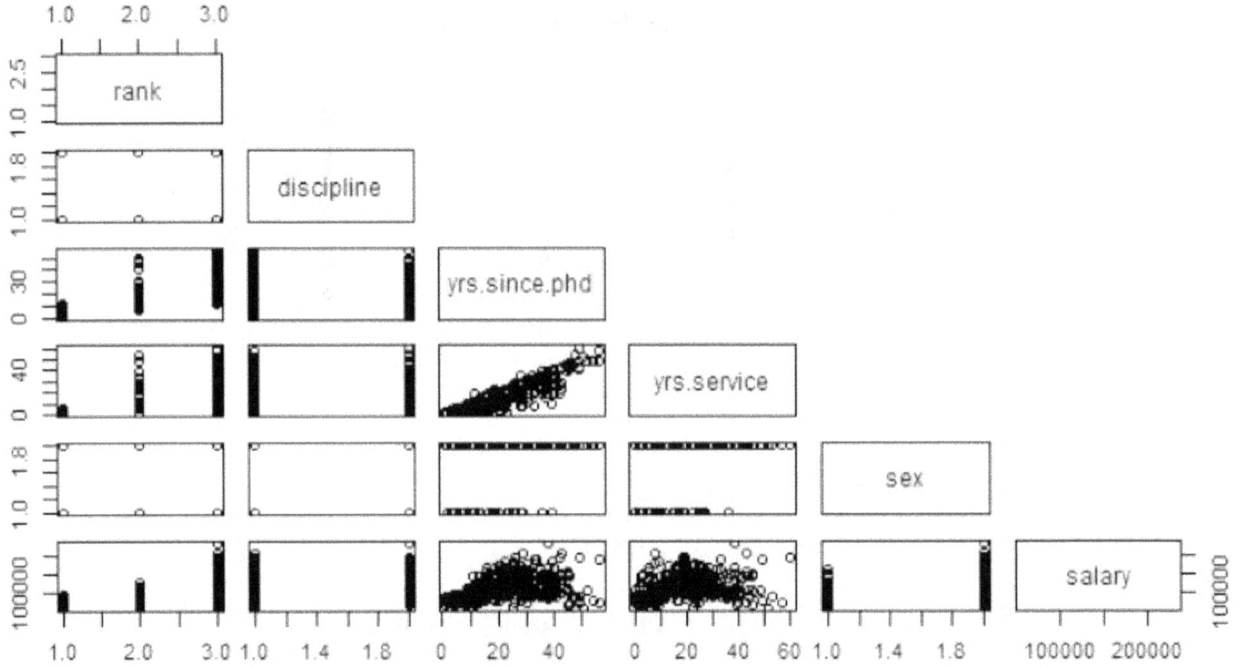

Figure 3.11 Scatter plot matrix of *Salaries*

7. ***Cook's Distance***

In linear regression set up, cooks distance tells us the extent of influence a particular observation has on the model. Cook's distance should be less than 0.1, which is the scenario in our case, as shown below in figure 3.12.

R Functions Used for Generating the Output

- *Cutoff()*
- *nrow()*
- *length()*
- *plot()*

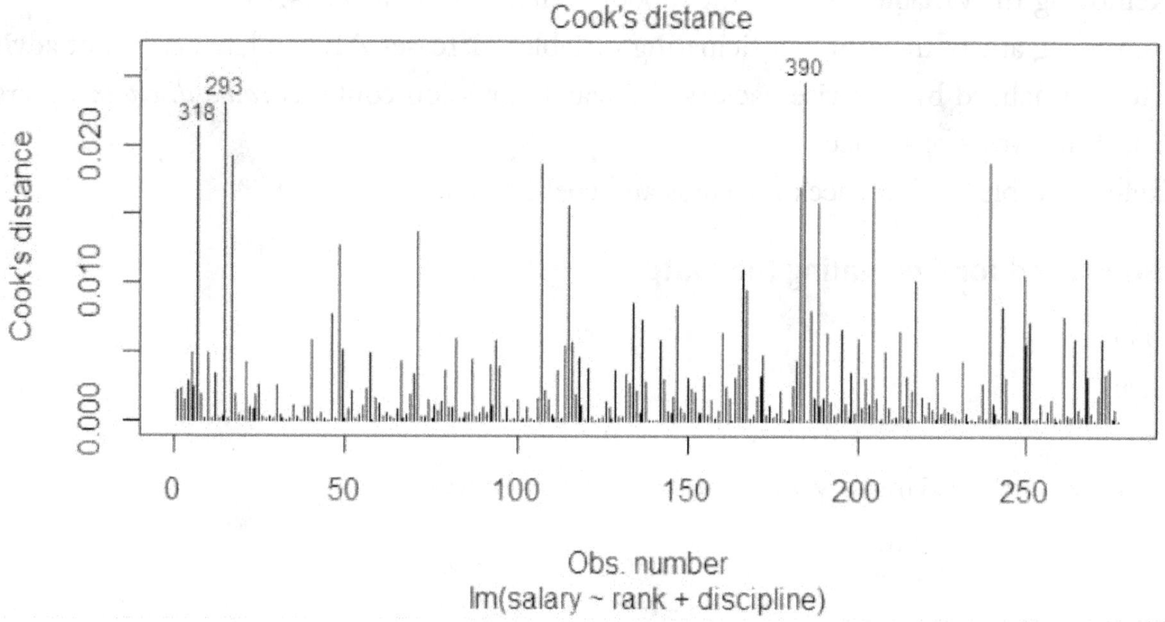

Figure 3.12 Cook's distance

8. ***Outliers***

R Function Used for Generating the Output

- *outlierTest()*

```
     rstudent unadjusted p-value Bonferonni p
390  3.28663           0.0011472      0.31776
```

Table 3.16 Outliers

These outliers are outliers in residuals, which are calculated after building the model.

The linear relationship between independent and dependent variables, the absence of multicollinearity, homoscedasticity and the normality of studentized residuals are often treated as assumptions of the linear regression exercise.

Stepwise Linear Regression

Stepwise Linear Regression (Backward)

As depicted in Table 3.17 below, the following steps are:

- Akaike information criterion (AIC) is the parameter used for comparing the relative quality of models.
- With all five variables used in the model building, AIC is 7965.19.

- Removing the variable *sex* from the model decreases AIC to 7964.75.
- Removing any of the other participating variables increases AIC and, hence, is not advisable.
- Model finalized by stepwise backward linear Regression contains *rank*, *discipline*, years since Ph.D. and years of service.
- Refer to Table 3.17 to check the steps and coefficients.

R Functions Used for Generating the Output

- *lm()*
- *step()*

```
Start:  AIC=7965.19
salary ~ rank + discipline + yrs.since.phd + yrs.service + sex

                Df  Sum of Sq        RSS    AIC
- sex            1 7.8068e+08 1.9890e+11 7964.8
<none>                        1.9812e+11 7965.2
- yrs.since.phd  1 2.5041e+09 2.0062e+11 7968.2
- yrs.service    1 2.7100e+09 2.0083e+11 7968.6
- discipline     1 1.9237e+10 2.1735e+11 8000.0
- rank           2 6.9508e+10 2.6762e+11 8080.6

Step:  AIC=7964.75
salary ~ rank + discipline + yrs.since.phd + yrs.service

                Df  Sum of Sq        RSS    AIC
<none>                        1.9890e+11 7964.8
- yrs.since.phd  1 2.5001e+09 2.0140e+11 7967.7
- yrs.service    1 2.5763e+09 2.0147e+11 7967.9
- discipline     1 1.9489e+10 2.1839e+11 7999.9
- rank           2 7.0679e+10 2.6958e+11 8081.5

Call:
lm(formula = salary ~ rank + discipline + yrs.since.phd + yrs.service,
    data = Salaries)

Coefficients:
  (Intercept)  rankAssocProf       rankProf    disciplineB  yrs.since.phd    yrs.service
      69869.0        12831.5        45287.7        14505.2          534.6         -476.7
```

Table 3.17 Backward stepwise linear Regression

Stepwise Linear Regression (Forward)

- With no variables used in the model building, AIC is 8193.92.
- With adding variable *rank* to the model, AIC decreases to 7998.9.
- With adding variable *discipline* to the model, AIC decreases to 7966.19.
- Adding any of the other potential variables increases AIC and, hence, is not advisable.
- Model finalized by stepwise backward linear Regression contains *rank* and *discipline.*
- Refer to Table 3.18 to check the steps and coefficients.

R Functions Used for Generating the Output

- *lm()*
- *step()*

```
Start:  AIC=8193.92
salary ~ 1

                   Df  Sum of Sq        RSS    AIC
+ rank              2 1.4323e+11 2.2007e+11 7998.9
+ yrs.since.phd     1 6.3852e+10 2.9945e+11 8119.2
+ yrs.service       1 4.0709e+10 3.2259e+11 8148.7
+ discipline        1 8.8508e+09 3.5445e+11 8186.1
+ sex               1 6.9800e+09 3.5632e+11 8188.2
<none>                           3.6330e+11 8193.9

Step:  AIC=7998.91
salary ~ rank

                   Df  Sum of Sq        RSS    AIC
+ discipline        1 1.8430e+10 2.0164e+11 7966.2
<none>                           2.2007e+11 7998.9
+ yrs.service       1 1.0546e+09 2.1901e+11 7999.0
+ sex               1 8.4082e+08 2.1923e+11 7999.4
+ yrs.since.phd     1 2.1559e+08 2.1985e+11 8000.5

Step:  AIC=7966.19
salary ~ rank + discipline

                   Df Sum of Sq        RSS    AIC
<none>                          2.0164e+11 7966.2
+ sex               1 694070191 2.0094e+11 7966.8
+ yrs.service       1 241866236 2.0140e+11 7967.7
+ yrs.since.phd     1 165649329 2.0147e+11 7967.9

Call:
lm(formula = salary ~ rank + discipline, data = Salaries)

Coefficients:
  (Intercept)  rankAssocProf       rankProf    disciplineB
        71944          13762          47844          13761
```

Table 3.18 Forward stepwise linear regression

Chapter 4

Logistic Regression

We will discuss the following items in this chapter:

- Brief mathematical understanding of logistic regression
- Understanding the Titanic dataset
- Data exploration
- Missing-ness map
- Model building
- The summary of the output of logistic regression
- Diagnostics
  - Confusion matrix
    - TP, TN, FP, FN
    - Sensitivity, specificity, precision, recall
    - True positive rate, False positive rate
    - F1 score
  - ROC curve. AUC
  - Precision/recall tradeoff
  - Accuracy plot
  - Deciding on an appropriate cut-off
  - Gains table
  - KS statistic
  - Concordance/discordance

When the outcome variable is dichotomous, as in it can accept one of two values – 0 and 1, got a job or didn't get a job, married or unmarried, approved or rejected, male or female – we cannot apply a linear function to model the behavior of the variables.

The scatter plot looks quite different from what it was for a continuous outcome. For the Titanic dataset that is available on Kaggle, if we were to draw a scatter plot of the age distribution of passengers, it looks as below.

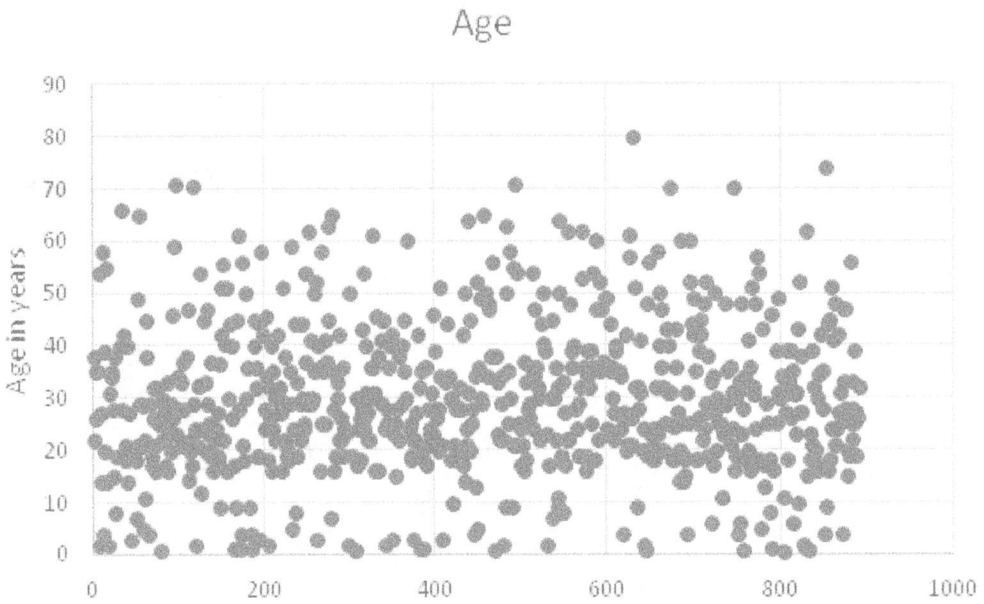

If we were to plot if the passenger survived or not, the scatter plot looks as below. Whether the passenger survived or not is a dichotomous variable.

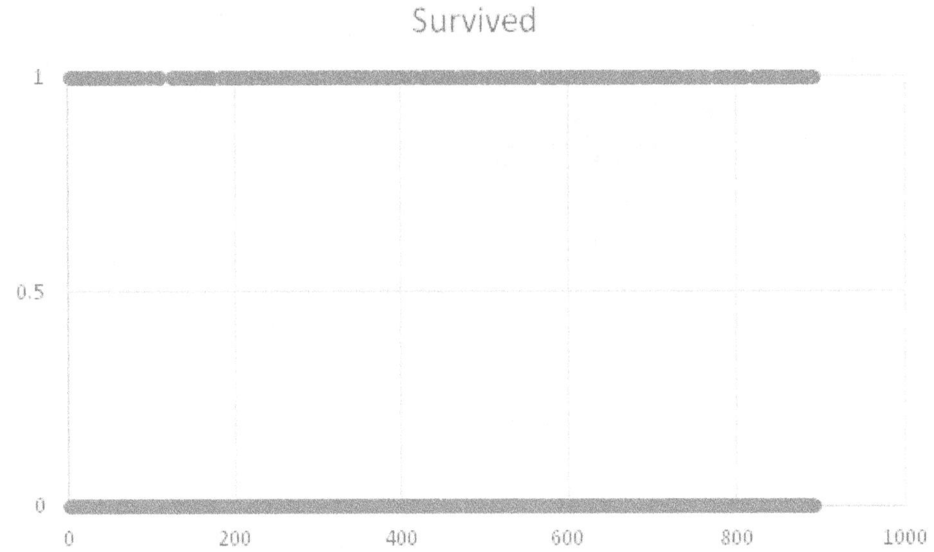

The distribution of passenger class in which they traveled looks as below. Passenger class variable is a categorical variable that is ordinal as it takes ranked values of 1, 2 and 3. Had the values been something like red, blue and green, such a categorical variable is nominal, as in there is no ordering between the different values it takes. If we were to predict the *Pclass* variable, we could apply a multinomial logistic regression model. This topic is out of scope for the current book. We discuss binary logistic regression.

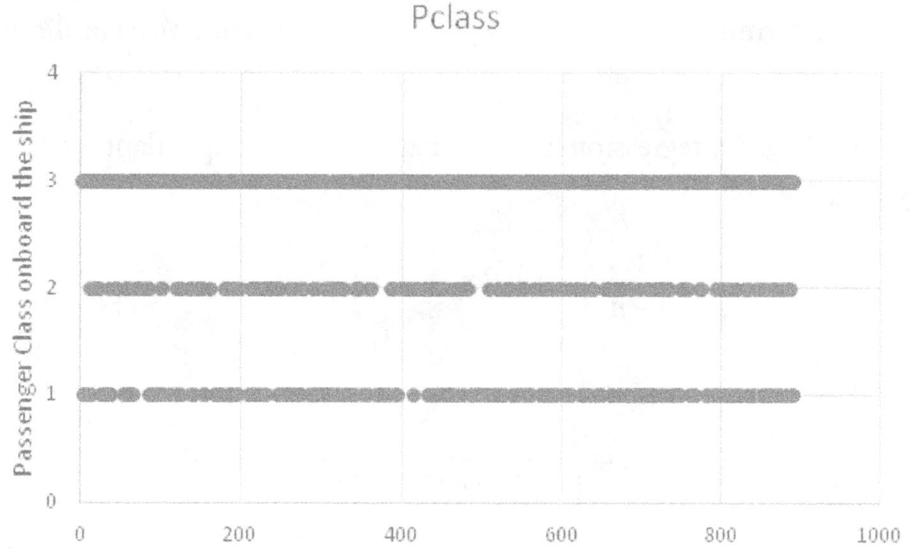

A linear model does not necessarily capture the relationship between the various factors influencing why a given passenger on Titanic survived. So what we then explore is the probability that a given passenger survived. This seemingly transforms the problem into a linear function. But the problem is only half solved.

Let us consider the case where you are told that the probability of a person A getting a job is twice the probability of a person B getting that job. Assuming that the probability of persons getting a job is a linear function. And if I have the probability of B getting the job as 0.4, the logic is simple. You would tell me that the probability of A getting the job is 0.8. But had the probability of B getting a job been 0.6, the same rule doesn't apply as the value would have been 0.6*2 = 1.2. Probability can take values between 0 and 1. So a probability value of 1.2 is an incorrect deduction. To solve this, the probability of an event occurring is converted into an odds ratio of an event occurring.

$$odds = p/(1-p)$$

Once you are given the odds of an event occurring, you could compute the probability of that event occurring as

$$p = odds/(1+odds)$$

For this given example, the probability of B getting a job is specified as 0.4. Following this, the odds of B getting a job can be computed as $0.4/(1-0.4)$. That would be 0.67. Based on this value, the odds of A getting a job is $2*0.67$, which is 1.33. Hence, the probability of A getting a job is $1.33/(1+1.33)$, which is 0.57.

But still, the problem is not solved. If the probability of an event occurring is 1, then the value of odds is undefined (divide by zero error). And if the probability of an event is 0, then the lower bound is still zero. To overcome these limitations, the natural log of the odds is calculated. This transformed value is called logit or log-odds. A linear function expects that the dependent variable can take values from -∞ to + ∞. By transforming probability to logit or log-odd values, we have eliminated both upper and lower bounds.

An equation of a logistic regression model that has k independent variables and $i=1 to n$ observations is given as below:

$$ln\left(\frac{p_i}{1-p_i}\right)=\alpha+\beta_1 x_{i1}+\beta_2 x_{i2}+\ldots+\beta_k x_{ik}$$

p_i can be given as:

$$p_i=\frac{e^{\alpha+\beta_1 x_{i1}+\beta_2 x_{i2}+\ldots+\beta_k x_{ik}}}{1+e^{\alpha+\beta_1 x_{i1}+\beta_2 x_{i2}+\ldots+\beta_k x_{ik}}}$$

By dividing both the numerator and denominator by the numerator, we can further simplify this equation to determine p_i:

$$p_i=\frac{1}{1+e^{-\alpha-\beta_1 x_{i1}-\beta_2 x_{i2}-\ldots-\beta_k x_{ik}}}$$

This ensures that no matter what the values of the coefficients, intercept and independent variables are, the value of probability always lies between 0 and 1.

Tabulated below are values of odds and log-odds given the probability.

p (probability)	**odds**	**logit or log-odds**
0	0	Undefined
0.1	0.111111111	-2.197224577
0.2	0.25	-1.386294361
0.3	0.428571429	-0.84729786
0.4	0.666666667	-0.405465108
0.5	1	0
0.6	1.5	0.405465108
0.7	2.333333333	0.84729786
0.8	4	1.386294361
0.9	9	2.197224577
1	Upper limit breached	Undefined
	p/(1-p)	natural log (odds)
odds/(1 + odds)	exp(logit)	

For better illustration, we have calculated the probabilities of the event occurring, odds and corresponding log-odds. Tabulated below:

p	odds	logit
0.0000008	8.31529E-07	-14
0.0000023	2.26033E-06	-13
0.0000061	6.14421E-06	-12
0.0000167	1.67017E-05	-11
0.0000454	4.53999E-05	-10
0.0001234	0.00012341	-9
0.0003354	0.000335463	-8
0.0009111	0.000911882	-7
0.0024726	0.002478752	-6
0.0024726	0.002478752	-6
0.0179862	0.018315639	-4
0.0474259	0.049787068	-3
0.0758582	0.082084999	-2.5
0.1192029	0.135335283	-2
0.2689414	0.367879441	-1
0.5000000	1	0
0.7310586	2.718281828	1
0.8807971	7.389056099	2
0.9241418	12.18249396	2.5
0.9525741	20.08553692	3
0.9706878	33.11545196	3.5
0.9820138	54.59815003	4
0.9933071	148.4131591	5
0.9975274	403.4287935	6
0.9990889	1096.633158	7
0.9996646	2980.957987	8
0.9998766	8103.083928	9
0.9999546	22026.46579	10
0.9999833	59874.14172	11
0.9999939	162754.7914	12
0.9999977	442413.392	13
0.9999992	1202604.284	14

These values, when plotted, come up as an S curve.

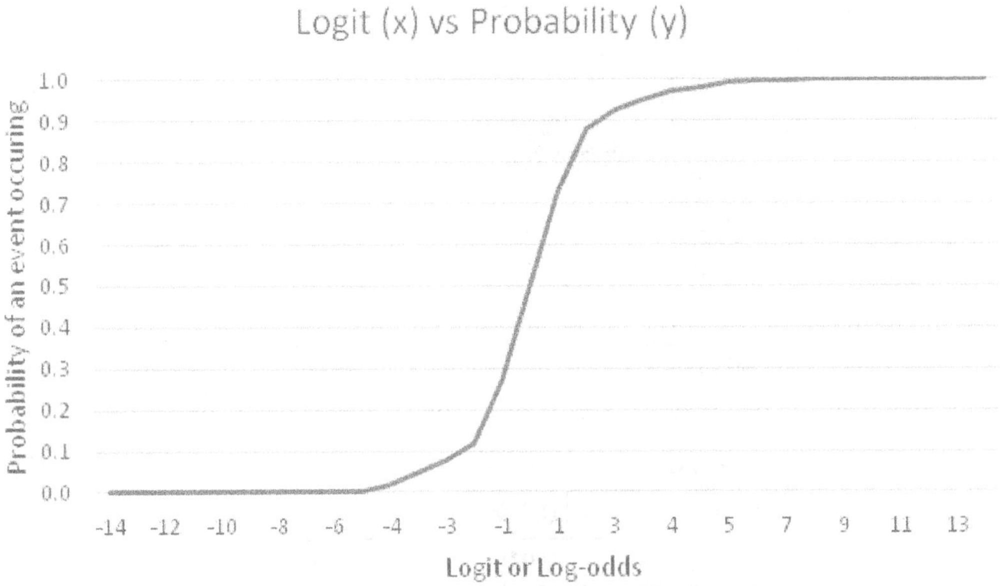

The Titanic dataset has 891 observations with 12 variables. The following is a description of each variable.

PassengerId	Unique identifier for a passenger
Survived	Survival indicator
Pclass	Passenger class
Name	Name of passenger
Sex	Gender of passenger
Age	Age of passenger
SibSp	Number of siblings/spouses aboard
Parch	Number of parents/children aboard
Ticket	Ticket number
Fare	Passenger fare
Cabin	Cabin of passenger
Embarked	Port of embarking (C = Cherbourg; Q = Queenstown; S = Southampton)

The task at hand is to be able to predict the survival of a passenger using passenger attributes. Let's check how the values look like.

R Function Used for Generating the Output

- *head()*

PassengerId	Survived	Pclass	Name	Sex	Age	SibSp	Parch	Ticket	Fare	Cabin	Embarked
1	0	3	Braund, Mr. Owen Harris	male	22	1	0	A/5 21171	7.2500		S
2	1	1	Cumings, Mrs. John Bradley (Florence Briggs Thayer)	female	38	1	0	PC 17599	71.2833	C85	C
3	1	3	Heikkinen, Miss. Laina	female	26	0	0	STON/O2. 3101282	7.9250		S
4	1	1	Futrelle, Mrs. Jacques Heath (Lily May Peel)	female	35	1	0	113803	53.1000	C123	S
5	0	3	Allen, Mr. William Henry	male	35	0	0	373450	8.0500		S
6	0	3	Moran, Mr. James	male	NA	0	0	330877	8.4583		Q

Table 4.1 Head of Titanic dataset

R Function Used for Generating the Output

- *summary()*

Next, let's see the summary of the dataset.

```
  PassengerId       Survived          Pclass          Name                Sex                   Age             SibSp           Parch             Ticket
 Min.   :  1.0   Min.   :0.0000   Min.   :1.000   Length:891         Length:891         Min.   : 0.42   Min.   :0.000   Min.   :0.0000   Length:891
 1st Qu.:223.5   1st Qu.:0.0000   1st Qu.:2.000   Class :character   Class :character   1st Qu.:20.12   1st Qu.:0.000   1st Qu.:0.0000   Class :character
 Median :446.0   Median :0.0000   Median :3.000   Mode  :character   Mode  :character   Median :28.00   Median :0.000   Median :0.0000   Mode  :character
 Mean   :446.0   Mean   :0.3838   Mean   :2.309                                         Mean   :29.70   Mean   :0.523   Mean   :0.3816
 3rd Qu.:668.5   3rd Qu.:1.0000   3rd Qu.:3.000                                         3rd Qu.:38.00   3rd Qu.:1.000   3rd Qu.:0.0000
 Max.   :891.0   Max.   :1.0000   Max.   :3.000                                         Max.   :80.00   Max.   :8.000   Max.   :6.0000
                                                                                        NA's   :177
      Fare            Cabin              Embarked
 Min.   :  0.00   Length:891         Length:891
 1st Qu.:  7.91   Class :character   Class :character
 Median : 14.45   Mode  :character   Mode  :character
 Mean   : 32.20
 3rd Qu.: 31.00
 Max.   :512.33
```

Table 4.2 Summary of Titanic dataset with numeric *Pclass*

Think. Do all columns have the appropriate data types based on our understanding of what the variables mean? *Survived*? *Pclass*? We will have to convert *Survived* to a categorical variable. However, you can argue why *Pclass* should be a categorical variable when there is a clear order in *Pclass* (1 → First class, 2 → Second class, 3 → Third class). Our argument is, why 1, 2, 3? Why not 10, 20, 30 to represent *Pclass* in a numeric form? For the moment, we will go ahead with converting *Pclass* to a categorical and ordinal variable. Categorical variables could be binary, nominal or ordinal.

Notice the variable *PassengerId*. Does it make any sense as numeric? Not at all. There is nothing like an average of *PassengerId*. It's a unique identifier of a passenger. Even though we are not going to use *PassengerId* during our analysis, for the sake of clarity, we will keep it converted to a categorical variable.

Let's take another look at the summary.

R Function Used for Generating the Output

- *summary()*

```
 PassengerId  Survived Pclass      Name                Sex                   Age            SibSp           Parch            Ticket               Fare
1      :  1   0:549    1:216   Length:891         Length:891         Min.   : 0.42   Min.   :0.000   Min.   :0.0000   Length:891         Min.   :  0.00
2      :  1   1:342    2:184   Class :character   Class :character   1st Qu.:20.12   1st Qu.:0.000   1st Qu.:0.0000   Class :character   1st Qu.:  7.91
3      :  1            3:491   Mode  :character   Mode  :character   Median :28.00   Median :0.000   Median :0.0000   Mode  :character   Median : 14.45
4      :  1                                                          Mean   :29.70   Mean   :0.523   Mean   :0.3816                      Mean   : 32.20
5      :  1                                                          3rd Qu.:38.00   3rd Qu.:1.000   3rd Qu.:0.0000                      3rd Qu.: 31.00
6      :  1                                                          Max.   :80.00   Max.   :8.000   Max.   :6.0000                      Max.   :512.33
(Other):885                                                          NA's   :177
   Cabin             Embarked
Length:891         Length:891
Class :character   Class :character
Mode  :character   Mode  :character
```

Table 4.3 Summary of Titanic dataset with categorical *Pclass*

Exploratory Data Analysis

Let's play around with some data exploration to understand what's happening. Do we agree that Survived is our dependent variable? Yes.

Refer to Table 4.4 showing a cross-tabulation between passenger class and survived indicator. The survival rate is highest for Pclass 1 (63%) and lowest for Pclass 3 (24%). We did have the understanding that *Pclass* 1 is the topmost class. Let's confirm our understanding by using *Fare*.

R Function Used for Generating the Output

- *table()*

		Survived 0	Survived 1	Survival rate
Pclass	1	80	136	63%
	2	97	87	47%
	3	372	119	24%

Table 4.4 Cross-tabulation of *Pclass* with *Survived*

R Function Used for Generating the Output

- *boxplot()*

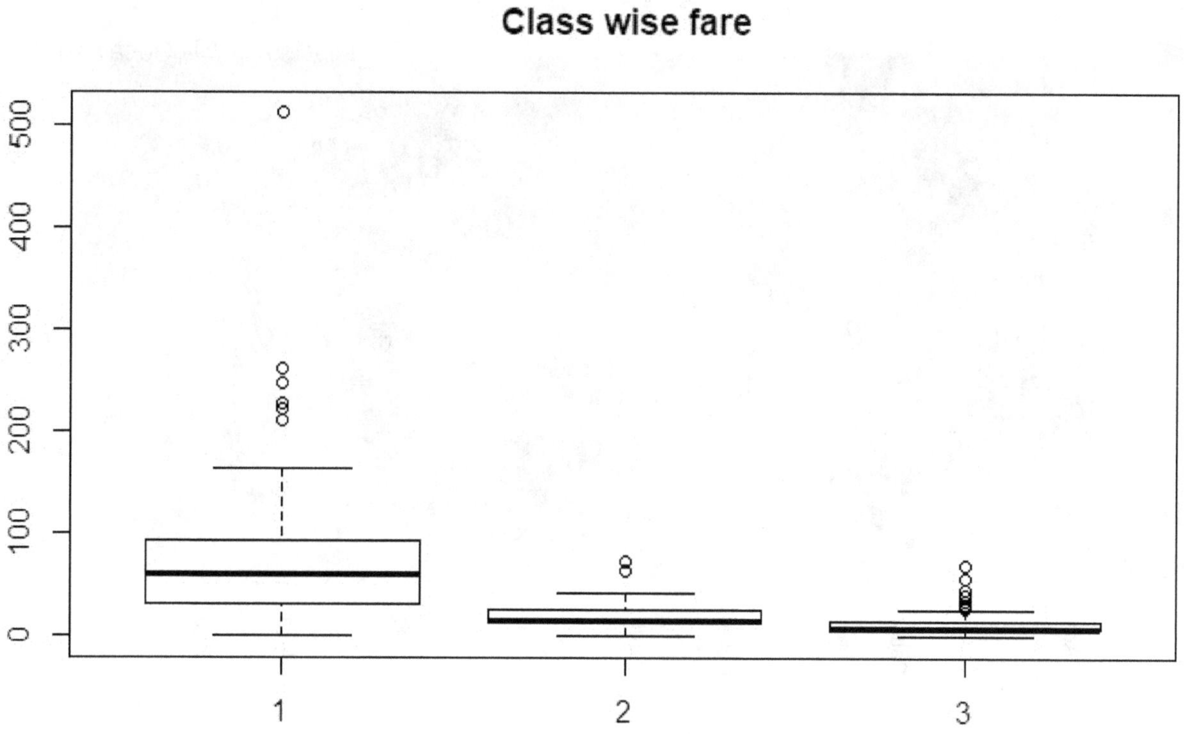

Figure 4.1 Box plot of class-wise fare

Indeed, Pclass 1 seems to be the costliest, and hence, our understanding is correct. Do you get an idea that class 1, being the costliest, had better safety measures than the other two classes? It could be true.

But we still have not taken care of the missing values. Figure 4.2 shows that there are missing values in the column *Age* for a few records. Missing values can be treated by either removing the observations having them from the dataset or by imputing them. One way of imputing is to fill up all missing ages with the average of the non-missing age values.

R Function Used for Generating the Output

- *missmap()*

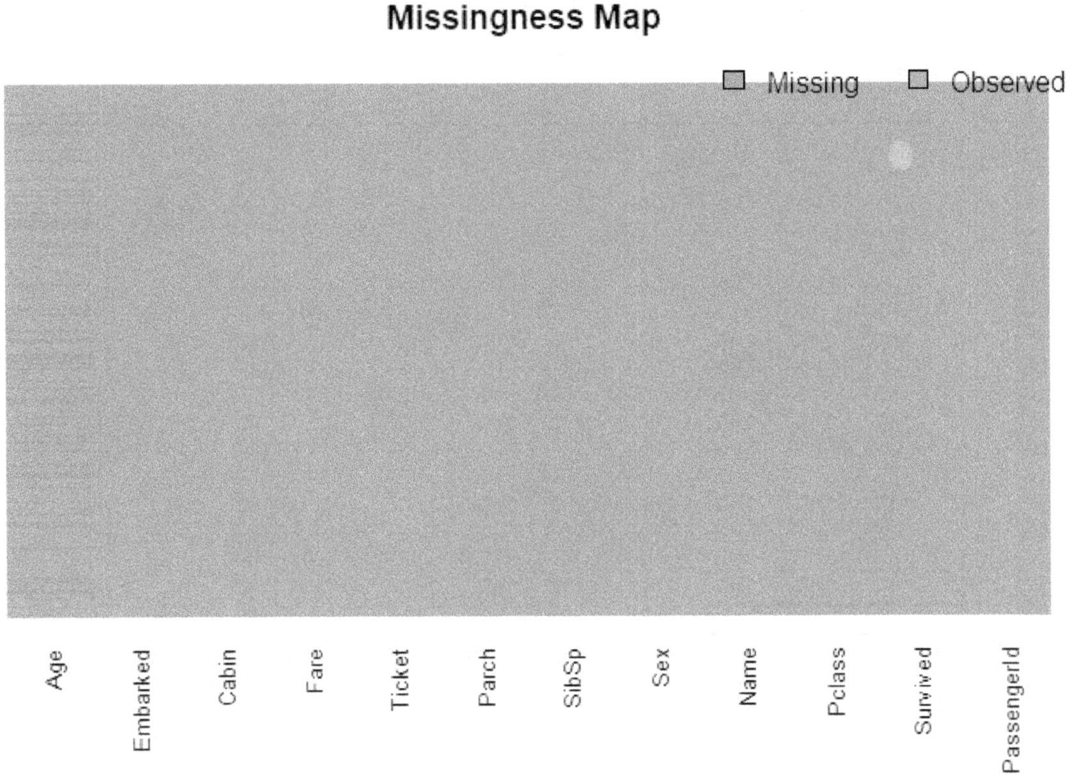

Figure 4.2 Missing-ness map of Titanic dataset (before handling missing values)

For the sake of simplicity, let's remove the observations having missing values in them. You have to be careful about the volume of information we are losing by removing the rows. The original dataset had 891 observations, which went down to 714 after the removal. This is a loss of around 20% of the observations, which is on the higher side. However, let's move on. Figure 4.3 shows the missing-ness of the resulting dataset. It is perfect. There are no missing values now.

R Function Used for Generating the Output

- *missmap()*

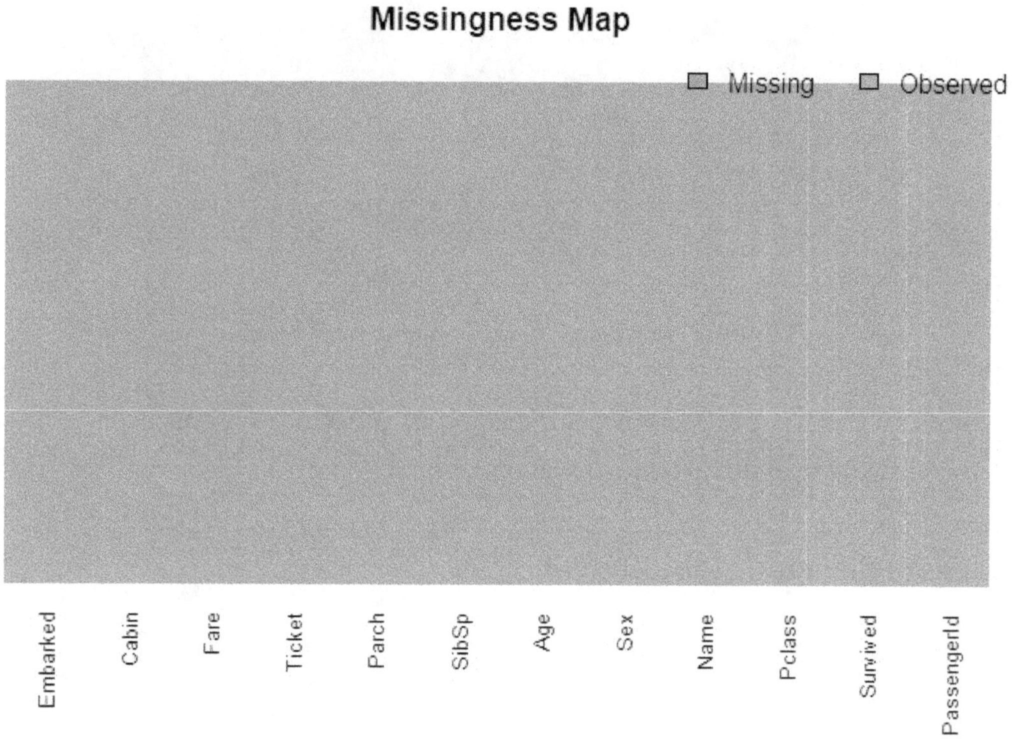

Figure 4.3 Missing-ness map of Titanic dataset (after handling missing values)

We have already seen the relationship between passenger class and survival. Let's do the same for other variables with survival.

R Function Used for Generating the Output

- *table()*

	Survived		Survival rate
	0	1	
female	64	197	75%
male	360	93	21%

Table 4.5 Survival rate of males versus females

According to Table 4.5 above, the survival chances of women are much higher than that of men.

R Function Used for Generating the Output

- *table()*

		Survived 0	Survived 1	Survival rate
Embarked	C	51	79	61%
	Q	20	8	29%
	S	353	201	36%

Table 4.6 Survival rate based on embarked location

See Table 4.6 above. Does the port of embarking have an influence on survival? What could be the reason behind the survival of many passengers embarking at C?

R Function Used for Generating the Output

- *boxplot()*

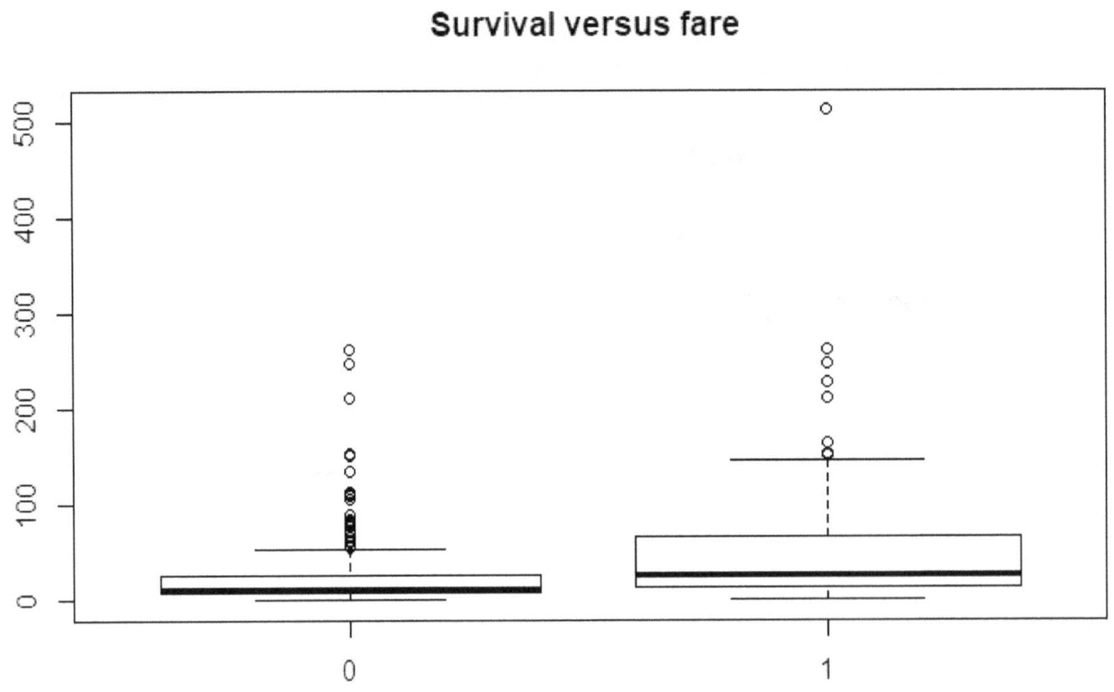

Figure 4.4 Box plot of survival versus fare

Refer to figure 4.4 above. The survival rate is generally higher for passengers whose fare was more. This is in line with our understanding of *Pclass* versus *Fare*. Many class 1 passengers survived and had paid more.

R Function Used for Generating the Output

- *boxplot()*

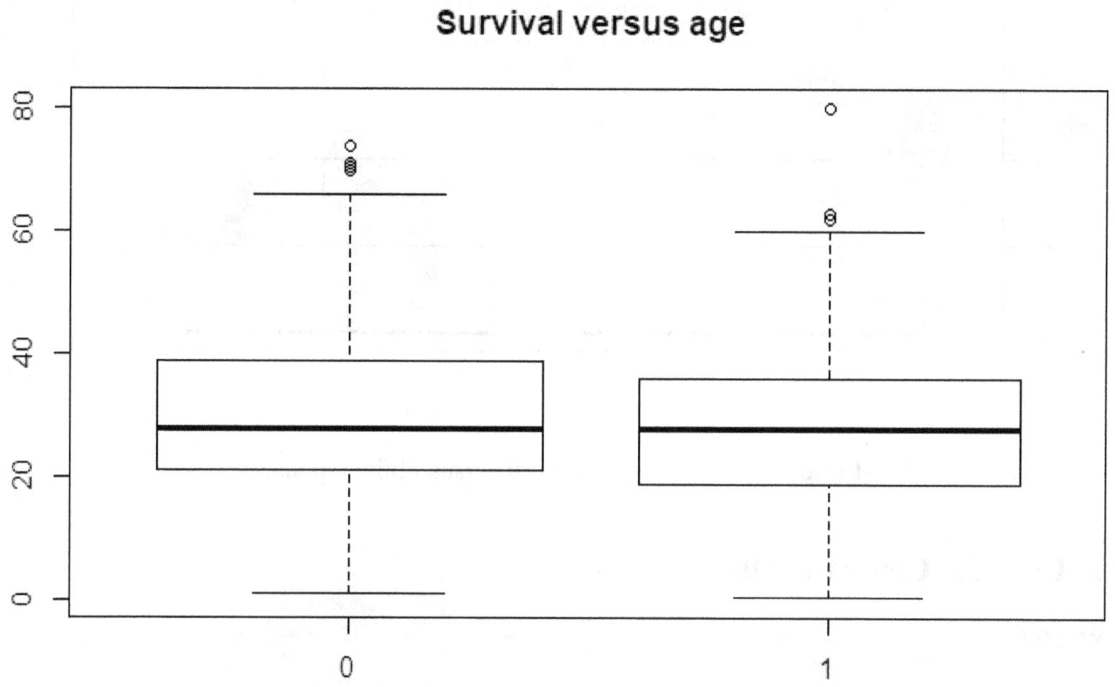

Figure 4.5 Box plot of survival versus age

As seen in figure 4.5 above, *age* does not seem to have any significant impact on survival ability. Both the box plots look similar.

We will leave you here and let you derive an understanding of the next two plots shown below (figures 4.6 and 4.7).

R Function Used for Generating the Output

- *boxplot()*

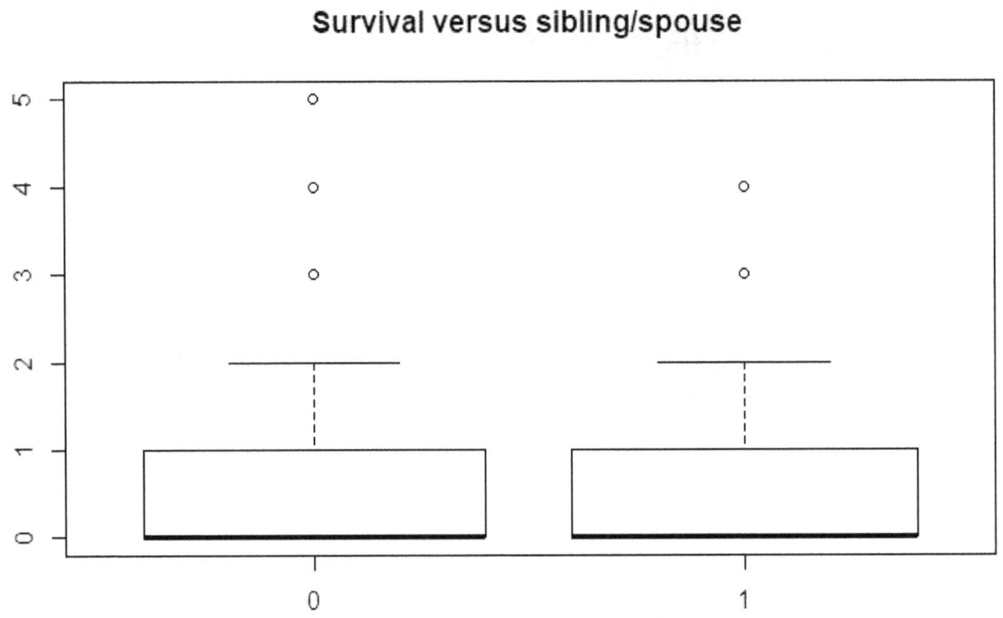

Figure 4.6 Box plot of survival versus sibling/spouse

R Function Used for Generating the Output

- *Boxplot()*

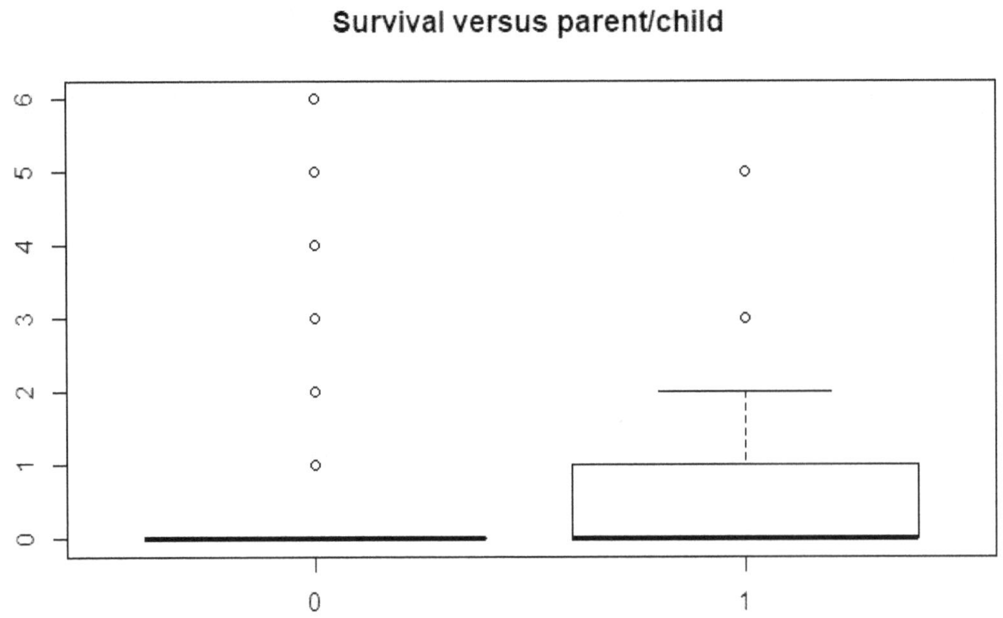

Figure 4.7 Box plot of survival versus parent/child

Model Building

Number of non-null rows in Titanic = 714

Number of rows in Train = 499 (70%)

Number of rows in Test = 215 (30%)

One important thing to note here, while dividing the dataset into train and test sets, is that the test set should be a good representative of the train set. This will ensure that we have given the same playing field while comparing the train performance with the test performance. One straightforward way of comparing the train set with the test set is shown below.

R Function Used for Generating the Output

- *summary()*

Train set profile

```
  PassengerId  Survived Pclass      Name               Sex                  Age            SibSp            Parch
 1      :  1   0:298    1:127   Length:499         Length:499         Min.   : 0.75   Min.   :0.0000   Min.   :0.0000
 2      :  1   1:201    2:121   Class :character   Class :character   1st Qu.:20.00   1st Qu.:0.0000   1st Qu.:0.0000
 7      :  1            3:251   Mode  :character   Mode  :character   Median :28.00   Median :0.0000   Median :0.0000
 8      :  1                                                          Mean   :29.44   Mean   :0.5251   Mean   :0.4329
 9      :  1                                                          3rd Qu.:38.00   3rd Qu.:1.0000   3rd Qu.:1.0000
 10     :  1                                                          Max.   :80.00   Max.   :5.0000   Max.   :5.0000
 (Other):493
    Ticket               Fare             Cabin             Embarked
 Length:499         Min.   :  0.00   Length:499         Length:499
 Class :character   1st Qu.:  8.05   Class :character   Class :character
 Mode  :character   Median : 15.85   Mode  :character   Mode  :character
                    Mean   : 34.58
                    3rd Qu.: 32.75
                    Max.   :512.33
```

R Function Used for Generating the Output

- *summary()*

Test set profile

```
  PassengerId  Survived Pclass      Name               Sex                  Age            SibSp            Parch
 3      :  1   0:126    1: 59   Length:215         Length:215         Min.   : 0.42   Min.   :0.0000   Min.   :0.0000
 4      :  1   1: 89    2: 52   Class :character   Class :character   1st Qu.:21.00   1st Qu.:0.0000   1st Qu.:0.0000
 5      :  1            3:104   Mode  :character   Mode  :character   Median :28.50   Median :0.0000   Median :0.0000
 16     :  1                                                          Mean   :30.31   Mean   :0.4837   Mean   :0.4279
 21     :  1                                                          3rd Qu.:39.00   3rd Qu.:1.0000   3rd Qu.:1.0000
 23     :  1                                                          Max.   :70.50   Max.   :5.0000   Max.   :6.0000
 (Other):209
    Ticket               Fare              Cabin             Embarked
 Length:215         Min.   :  0.000   Length:215         Length:215
 Class :character   1st Qu.:  8.383   Class :character   Class :character
 Mode  :character   Median : 15.046   Mode  :character   Mode  :character
                    Mean   : 34.969
                    3rd Qu.: 34.375
                    Max.   :512.329
```

Table 4.7 Train and test set profiles of Titanic

R Function Used for Generating the Output

- *Str()*

Let's check the structure of the Titanic dataset.

```
'data.frame':   714 obs. of  12 variables:
 $ PassengerId: Factor w/ 891 levels "1","2","3","4",..: 1 2 3 4 5 7 8 9 10 11 ...
 $ Survived   : Factor w/ 2 levels "0","1": 1 2 2 2 1 1 1 2 2 2 ...
 $ Pclass     : Factor w/ 3 levels "1","2","3": 3 1 3 1 3 1 3 3 2 3 ...
 $ Name       : chr  "Braund, Mr. Owen Harris" "Cumings, Mrs. John Bradley (Florence Briggs Thayer)"
s. Jacques Heath (Lily May Peel)" ...
 $ Sex        : chr  "male" "female" "female" "female" ...
 $ Age        : num  22 38 26 35 35 54 2 27 14 4 ...
 $ SibSp      : int  1 1 0 1 0 0 3 0 1 1 ...
 $ Parch      : int  0 0 0 0 0 0 1 2 0 1 ...
 $ Ticket     : chr  "A/5 21171" "PC 17599" "STON/O2. 3101282" "113803" ...
 $ Fare       : num  7.25 71.28 7.92 53.1 8.05 ...
 $ Cabin      : chr  "" "C85" "" "C123" ...
 $ Embarked   : chr  "S" "C" "S" "S" ...
```

Table 4.8 Structure of Titanic dataset

From an initial understanding point of view, let's pick the following independent variables. Survived is the dependent variable.

Pclass

Sex

Age

SibSp

Parch

Embarked

Fare

R Function Used for Generating the Output

- *glm()*

```
Call:
glm(formula = Survived ~ Pclass + Fare + Sex + Age + Embarked +
    SibSp + Parch, family = binomial, data = Train)

Deviance Residuals:
    Min       1Q   Median       3Q      Max
-2.7079  -0.6648  -0.3611   0.5488   2.4536

Coefficients:
              Estimate Std. Error z value Pr(>|z|)
(Intercept)  15.878413 882.743501   0.018 0.985649
Pclass2      -0.869125   0.394437  -2.203 0.027563 *
Pclass3      -2.360259   0.417228  -5.657 1.54e-08 ***
Fare          0.001260   0.003183   0.396 0.692218
Sexmale      -2.765431   0.276319 -10.008  < 2e-16 ***
Age          -0.037188   0.009945  -3.739 0.000184 ***
EmbarkedC   -11.715993 882.743470  -0.013 0.989411
EmbarkedQ   -12.530310 882.743663  -0.014 0.988675
EmbarkedS   -12.048841 882.743453  -0.014 0.989110
SibSp        -0.387433   0.151288  -2.561 0.010440 *
Parch         0.040816   0.157837   0.259 0.795948
---
Signif. codes:  0 '***' 0.001 '**' 0.01 '*' 0.05 '.' 0.1 ' ' 1

(Dispersion parameter for binomial family taken to be 1)

    Null deviance: 672.78  on 498  degrees of freedom
Residual deviance: 428.72  on 488  degrees of freedom
AIC: 450.72

Number of Fisher Scoring iterations: 13
```

Table 4.9 Summary of logistic regression output version 1

For the next iteration of building the model, pick the variables which are identified by a significant p-value (one, two or three stars).

R Function Used for Generating the Output

- *Glm()*

```
Call:
glm(formula = Survived ~ Pclass + Sex + Age + SibSp, family = binomial,
    data = Train)

Deviance Residuals:
    Min       1Q   Median       3Q      Max
-2.7100  -0.6583  -0.3730   0.5503   2.4584

Coefficients:
            Estimate Std. Error z value Pr(>|z|)
(Intercept)  4.08652    0.53791   7.597 3.03e-14 ***
Pclass2     -1.03379    0.34438  -3.002 0.002683 **
Pclass3     -2.57383    0.34785  -7.399 1.37e-13 ***
Sexmale     -2.77846    0.26661 -10.421  < 2e-16 ***
Age         -0.03791    0.00984  -3.853 0.000117 ***
SibSp       -0.36428    0.14074  -2.588 0.009644 **
---
Signif. codes:  0 '***' 0.001 '**' 0.01 '*' 0.05 '.' 0.1 ' ' 1

(Dispersion parameter for binomial family taken to be 1)

    Null deviance: 672.78  on 498  degrees of freedom
Residual deviance: 430.93  on 493  degrees of freedom
AIC: 442.93

Number of Fisher Scoring iterations: 5
```

Table 4.10 Summary of logistic regression output version 2

R Function Used for Generating the Output

- *Names()*

Names

```
"coefficients"  "residuals"  "fitted.values"      "effects"      "R"          "rank"
"qr"            "family"     "linear.predictors"  "deviance"     "aic"        "null.deviance"
"iter"          "weights"    "prior.weights"      "df.residual"  "df.null"    "y"
"converged"     "boundary"   "model"              "call"         "formula"    "terms"
"data"          "offset"     "control"            "method"       "contrasts"  "xlevels"
```

R Functions Used for Generating the Output

- *Model$fitted.values*
- *model$coefficients*
- *model$residuals*
- *model$aic*

Fitted (Predicted) Values

```
       105        559        546        890        766        573          8        207        595        451        620        481 
0.03238447 0.90409519 0.24629598 0.57988156 0.85675603 0.48578925 0.08058508 0.05502838 0.18349630 0.18924516 0.32926758 0.03142018 
       247        811        254        736        248        231        162        204        273        260        139         36 
0.63756963 0.09521660 0.05910718 0.08735812 0.89499286 0.91646336 0.82290501 0.04783982 0.81731183 0.76078882 0.13326476 0.34329992 
       190        704        450        789        718         41        390        226        258        433        153        653 
0.06718940 0.09853347 0.33995582 0.15869705 0.88381292 0.40898462 0.91744965 0.10910819 0.95022031 0.74951891 0.03324565 0.11284861 
```

Coefficients

```
(Intercept)      Pclass2      Pclass3      Sexmale          Age        SibSp 
 4.08652337  -1.03378676  -2.57382845  -2.77845781  -0.03791455  -0.36427734 
```

Residuals

```
      105       559       546       890       766       573         8       207       595       451       620       481 
-1.033468  1.106078 -1.326781  1.724490  1.167193  2.058506 -1.087648 -1.058233 -1.224734 -1.233418 -1.490908 -1.032439 
      247       811       254       736       248       231       162       204       273       260       139        36 
-2.759151 -1.105237 -1.062820 -1.095720  1.117327  1.091151  1.215207 -1.050243  1.223523  1.314425 -1.153755 -1.522765 
      190       704       450       789       718        41       390       226       258       433       153       653 
-1.072029 -1.109304  2.941559  6.301314  1.131461 -1.692003  1.089978 -1.122471  1.052388  1.334189 -1.034389 -1.127203 
```

Table 4.11 Summary of logistic regression output version 3

AIC = 443

Cut-off = 0.5. This is the threshold probability above which the observation is predicted as a 1 and below which the observation is predicted as a 0.

R Function Used for Generating the Output

- *head()*

```
PassengerId Survived Pclass                                Name    Sex Age SibSp Parch    Ticket    Fare Cabin Embarked
        105        0      3         Gustafsson, Mr. Anders Vilhelm   male  37     2     0   3101276  7.9250              S
        559        1      1 Taussig, Mrs. Emil (Tillie Mandelbaum) female  39     1     1    110413 79.6500   E67        S
        546        0      1           Nicholson, Mr. Arthur Ernest   male  64     0     0       693 26.0000              S
        890        1      1                  Behr, Mr. Karl Howell   male  26     0     0    111369 30.0000  C148        C
        766        1      1   Hogeboom, Mrs. John C (Anna Andrews) female  51     1     0     13502 77.9583   D11        S
        573        1      1          Flynn, Mr. John Irwin ("Irving")   male  36     0     0 PC 17474 26.3875   E25        S
predicted_binary
               0
               1
               0
               1
               1
               0
```

Table 4.12 Head of Titanic dataset

Diagnostics (Train Performance Measures)

1. *Confusion Matrix*

R Function Used for Generating the Output

- *table()*

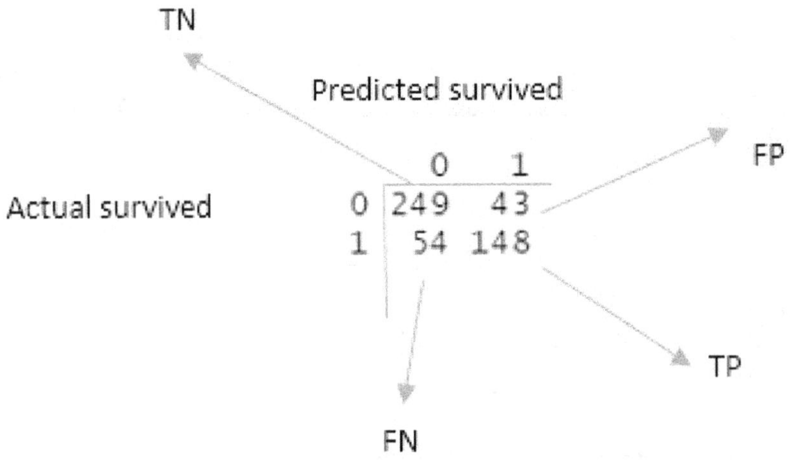

Table 4.13 Confusion matrix

Overall Accuracy

- (TN + TP)/(TN + TP + FN + FP)
- (The number of correct predictions)/(Total number of predictions)
- (249 + 148)/(249 + 148 + 54 + 43) = 80.4%

False Positives (FP)

- FPR = FP/(TN + FP)
- Actual dead passengers predicted as survived = 43
- FP Rate = 43/(249 + 43) = 14.7%

False Negatives (FN)

- FNR = FN/(FN + TP)
- Actual survived passengers predicted as dead = 54
- FN Rate = 54/(54 + 148) = 26.7%

True Positives (TP)

- TPR = TP/(FN + TP)
- Actual survived passengers predicted as survived = 249
- TP Rate = 148/(54 + 148) = 73.3%

True Negatives (TN)

- TNR = TN/(TN + FP)
- Actual dead passengers predicted as dead = 249
- TN Rate = 249/(249 + 43) = 63.5%

Sensitivity

- TP/(FN + TP)
- Out of actual survived, how many were predicted so
- Sensitivity = TP Rate = 148/(54 + 148) = 73.3%
- Also called TPR

Specificity

- TN/(TN + FP)
- Out of actual dead, how many were predicted so
- Specificity = TN Rate = 249/(249 + 43) = 63.5%
- Also called TNR

Precision

- TP/(FP + TP)
- Out of all predicted survived, how many actually survived
- 148/(43 + 148) = 77.5%

Recall

- TP/(TP + FN)
- Out of actual survived, how many were predicted so
- 148/(54 + 148) = 73.3%
- Also called TPR

Yes, you got it right. Sensitivity and recall have the same formula

F1 Score

- F1 = 2 * (Precision) * (Recall)/(Precision + Recall)
- 2 (0.775) (0.733)/(0.775 + 0.733) = 1.14/1.508 = 0.76

2. ***ROC Curve***

R Functions Used for Generating the Output

- *prediction()*
- *performance()*

- *slot()*
- *unlist()*
- *plot()*

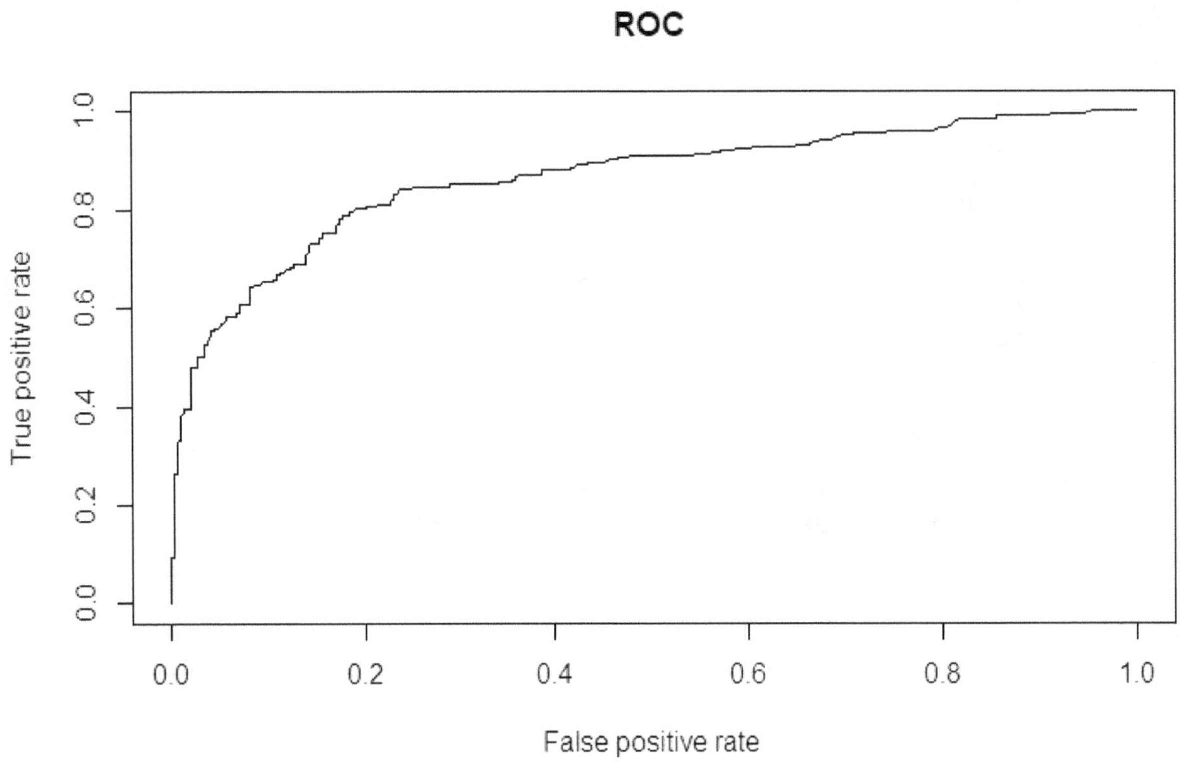

Figure 4.8 ROC curve

Let's discuss a few things on the ROC curve, as shown in figure 4.8 above. The X-axis denotes FPR and the Y-axis has TPR. What would be the favorable values of these two metrics? Obviously, FPR should be as low as possible and TPR should be as high as possible. A ROC curve covering a greater area around the top-left corner indicates a better model than a ROC curve that is flatter on the top-left corner.

For a single model built, there is one confusion matrix created for calculations of accuracy. One confusion matrix will produce one FPR-TPR pair. This gives us only a single point on the chart. How are we getting a continuous graph on the chart? Do you remember the function of the cut-off point? The output of logistic regression is not a binary 0 or 1. Instead, it is a continuous probability output, which indicates the probability of that row getting assigned a 1. For practical purposes, we will set a cut-off point (let's say 0.6). Anything equal to or above 0.6 is assigned a 1 and below 0.6 is assigned a 0. The decision of what value to set for the cut-off depends on the problem statement we are trying to solve. In use cases where false positives are dangerous, the cut-off point should be placed at a very high point (for example, 0.8). In other words, unless we are very sure that a row is a 1, we don't declare it a 1. The ROC curve is generated by taking the FPR-TPR pairs for different cut-off values.

Take the example of a person accused of committing a crime. We could argue that him getting wrongly convicted is far more disastrous than him getting acquitted by mistake. In this case, set the cut-off point very high.

Area under the curve (AUC) = 0.863. This is the area under the ROC curve. AUC ranges between 0 and 1. The values closer to 1 represent better models than those far below 1.

The Precision-recall Tradeoff

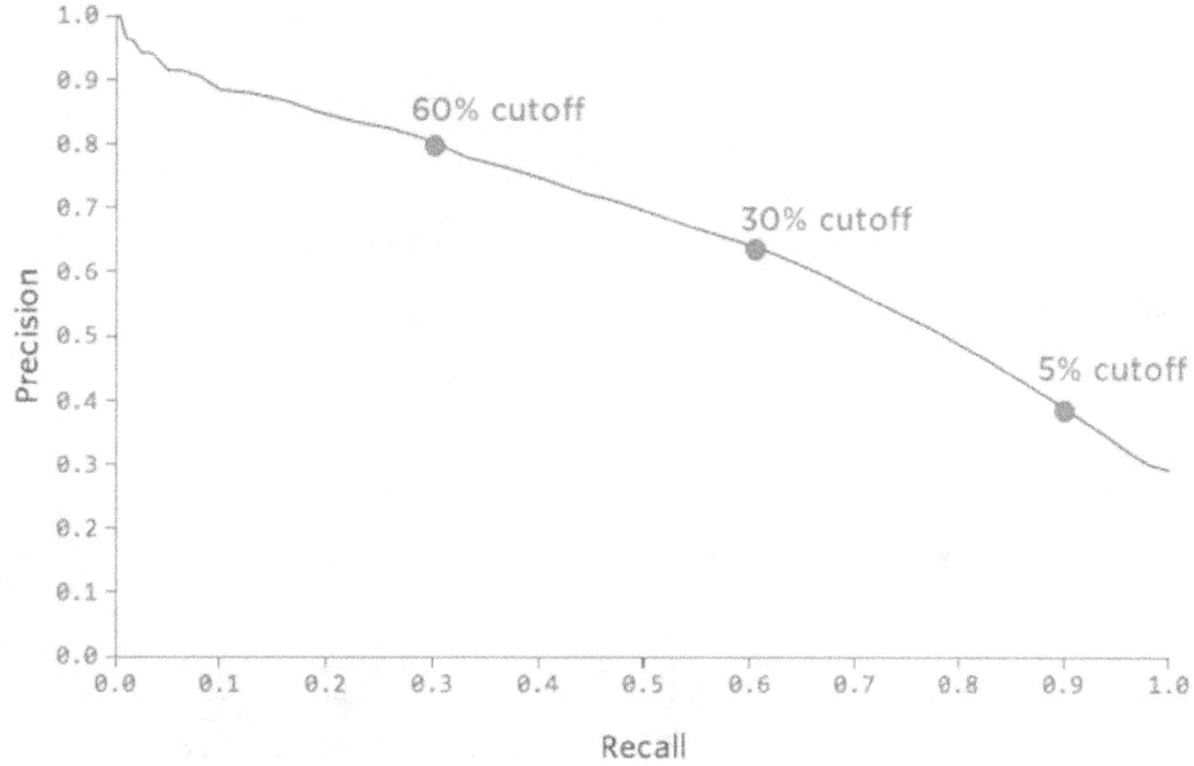

Figure 4.9 Precision-recall tradeoff

Figures 4.9 and 4.10 are dummy graphs used to drive home the concept. These two charts are not created from the logistic regression model built with the Titanic dataset. In figure 4.9 above, as we increase the recall by reducing the cut-off point, precision goes down. Similarly, when we tend to increase the precision by increasing the cut-off point, the recall goes down. Figure 4.10 below simply shows how a cut-off versus overall accuracy plot will look like. Such plots, along with sound domain knowledge, can be used to decide on an appropriate threshold.

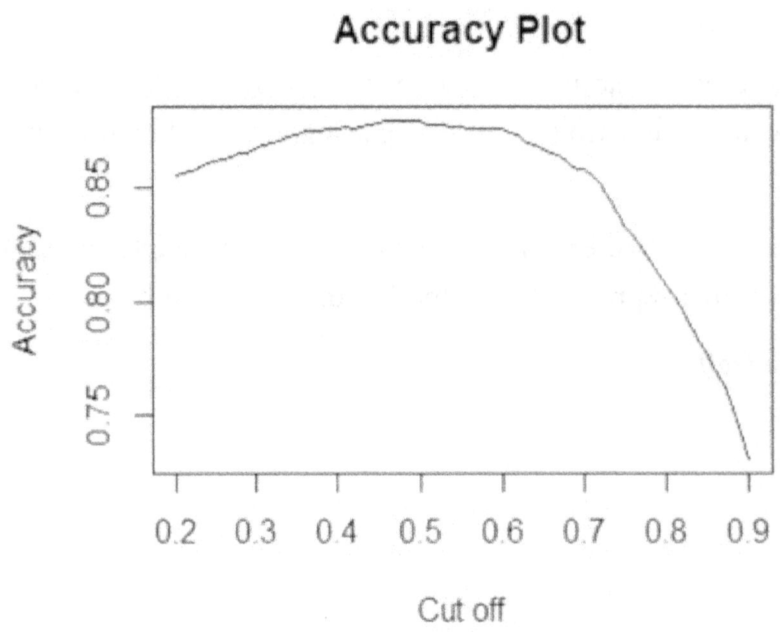

Figure 4.10 Plot of cut-off versus overall accuracy

3. ***Gains Table***

R Function Used for Generating the Output

- *A user-defined function is used*

bucket	total	totalresp	Cumresp	Gain	Cumlift
<dbl>	<int>	<dbl>	<dbl>	<dbl>	<dbl>
1	50	38	38	18.81188	1.881188
2	49	36	74	36.63366	1.831683
3	50	40	114	56.43564	1.881188
4	49	37	151	74.75248	1.868812
5	49	8	159	78.71287	1.574257
6	50	8	167	82.67327	1.377888
7	49	10	177	87.62376	1.251768
8	50	8	185	91.58416	1.144802
9	49	8	193	95.54455	1.061606
10	49	9	202	100.00000	1.000000

Table 4.14 Gains table

Table 4.14 shows the gains table for the logistic regression model we have built earlier. We will define each of the columns.

Bucket: This is also called a decile. The observations are divided into ten bins of equal size.

Total: The number of observations in each bucket

Total responses: In the gains table, the observations are arranged in decreasing order of probability predictions. This means that in the top deciles, we would find a high number of observations whose actual Y is a 1. There might be few records among the top deciles whose actual Y is a 0, but our model has given it a high probability by mistake. Similarly, in the lower deciles, we would expect a higher proportion of 0s and a smaller number of 1s if the model does well. In short, this column gives the number of actual 1s present in each decile.

Cumulative response: This column shows the cumulative number of actual 1s in each decile

Gain: This is a derived column that tells us the percentage of 1s covered in each decile. For example, the table indicates that 56.44% of 1s are covered by taking only 30% of the observations.

Cumulative lift: This column shows that the top 3 deciles using the model give us 1.88 times more 1s than simply randomly selecting 30% of observations from the dataset. Refer to figure 4.9 for details.

R Function Used for Generating the Output

- *Plot()*

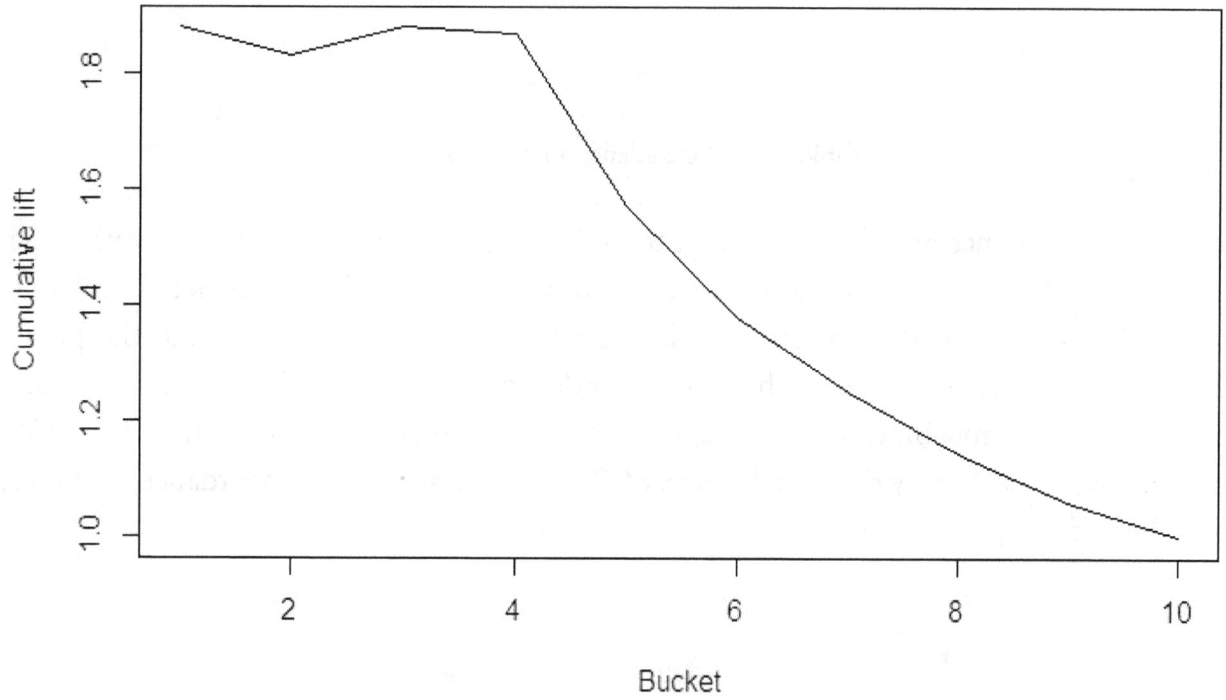

Figure 4.11 Cumulative lift

4. ***KS Statistic*** = 61.2

R Functions Used for Generating the Output

- *Performance()*
- *attr()*

The KS statistic is the maximum difference in percentage terms between the coverage of 1s and 0s in any of the deciles of the gains table.

5. ***Concordance/Discordance***

R Function Used for Generating the Output

- *A user-defined function*

```
$Concordance
[1] 0.862183

$Discordance
[1] 0.1362064

$Tied
[1] 0.001610606

$Pairs
[1] 58984
```

Table 4.15 Concordance analysis output

Let's explain concordance and discordance in the following way. Pair up each observation, which has an actual 0 with another observation that has an actual 1. Check the predicted probabilities of the two observations. If the predicted probability of the 1-record is more than the predicted probability of the 0- record, then we have a concordance pair. Else, we have a discordance pair. When the predicted probabilities are equal, we get a tie. As seen from Table 4.15 above, 58984 pairs were analyzed in the way described above. 86.2% of pairs displayed concordance, while 13.6% displayed discordance.

Diagnostics (Test Performance Measures)

View test data

R Function Used for Generating the Output

- *Head()*

	PassengerId	Survived	Pclass	Name	Sex	Age	SibSp	Parch	Ticket	Fare	Cabin	Embarked
	5	0	3	Allen, Mr. William Henry	male	35	0	0	373450	8.0500		S
	7	0	1	McCarthy, Mr. Timothy J	male	54	0	0	17463	51.8625	E46	S
	8	0	3	Palsson, Master. Gosta Leonard	male	2	3	1	349909	21.0750		S
	11	1	3	Sandstrom, Miss. Marguerite Rut	female	4	1	1	PP 9549	16.7000	G6	S
	13	0	3	Saundercock, Mr. William Henry	male	20	0	0	A/5. 2151	8.0500		S
	17	0	3	Rice, Master. Eugene	male	2	4	1	382652	29.1250		Q

With binary prediction

R Function Used for Generating the Output

- *Head()*

	PassengerId	Survived	Pclass	Name	Sex	Age	SibSp	Parch	Ticket	Fare	Cabin	Embarked	test_prediction_binary
	5	0	3	Allen, Mr. William Henry	male	35	0	0	373450	8.0500		S	0
	7	0	1	McCarthy, Mr. Timothy J	male	54	0	0	17463	51.8625	E46	S	0
	8	0	3	Palsson, Master. Gosta Leonard	male	2	3	1	349909	21.0750		S	0
	11	1	3	Sandstrom, Miss. Marguerite Rut	female	4	1	1	PP 9549	16.7000	G6	S	1
	13	0	3	Saundercock, Mr. William Henry	male	20	0	0	A/5. 2151	8.0500		S	0
	17	0	3	Rice, Master. Eugene	male	2	4	1	382652	29.1250		Q	0

Table 4.16 Test prediction in binary form

R Function Used for Generating the Output

- *Table()*

Confusion Matrix

	0	1
0	105	27
1	20	68

Table 4.17 Confusion matrix

Using the test confusion matrix, calculate the following metrics – Overall accuracy, FP, FN, TP, TN, Sensitivity, Specificity, Recall, Precision and F1 score.

In addition, create the ROC curve, AUC, gains table, KS statistic and concordance/discordance for the prediction on test data. Keep in mind that a good model will keep all test performance metrics close to train performance metrics. Moreover, both the sets of metrics should be within acceptable ranges.

Chapter 5

Decision Trees

We will discuss the following items in this chapter:

- Interpreting a decision tree model
- Zero-nodes and one-nodes
- The classification tree
  - Understand the *Carseats* dataset
  - Introduce a new categorical column for sales (high/low)
  - Interpreting textual representation of decision tree
  - Bias/variance
  - Tree pruning
  - Diagnostics – confusion matrix, overall accuracy, class accuracy
- The regression tree
  - Understand the Boston dataset
  - Tree pruning
  - Root Mean Square Error (RMSE)
- The random forest
- Variable importance plots

Let's use the Titanic dataset again. The Titanic dataset has 891 observations with 12 variables. The following is a description of each variable.

PassengerId	Unique identifier for a passenger
Survived	Survival indicator
Pclass	Passenger class
Name	Name of passenger
Sex	Gender of passenger
Age	Age of passenger
SibSp	Number of siblings/spouses aboard

Parch	Number of parents/children aboard
Ticket	Ticket number
Fare	Passenger fare
Cabin	Cabin of passenger
Embarked	Port of embarking (C = Cherbourg; Q = Queenstown; S = Southampton)

The task at hand is to be able to predict the survival of a passenger using passenger attributes. Let's check how the values look.

R Function Used for Generating the Output

- *head()*

PassengerId	Survived	Pclass	Name	Sex	Age	SibSp	Parch	Ticket	Fare	Cabin	Embarked
1	0	3	Braund, Mr. Owen Harris	male	22	1	0	A/5 21171	7.2500		S
2	1	1	Cumings, Mrs. John Bradley (Florence Briggs Thayer)	female	38	1	0	PC 17599	71.2833	C85	C
3	1	3	Heikkinen, Miss. Laina	female	26	0	0	STON/O2. 3101282	7.9250		S
4	1	1	Futrelle, Mrs. Jacques Heath (Lily May Peel)	female	35	1	0	113803	53.1000	C123	S
5	0	3	Allen, Mr. William Henry	male	35	0	0	373450	8.0500		S
6	0	3	Moran, Mr. James	male	NA	0	0	330877	8.4583		Q

Table 5.1 Top six rows of Titanic

R Function Used for Generating the Output

- *Summary()*

Next, let's see the summary of the dataset.

PassengerId	Survived	Pclass	Name	Sex	Age	SibSp	Parch	Ticket
Min. : 1.0	Min. :0.0000	Min. :1.000	Length:891	Length:891	Min. : 0.42	Min. :0.000	Min. :0.0000	Length:891
1st Qu.:223.5	1st Qu.:0.0000	1st Qu.:2.000	Class :character	Class :character	1st Qu.:20.12	1st Qu.:0.000	1st Qu.:0.0000	Class :character
Median :446.0	Median :0.0000	Median :3.000	Mode :character	Mode :character	Median :28.00	Median :0.000	Median :0.0000	Mode :character
Mean :446.0	Mean :0.3838	Mean :2.309			Mean :29.70	Mean :0.523	Mean :0.3816	
3rd Qu.:668.5	3rd Qu.:1.0000	3rd Qu.:3.000			3rd Qu.:38.00	3rd Qu.:1.000	3rd Qu.:0.0000	
Max. :891.0	Max. :1.0000	Max. :3.000			Max. :80.00	Max. :8.000	Max. :6.0000	
					NA's :177			

Fare	Cabin	Embarked
Min. : 0.00	Length:891	Length:891
1st Qu.: 7.91	Class :character	Class :character
Median : 14.45	Mode :character	Mode :character
Mean : 32.20		
3rd Qu.: 31.00		
Max. :512.33		

Table 5.2 Summary of Titanic dataset

Carry out a similar data exploration, as discussed in chapter four (Logistic Regression). Convert data types of variables as necessary.

R Function Used for Generating the Output

- *Rpart.plot()*

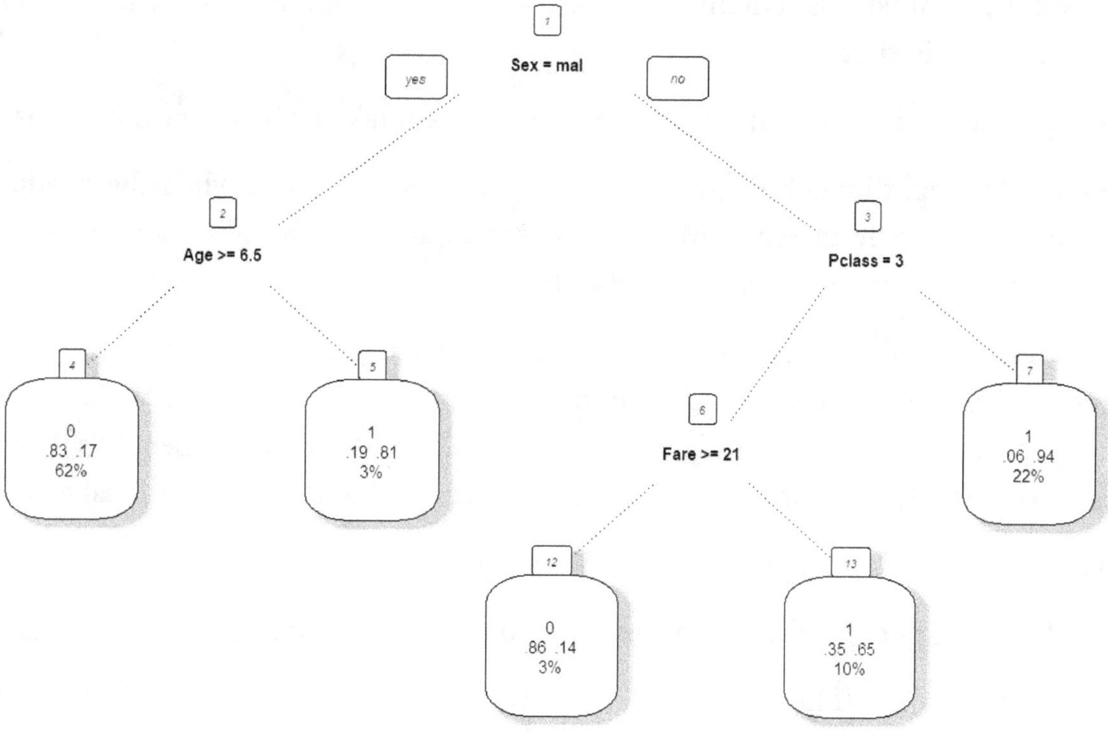

Figure 5.1 Decision tree model on Titanic dataset

What's the way to interpret such a tree? Instead, we should ask how many different ways are there to represent the output of a tree-based model – the answer is many. The pictorial representation and details mentioned in each node could vary from tool to tool or from package to package within the same tool. However, irrespective of the visualization, the underlying structure of the tree-based model remains the same.

The following explanation is based on figure 5.1 shown above. Let's understand a few terminologies related to a tree.

Decision node: Any intermediate node that is further split into two or more nodes is called a decision node.

Terminal node: A terminal node is a node where the splitting ends. Any node that is not a decision node has to be a terminal node (also called a leaf node).

Root node: The first node where splitting starts is the root node.

Parent/child node: A node that gets split into two or more nodes is called a parent node. The resulting nodes, which are outcomes of the split, are known as child nodes. Note that a particular node can very well be a parent node and a child node, too, when seen in different contexts.

Condition: A parent node is split into child nodes based on a condition involving the most eligible variable at that point in time.

Yes branch: The left branch of the split stands for the path taken when the condition is satisfied.

No branch: The right branch of the split stands for the path taken when the condition is not satisfied. This is a generally agreed convention. Interchanging left and right branches does not cause a problem as long as the branches are explicitly labeled.

Zero/one node: In the case of a binary tree, a terminal node must be tagged as either 0 or 1 node. Traveling down the tree, we should end up in one of the terminal nodes. The tagging should let us know the class of the dependent variable. If a terminal node has a higher number of 0s than 1s, then it is called a 'zero node'. The terminal node that has a higher number of 1s than 0s is called a 'one node'.

Binary tree: If a parent node can be split into exactly two child nodes, then it's called a binary tree.

Tagging: The assignment of the dominant class to the terminal node is called tagging.

Split stopping criterion: This is a condition, which, when satisfied, stops further splitting of the node. An example is 'the minimum number of observations in a node should be 50'. Another example could be 'maximum depth of the tree should be 5'.

Depth of a tree: The maximum number of branches we can traverse from top to bottom indicates the depth of the tree.

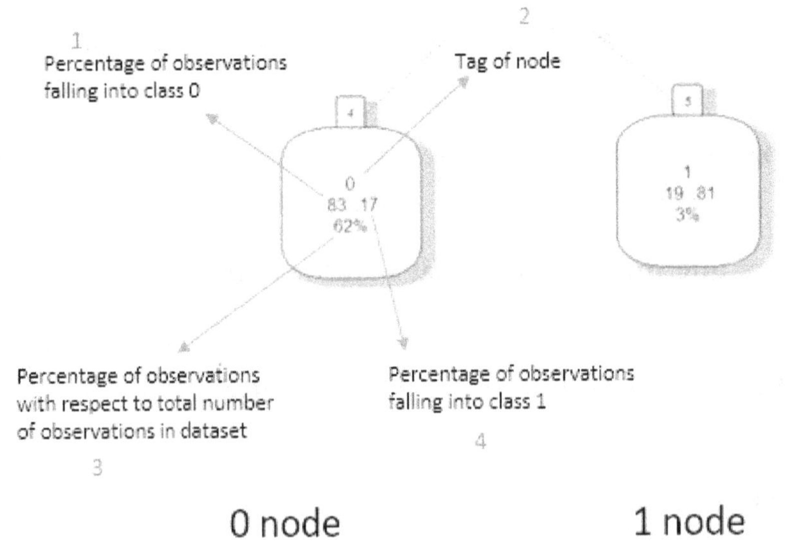

Figure 5.2 Decision tree nodes

R Function Used for Generating the Output

- *rpart.plot()*

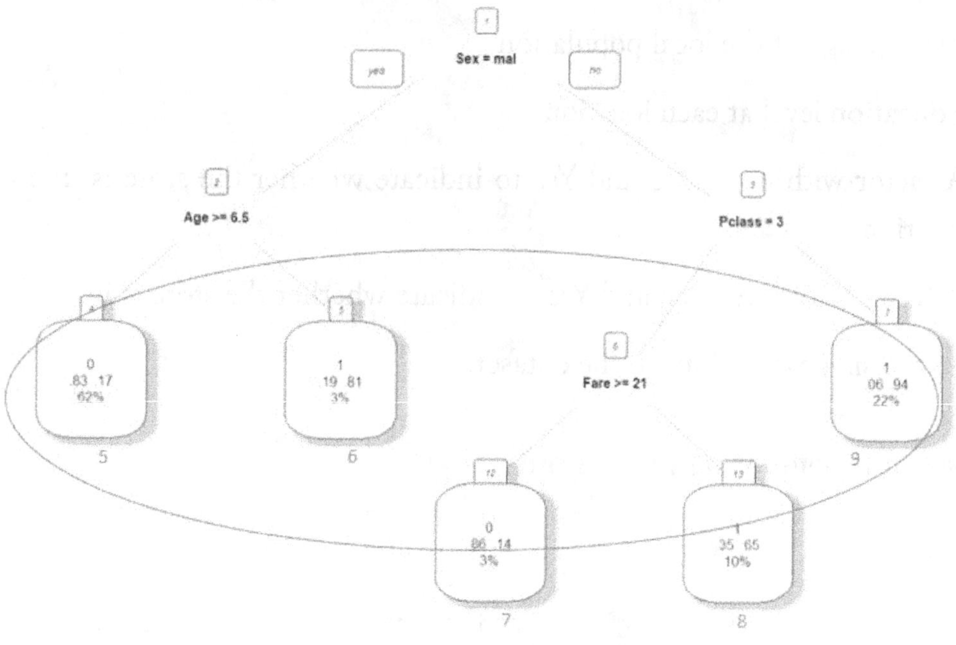

Figure 5.3 Terminal nodes

Refer to figure 5.2, which mentions the significance of each value in a node. The sum of the fraction of observations falling into class 0 and the fraction of observations falling into class 1 is 1. As seen in figure 5.3, the sum of the percentage of observations distributed across all terminal nodes is 100%.

Classification Tree

Package: ISLR

Dataset: Carseats

Carseats is a simulated dataset containing sales of child car seats at 400 different stores. Check the columns found in the dataset.

A data frame with 400 observations on the following 11 variables.

Sales	Unit sales (in thousands) at each location
CompPrice	Price charged by competitor at each location
Income	Community income level (in thousands of dollars)
Advertising	Local advertising budget for company at each location (in thousands of dollars)
Population	Population size in region (in thousands)

Price	Price the company charges for car seats at each site
ShelveLoc	A factor with levels Bad, Good and Medium indicating the quality of the shelving location for the car seats at each site
Age	Average age of the local population
Education	Education level at each location
Urban	A factor with levels No and Yes to indicate whether the store is in an urban or rural location
US	A factor with levels No and Yes to indicate whether the store is in the US or not

Let's look at the top six observations of the dataset.

R Function Used for Generating the Output

- *Head()*

```
Sales CompPrice Income Advertising Population Price ShelveLoc Age Education Urban  US
 9.50       138     73          11        276   120       Bad  42        17   Yes Yes
11.22       111     48          16        260    83      Good  65        10   Yes Yes
10.06       113     35          10        269    80    Medium  59        12   Yes Yes
 7.40       117    100           4        466    97    Medium  55        14   Yes Yes
 4.15       141     64           3        340   128       Bad  38        13   Yes  No
10.81       124    113          13        501    72       Bad  78        16    No Yes
```

R Function Used Ffor Generating the Output

- *Summary()*

Summary of Sales

```
  Min. 1st Qu.  Median    Mean 3rd Qu.    Max.
 0.000   5.390   7.490   7.496   9.320  16.270
```

Table 5.3 View of *Carseats* dataset and summary of sales

What could be a good problem statement that can be solved using the *Carseats* dataset shown in Table 5.3 above? The analytics problem statement is to predict sales when other attributes are known to us?

Given the dataset, can you guess which is the dependent variable and which are the independent variables? Your answer might be *Sales* for the dependent variable. All others are independent variables. Indeed, *Sales* is the dependent variable when we want to predict sales.

Can we say that *Age* could be a dependent variable? Yes, we can. However, it will very well be an outcome variable for a different problem statement. Analytics problem statement: Can we predict the average age of the local population given all other data related to sales of car seats? Why someone would like to predict the average age of the local population. But technically, it still makes sense. Any regression model will easily predict the age for you. So what did we learn? The identification of a target variable depends on the business problem statement we are trying to solve.

R Function Used for Generating the Output

- *Hist()*

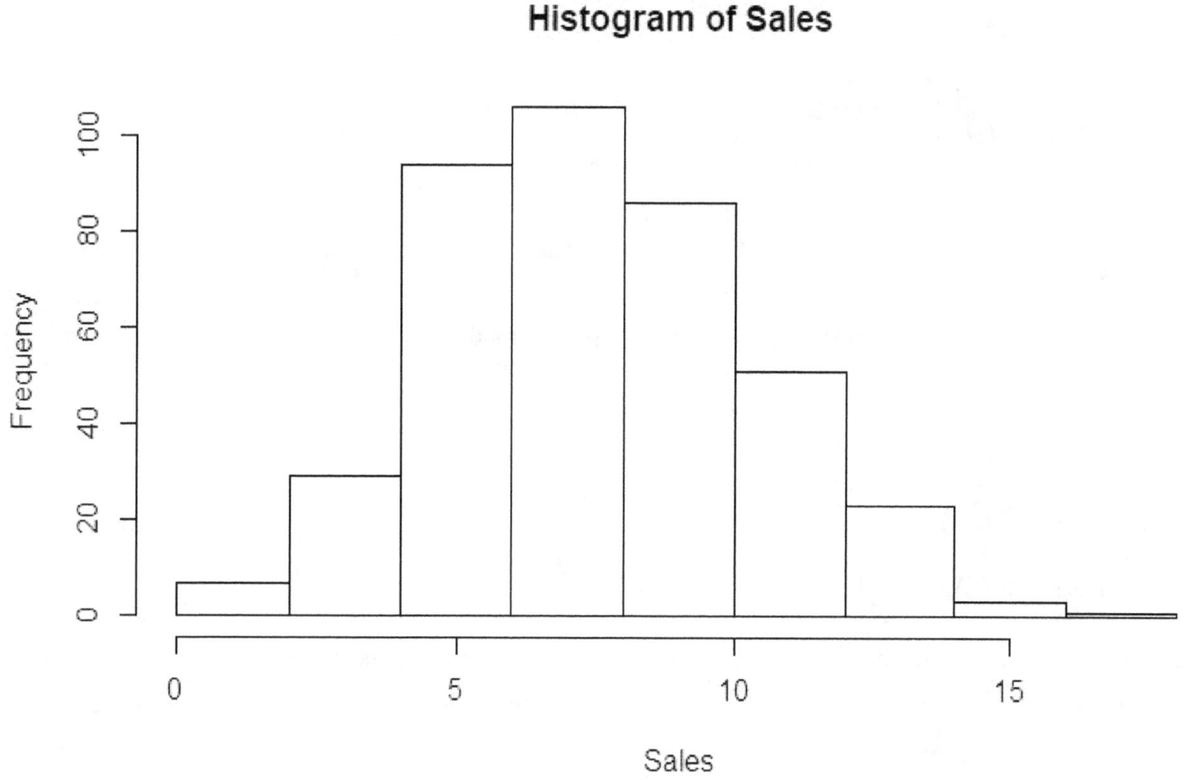

Figure 5.4 Histogram of sales

Wait for a second! We are demonstrating a classification modeling technique. Hence, the outcome variable should be categorical in nature. *Sales* is a continuous variable. We have to convert *Sales* into a binary categorical target. Look at the histogram in figure 5.4 above, showing the distribution of *Sales*. To make it work, let's take all sales below eight as low and those above or equal to eight as high. As seen in Table 5.4 below, we have added a new column to the dataset called '*High*' having values 'Yes' and 'No'.

R Function Used for Generating the Output

- *Head()*

Sales	CompPrice	Income	Advertising	Population	Price	ShelveLoc	Age	Education	Urban	US	High
9.50	138	73	11	276	120	Bad	42	17	Yes	Yes	Yes
11.22	111	48	16	260	83	Good	65	10	Yes	Yes	Yes
10.06	113	35	10	269	80	Medium	59	12	Yes	Yes	Yes
7.40	117	100	4	466	97	Medium	55	14	Yes	Yes	No
4.15	141	64	3	340	128	Bad	38	13	Yes	No	No
10.81	124	113	13	501	72	Bad	78	16	No	Yes	Yes

R Function Used for Generating the Output

- *table()*

No	Yes
236	164

Table 5.4 Conversion of *Sales* to High/Low

While the original analytics problem statement was 'predict sales', the new problem statement becomes 'predict sales category – high or low'.

Carseats: 400 rows

Train: 280 rows (70%)

Test: 120 rows (30%)

We have taken a 70-30 distribution of train-test datasets, which is usually what is taken. The idea is that we will build a model using 280 observations and test the performance of the model using 120 rows of the *Carseats* dataset.

R Function Used for Generating the Output

- *Plot()*

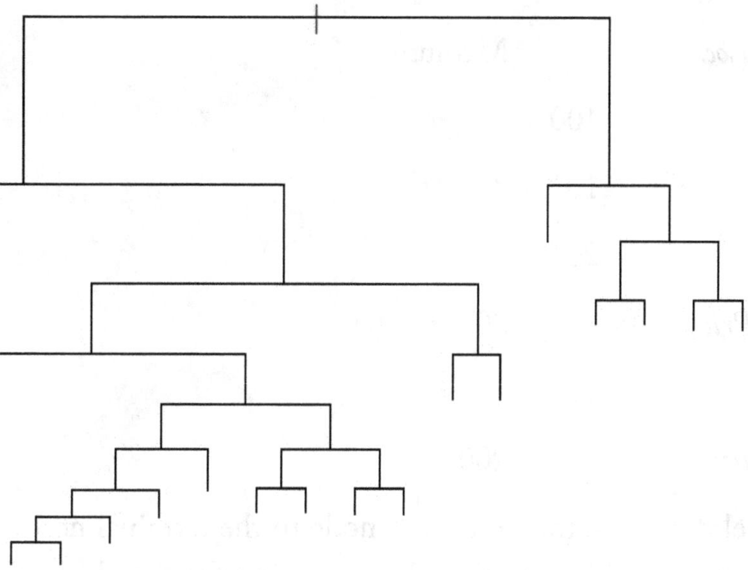

A

R Function Used for Generating the Output

- *text()*

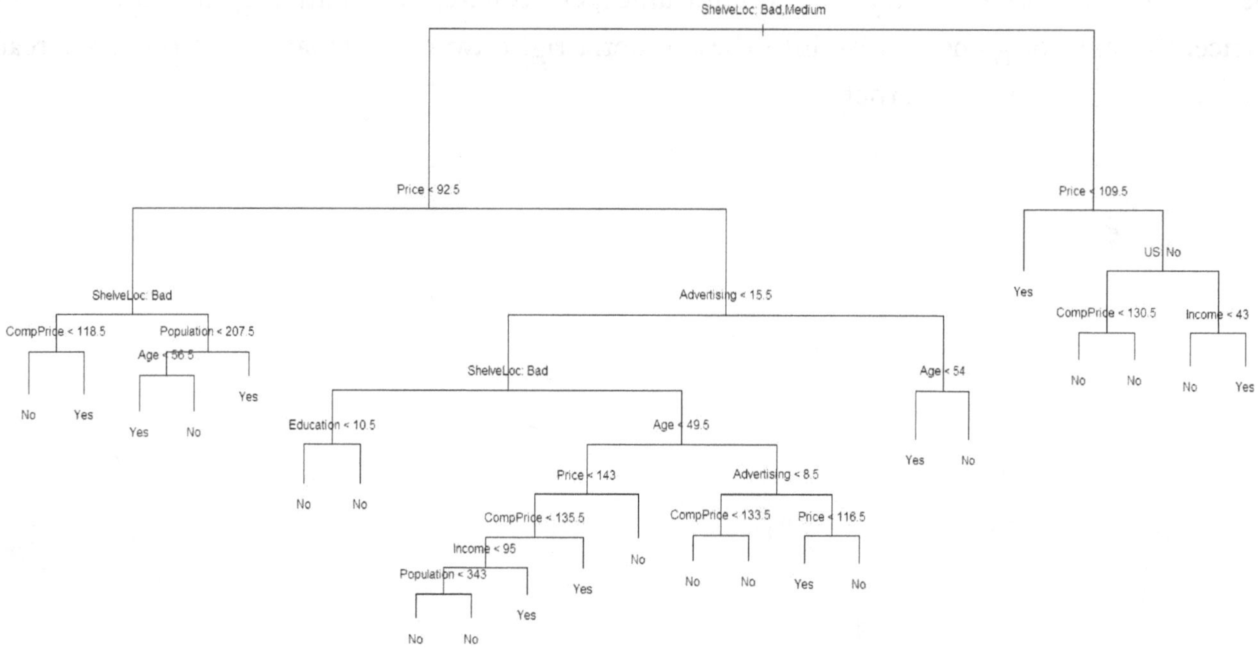

B

Figure 5.5 Decision tree for *Carseats* use case

As depicted in figure 5.5, we first see a skeleton of the tree model we have built (A). Then we see the tree with annotation (B). The tree has 23 terminal nodes. The good thing with decision trees is that they lay open the internal working of the tree. It is not a black-box model. Let's see how a prediction is made using the model. Consider an observation which has the following feature values.

ShelveLoc: Medium

Price: 100

Advertising: 10

Age: 20

CompPrice: 30

Income: 90

Population: 200

If we travel down the tree from root node to the terminal node through the branches satisfying the conditions, we would know that the prediction for the above observation is 'No', which stands for low sales. Similarly, we can bring in any observation, and our tree will be able to predict manually by traveling down the tree. However, we don't have to do the exercise manually every time as the analytics tool will usually have a function for predicting for an observation using the tree model. The manual flow was demonstrated to let you know how a tree prediction works.

Keep in mind that a parent node of a tree is split into two child nodes based on four criteria (not depending on each other). They are the Gini index, chi-square, information gain and reduction in variance. We are not going to dive into these criteria right away. Explanations of them are readily available in books and the internet.

R Function Used for Generating the Output

- *tree()*

```
1) root 280 378.400 No ( 0.59286 0.40714 )
  2) ShelveLoc: Bad,Medium 217 266.600 No ( 0.69585 0.30415 )
    4) Price < 92.5 38  48.820 Yes ( 0.34211 0.65789 )
      8) ShelveLoc: Bad 14  18.250 No ( 0.64286 0.35714 )
       16) CompPrice < 118.5 7   0.000 No ( 1.00000 0.00000 ) *
       17) CompPrice > 118.5 7   8.376 Yes ( 0.28571 0.71429 ) *
      9) ShelveLoc: Medium 24  21.630 Yes ( 0.16667 0.83333 )
       18) Population < 207.5 13  16.050 Yes ( 0.30769 0.69231 )
         36) Age < 56.5 7   0.000 Yes ( 0.00000 1.00000 ) *
         37) Age > 56.5 6   7.638 No ( 0.66667 0.33333 ) *
       19) Population > 207.5 11   0.000 Yes ( 0.00000 1.00000 ) *
    5) Price > 92.5 179 192.600 No ( 0.77095 0.22905 )
     10) Advertising < 15.5 161 151.800 No ( 0.81988 0.18012 )
       20) ShelveLoc: Bad 52  16.950 No ( 0.96154 0.03846 )
         40) Education < 10.5 6   7.638 No ( 0.66667 0.33333 ) *
         41) Education > 10.5 46   0.000 No ( 1.00000 0.00000 ) *
       21) ShelveLoc: Medium 109 122.000 No ( 0.75229 0.24771 )
         42) Age < 49.5 42  57.360 No ( 0.57143 0.42857 )
           84) Price < 143 34  47.020 Yes ( 0.47059 0.52941 )
            168) CompPrice < 135.5 25  33.650 No ( 0.60000 0.40000 )
              336) Income < 95 19  21.900 No ( 0.73684 0.26316 )
                672) Population < 343 12  16.300 No ( 0.58333 0.41667 ) *
                673) Population > 343 7   0.000 No ( 1.00000 0.00000 ) *
              337) Income > 95 6   5.407 Yes ( 0.16667 0.83333 ) *
            169) CompPrice > 135.5 9   6.279 Yes ( 0.11111 0.88889 ) *
           85) Price > 143 8   0.000 No ( 1.00000 0.00000 ) *
         43) Age > 49.5 67  52.870 No ( 0.86567 0.13433 )
           86) Advertising < 8.5 46  16.450 No ( 0.95652 0.04348 )
            172) CompPrice < 133.5 35   0.000 No ( 1.00000 0.00000 ) *
            173) CompPrice > 133.5 11  10.430 No ( 0.81818 0.18182 ) *
           87) Advertising > 8.5 21  26.730 No ( 0.66667 0.33333 )
            174) Price < 116.5 10  13.460 Yes ( 0.40000 0.60000 ) *
            175) Price > 116.5 11   6.702 No ( 0.90909 0.09091 ) *
     11) Advertising > 15.5 18  22.910 Yes ( 0.33333 0.66667 )
       22) Age < 54 9   0.000 Yes ( 0.00000 1.00000 ) *
       23) Age > 54 9  11.460 No ( 0.66667 0.33333 ) *
  3) ShelveLoc: Good 63  69.160 Yes ( 0.23810 0.76190 )
    6) Price < 109.5 21   0.000 Yes ( 0.00000 1.00000 ) *
    7) Price > 109.5 42  54.750 Yes ( 0.35714 0.64286 )
     14) US: No 15  17.400 No ( 0.73333 0.26667 )
       28) CompPrice < 130.5 7   0.000 No ( 1.00000 0.00000 ) *
       29) CompPrice > 130.5 8  11.090 No ( 0.50000 0.50000 ) *
     15) US: Yes 27  22.650 Yes ( 0.14815 0.85185 )
       30) Income < 43 5   6.730 No ( 0.60000 0.40000 ) *
       31) Income > 43 22   8.136 Yes ( 0.04545 0.95455 ) *
```

A

R Functions Used for Generating the Output

- *cbind()*
- *head()*
- *table()*

Sales	CompPrice	Income	Advertising	Population	Price	ShelveLoc	Age	Education	Urban	US	High	tree.pred
9.50	138	73	11	276	120	Bad	42	17	Yes	Yes	Yes	No
4.15	141	64	3	340	128	Bad	38	13	Yes	No	No	No
4.69	132	113	0	131	124	Medium	76	17	No	Yes	No	No
3.98	122	35	2	393	136	Medium	62	18	Yes	No	No	No
11.17	107	117	11	148	118	Good	52	18	Yes	Yes	Yes	Yes
8.71	149	95	5	400	144	Medium	76	18	No	No	Yes	No

B

		Predicted	
		No	Yes
Actual	No	61	9
	Yes	18	32

C

Table 5.5

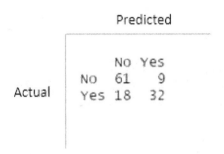

A. Decision tree represented in textual form
B. Check predictions
C. Confusion matrix

Table 5.5A shows the same tree represented in the text form. The nodes where we see a star are the terminal nodes.

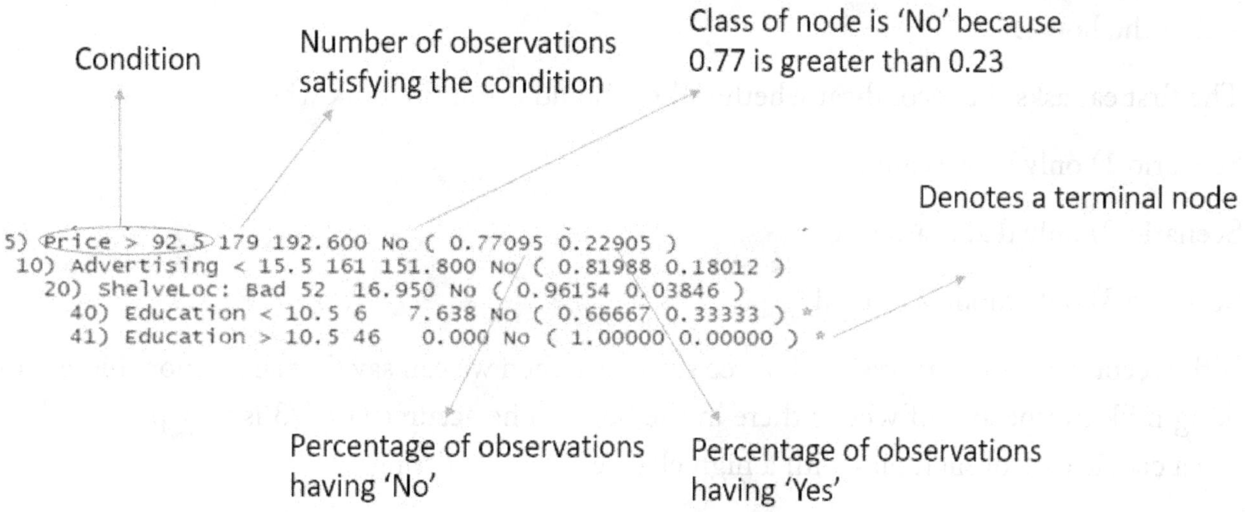

Table 5.5A.5 Interpreting textual representation of decision tree

Table 5.5B displays an additional column that corresponds to the prediction of the test data. The confusion matrix from the model performance is shown in Table 5.5C. The accuracy of prediction is approximately 78%.

Let us think about what the ideal number of terminal nodes is that a tree should have. Too many terminal nodes will make the model very complicated and will lead to overfitting. In the presence of overfitting, the model tends to perform very well on the train data but performs poorly on the test data. Optimum generalization is key to the concept of modeling. The model should be neither too generic nor too specific. It is the right time now to talk about the bias-variance tradeoff.

The bias-variance tradeoff is pivotal for arriving at an optimally performing supervised learning model. Bias is the difference between the average prediction of a model and the actual value. The model with high bias oversimplifies the model and pays little attention to train data points, thereby leading to high approximations and hence, high errors on train and test datasets. Variance, on the other hand, is a measure of how well spread the data is. It pays a lot of attention to train data points but does poorly on the data, which it has never seen. So which is better? Neither. Both are errors. When we add up the bias and variance, we get a total error. And what is the way to play with the bias-variance tradeoff space? Increase or decrease the complexity of the model. If your question is how to recognize a complex model, then try adding an insane number of independent variables or try increasing the depth of a decision tree to 30 levels.

In other words, bias represents how unfair something is with respect to others. Variance represents how likely some things change with respect to others. Let us take an example of two cats discussing whether they should drink milk, assuming that they can drink milk only when the baby alone is around in the house.

The first cat asks the second cat whether they should drink the milk when

Scenario 1) only baby is around

Scenario 2) only dad is around

Scenario 3) only mom is around

If the second cat answers 'yes' to all three scenarios, then we can say that she is more biased toward drinking milk irrespective of who is there in the house. The accuracy of 1/3 is very poor in this case. This is a classic case of high bias with a high chance of under-fitting.

If the second cat answers 'yes' to scenario one alone, that means she is following the assumption condition cent percent. She has learned the correct answer so much that if you twist and ask her a question such as 'Can we drink milk when baby sister is around?', her answer might as well be in the negative. This is a classic case of high variance with a high chance of overfitting where there is no generalization.

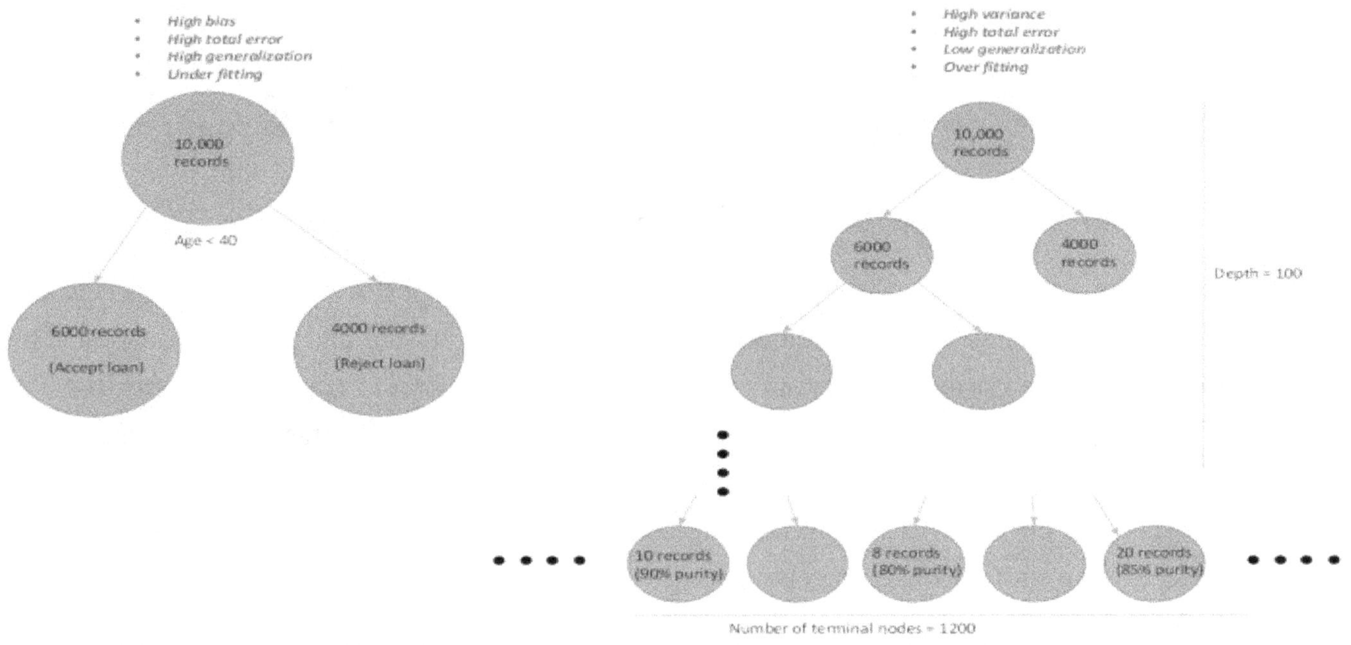

A

R Functions Used for Generating the Output

- *Cv.tree()*
- *plot()*

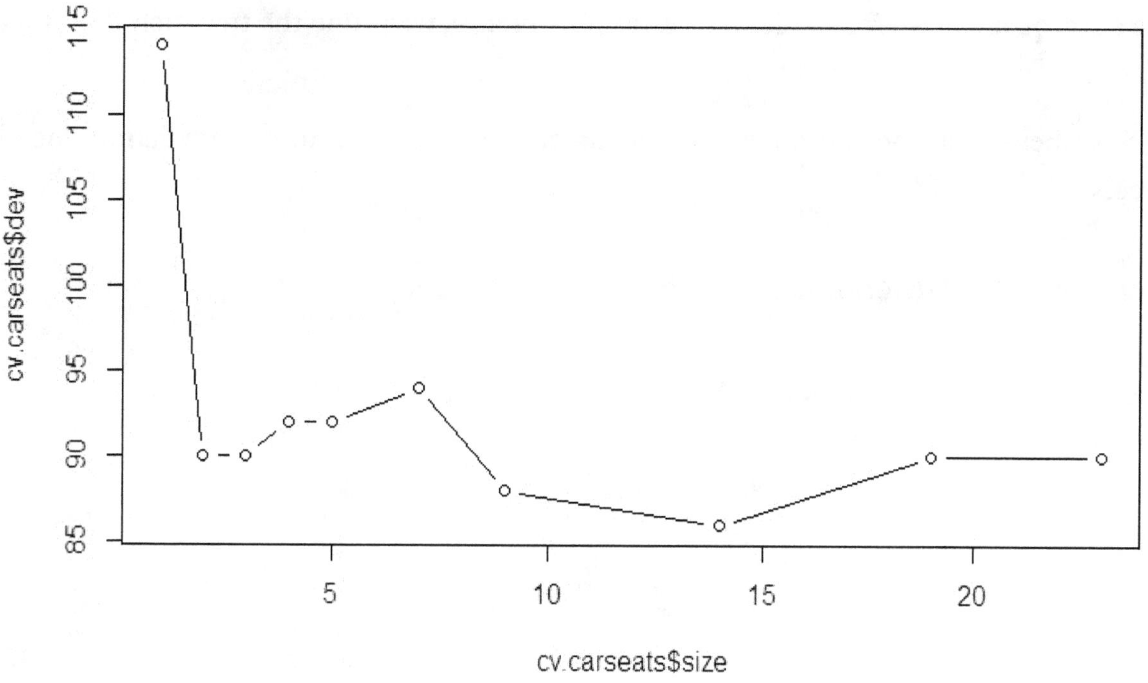

B

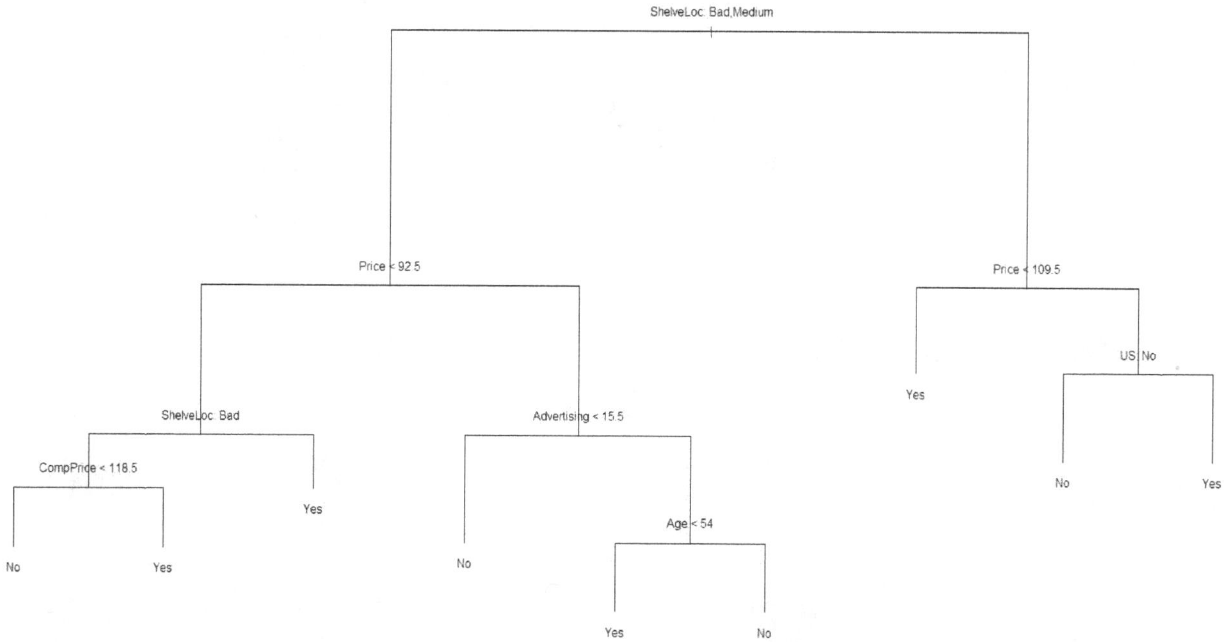

C

Figure 5.6

A. Bias-variance tradeoff
B. Choosing the right number of terminal nodes
C. Pruned decision tree model

Figure 5.6A displays two scenarios: under-fitting and overfitting. From figure 5.6B, we can roughly determine that the ideal number of terminal nodes for our tree should be nine. That is where the model has a reasonably low cross-validation error rate. Hence, we prune the tree such that it has nine terminal nodes. The decision tree is plotted in figure 5.6C above.

Table 5.6A below has the additional column added corresponding to the prediction done by the pruned tree.

R Functions Used for Generating the Output

- *Head()*
- *table()*

Sales	CompPrice	Income	Advertising	Population	Price	ShelveLoc	Age	Education	Urban	US	High	tree.pred	prune.pred
9.50	138	73	11	276	120	Bad	42	17	Yes	Yes	Yes	No	No
4.15	141	64	3	340	128	Bad	38	13	Yes	No	No	No	No
4.69	132	113	0	131	124	Medium	76	17	No	Yes	No	No	No
3.98	122	35	2	393	136	Medium	62	18	Yes	No	No	No	No
11.17	107	117	11	148	118	Good	52	18	Yes	Yes	Yes	Yes	Yes
8.71	149	95	5	400	144	Medium	76	18	No	No	Yes	No	No

A

Predicted

		No	Yes
Actual	No	63	7
	Yes	23	27

Accuracy = 75% (pruned to 9 nodes)

B

		Predicted	
		No	Yes
Actual	No	62	8
	Yes	16	34

Accuracy = 80% (pruned to 14 nodes)

C

Table 5.6 Decision tree pruning

We have realized that when the tree is pruned to 14 nodes, we get better accuracy than when it is pruned to 9 nodes. What conclusions are you able to draw from this analysis?

Regression Tree

Package: MASS

Dataset: Boston

This data frame contains the following columns:

crim	Per capita crime rate by town.
zn	Proportion of residential land zoned for lots over 25,000 square feet
indus	Proportion of non-retail business acres per town.
chas	Charles River dummy variable (= 1 if tract bounds river; 0 otherwise).
nox	Nitrogen oxides concentration (parts per 10 million).
rm	Average number of rooms per dwelling.
age	Proportion of owner-occupied units built prior to 1940.
dis	Weighted mean of distances to five Boston employment centers.
rad	Index of accessibility to radial highways.
tax	Full-value property-tax rate per \$10,000.
ptratio	Pupil-teacher ratio by town.
black	$1000(Bk - 0.63)^2$ where Bk is the proportion of blacks by town.

lstat Lower status of the population (percent).

medv Median value of owner-occupied homes in \$1000s.

Let's build a decision tree to predict the house prices (*medv*) using the rest of the variables available with us.

R Function Used for Generating the Output

- *Head()*

```
     crim zn indus chas   nox    rm  age    dis rad tax ptratio  black lstat medv
0.00632 18  2.31    0 0.538 6.575 65.2 4.0900   1 296    15.3 396.90  4.98 24.0
0.02731  0  7.07    0 0.469 6.421 78.9 4.9671   2 242    17.8 396.90  9.14 21.6
0.02729  0  7.07    0 0.469 7.185 61.1 4.9671   2 242    17.8 392.83  4.03 34.7
0.03237  0  2.18    0 0.458 6.998 45.8 6.0622   3 222    18.7 394.63  2.94 33.4
0.06905  0  2.18    0 0.458 7.147 54.2 6.0622   3 222    18.7 396.90  5.33 36.2
0.02985  0  2.18    0 0.458 6.430 58.7 6.0622   3 222    18.7 394.12  5.21 28.7
```

A

R Function Used for Generating the Output

- *Summary()*

```
     crim               zn              indus            chas              nox               rm             age              dis
Min.   : 0.00632   Min.   :  0.00   Min.   : 0.46   Min.   :0.00000   Min.   :0.3850   Min.   :3.561   Min.   :  2.90   Min.   : 1.130
1st Qu.: 0.08204   1st Qu.:  0.00   1st Qu.: 5.19   1st Qu.:0.00000   1st Qu.:0.4490   1st Qu.:5.886   1st Qu.: 45.02   1st Qu.: 2.100
Median : 0.25651   Median :  0.00   Median : 9.69   Median :0.00000   Median :0.5380   Median :6.208   Median : 77.50   Median : 3.207
Mean   : 3.61352   Mean   : 11.36   Mean   :11.14   Mean   :0.06917   Mean   :0.5547   Mean   :6.285   Mean   : 68.57   Mean   : 3.795
3rd Qu.: 3.67708   3rd Qu.: 12.50   3rd Qu.:18.10   3rd Qu.:0.00000   3rd Qu.:0.6240   3rd Qu.:6.623   3rd Qu.: 94.08   3rd Qu.: 5.188
Max.   :88.97620   Max.   :100.00   Max.   :27.74   Max.   :1.00000   Max.   :0.8710   Max.   :8.780   Max.   :100.00   Max.   :12.127
      rad              tax           ptratio          black             lstat            medv
Min.   : 1.000   Min.   :187.0   Min.   :12.60   Min.   :  0.32   Min.   : 1.73   Min.   : 5.00
1st Qu.: 4.000   1st Qu.:279.0   1st Qu.:17.40   1st Qu.:375.38   1st Qu.: 6.95   1st Qu.:17.02
Median : 5.000   Median :330.0   Median :19.05   Median :391.44   Median :11.36   Median :21.20
Mean   : 9.549   Mean   :408.2   Mean   :18.46   Mean   :356.67   Mean   :12.65   Mean   :22.53
3rd Qu.:24.000   3rd Qu.:666.0   3rd Qu.:20.20   3rd Qu.:396.23   3rd Qu.:16.95   3rd Qu.:25.00
Max.   :24.000   Max.   :711.0   Max.   :22.00   Max.   :396.90   Max.   :37.97   Max.   :50.00
```

B

Table 5.7 Sample and summary of *Boston* dataset

Table 5.7A is a sample set of first six observations from the *Boston* dataset. Moreover, Table 5.7B gives us a summary of the dataset.

Boston: 506 rows

Train: 354 rows (70%)

Test: 152 rows (30%)

Refer to the tree shown in figure 5.7 below, having ten terminal nodes. This time the terminal nodes have continuous numeric values instead of classes from a categorical dependent variable.

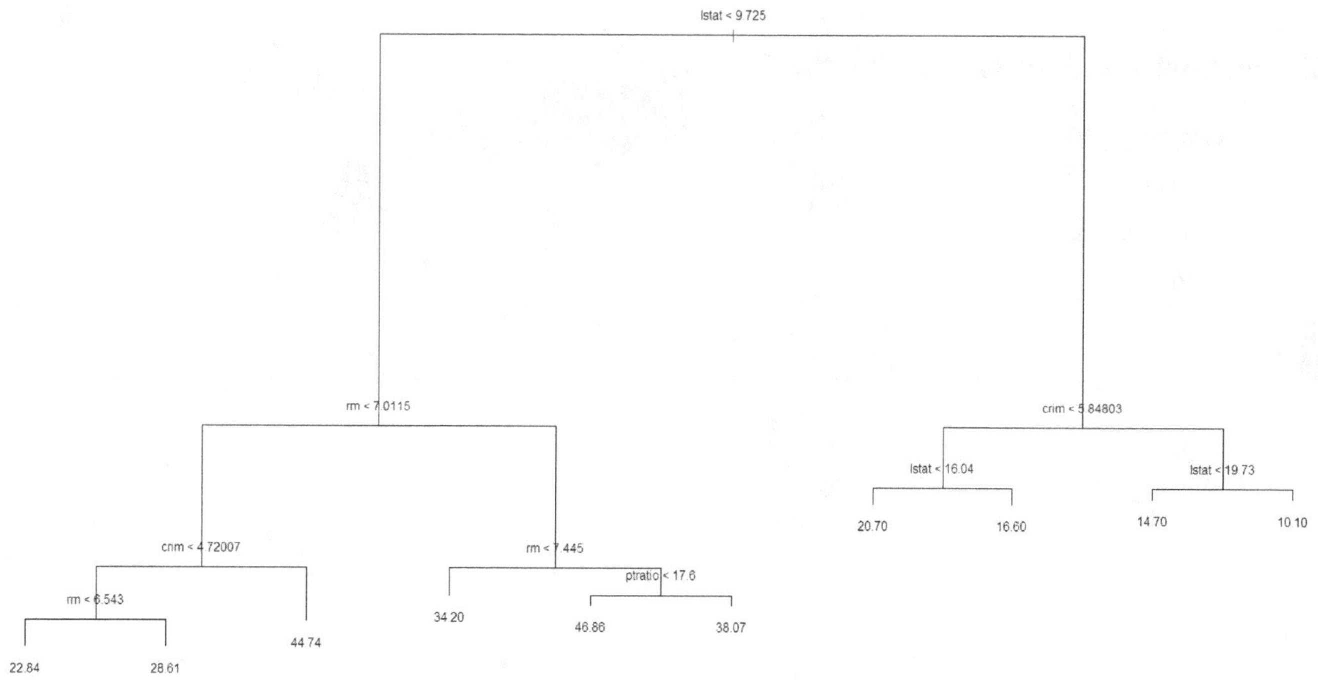

Figure 5.7 Decision tree with ten terminal nodes

```
1) root 354 29880.0 22.40
  2) lstat < 9.725 152 11560.0 29.46
    4) rm < 7.0115 113  4562.0 26.16
      8) crim < 4.72007 108  2203.0 25.30
       16) rm < 6.543 62    600.5 22.84 *
       17) rm > 6.543 46    722.4 28.61 *
      9) crim > 4.72007 5    553.4 44.74 *
    5) rm > 7.0115 39  2204.0 39.02
     10) rm < 7.445 20    364.8 34.20 *
     11) rm > 7.445 19    887.6 44.08
       22) ptratio < 17.6 13    132.3 46.86 *
       23) ptratio > 17.6 6    437.8 38.07 *
  3) lstat > 9.725 202  5072.0 17.10
    6) crim < 5.84803 138  2077.0 19.27
     12) lstat < 16.04 90    852.4 20.70 *
     13) lstat > 16.04 48    698.6 16.60 *
    7) crim > 5.84803 64   930.4 12.40
     14) lstat < 19.73 32    331.0 14.70 *
     15) lstat > 19.73 32    260.8 10.10 *
```

Table 5.8 Decision tree with ten terminal nodes (textual representation)

Table 5.8 is the textual representation of the original tree. We understand that we can prune the tree to have five terminal nodes instead of the ten terminal nodes for a better performance of the model. At the least, that is what we have assumed as of now. Let's explore.

R Functions Used for Generating the Output

- *Cv.tree()*
- *plot()*
- *prune.misclass()*
- *text()*

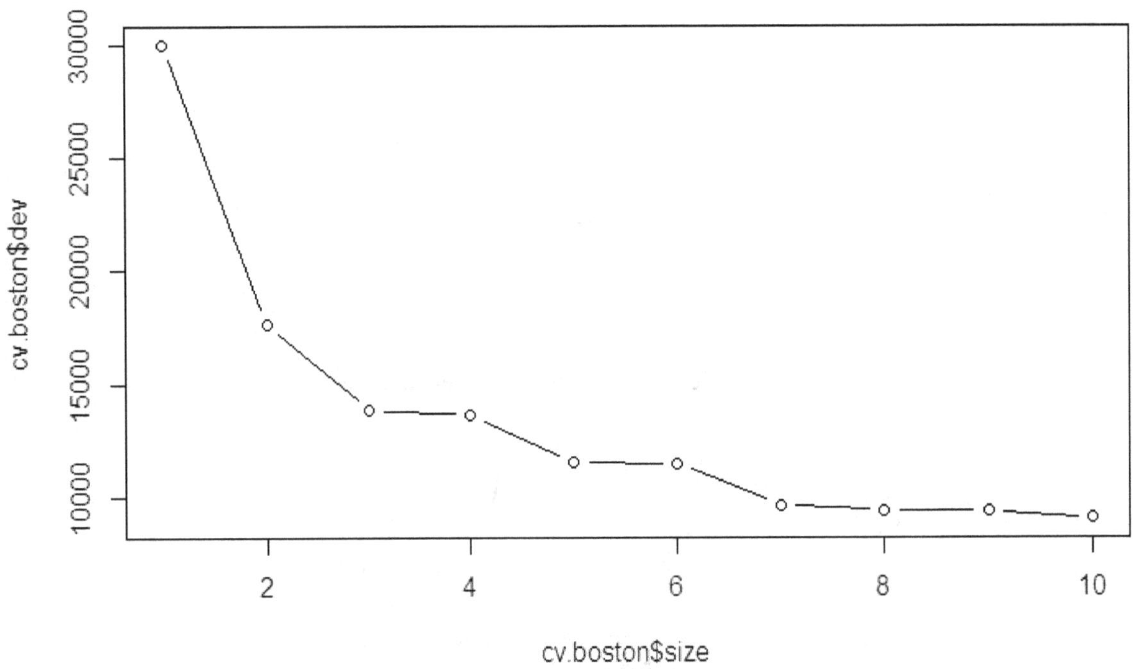

A

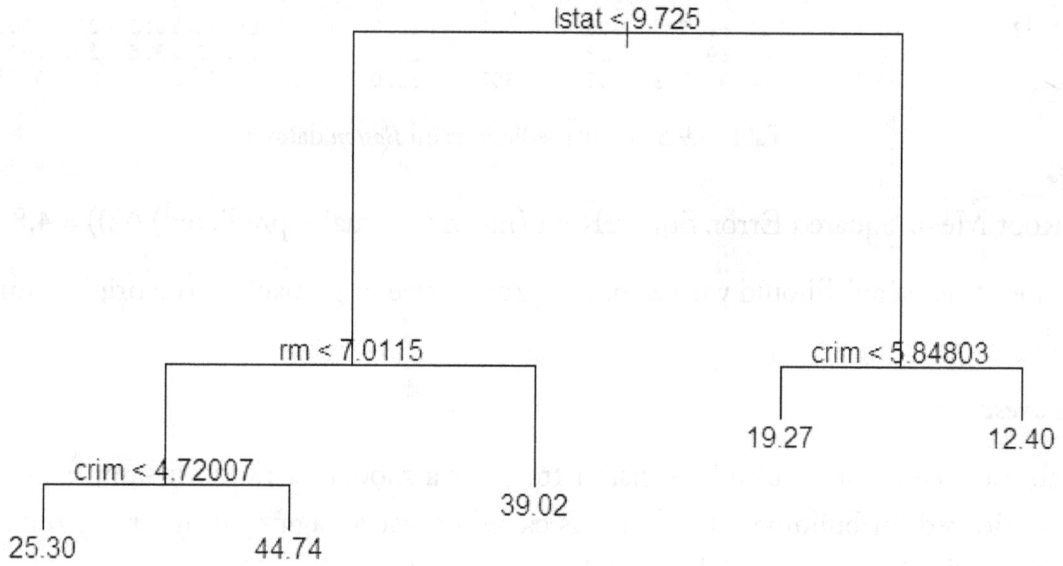

B

Figure 5.8

A. Determining the ideal number of terminal nodes

B. Pruned tree with five terminal nodes

Use the unpruned tree to make predictions on the test set. We already see 'tree.pred' added to the original test dataset as a new column, as shown in Table 5.9 below.

crim	zn	indus	chas	nox	rm	age	dis	rad	tax	ptratio	black	lstat	medv	tree.pred
0.00632	18	2.31	0	0.538	6.575	65.2	4.0900	1	296	15.3	396.90	4.98	24.0	28.61304
0.02731	0	7.07	0	0.469	6.421	78.9	4.9671	2	242	17.8	396.90	9.14	21.6	22.84032
0.02729	0	7.07	0	0.469	7.185	61.1	4.9671	2	242	17.8	392.83	4.03	34.7	34.20000
0.72580	0	8.14	0	0.538	5.727	69.5	3.7965	4	307	21.0	390.95	11.28	18.2	20.70000
0.85204	0	8.14	0	0.538	5.965	89.2	4.0123	4	307	21.0	392.53	13.83	19.6	20.70000
1.23247	0	8.14	0	0.538	6.142	91.7	3.9769	4	307	21.0	396.90	18.72	15.2	16.60208

Table 5.9 View *Boston* dataset

The Root Mean Squared Error is calculated. SquareRoot (mean ((Actual – predicted) ^2)) = 3.6

Then achieve the tree pruning as displayed in figures 5.8A and 5.8B. Use the pruned tree to make predictions on the test set. Now we have another column added called 'tree.pred1'.

```
    crim zn indus chas   nox    rm  age    dis rad tax ptratio  black lstat medv tree.pred tree.pred1
0.00632 18  2.31    0 0.538 6.575 65.2 4.0900   1 296    15.3 396.90  4.98 24.0  28.61304   25.29907
0.02731  0  7.07    0 0.469 6.421 78.9 4.9671   2 242    17.8 396.90  9.14 21.6  22.84032   25.29907
0.02729  0  7.07    0 0.469 7.185 61.1 4.9671   2 242    17.8 392.83  4.03 34.7  34.20000   39.01538
0.72580  0  8.14    0 0.538 5.727 69.5 3.7965   4 307    21.0 390.95 11.28 18.2  20.70000   19.27464
0.85204  0  8.14    0 0.538 5.965 89.2 4.0123   4 307    21.0 392.53 13.83 19.6  20.70000   19.27464
1.23247  0  8.14    0 0.538 6.142 91.7 3.9769   4 307    21.0 396.90 18.72 15.2  16.60208   19.27464
```

Table 5.9.5 View predictions on *Boston* dataset

Find the Root Mean Squared Error. SquareRoot (mean ((Actual – predicted) ^2)) = 4.8

What does this mean? Should we accept the pruned tree or go back to the original unpruned tree. Take a call.

Random Forest

Random forest arises from multiple decision trees for a model. A random sample of training data points is considered for building a tree. This is called bootstrap aggregating or bagging. Moreover, a random subset of independent variables is taken for each tree.

From Table 5.10A, we see that our random forest model is built with 1000 trees specified by the parameter *ntree*. 6 out of 13 variables are considered at each split, as denoted by the parameter *mtry*.

R Functions Used for Generating the Output

- *RandomForest ()*
- *head()*

```
Call:
 randomForest(formula = medv ~ ., data = Train, mtry = 6, importance = TRUE,      ntree = 1000)
               Type of random forest: regression
                     Number of trees: 1000
No. of variables tried at each split: 6

          Mean of squared residuals: 12.75937
                    % Var explained: 84.88
```

A

```
    crim zn indus chas   nox    rm  age    dis rad tax ptratio  black lstat medv forest.pred
0.00632 18  2.31    0 0.538 6.575 65.2 4.0900   1 296    15.3 396.90  4.98 24.0    27.42550
0.02731  0  7.07    0 0.469 6.421 78.9 4.9671   2 242    17.8 396.90  9.14 21.6    22.54464
0.02729  0  7.07    0 0.469 7.185 61.1 4.9671   2 242    17.8 392.83  4.03 34.7    34.69355
0.72580  0  8.14    0 0.538 5.727 69.5 3.7965   4 307    21.0 390.95 11.28 18.2    19.82857
0.85204  0  8.14    0 0.538 5.965 89.2 4.0123   4 307    21.0 392.53 13.83 19.6    18.63098
1.23247  0  8.14    0 0.538 6.142 91.7 3.9769   4 307    21.0 396.90 18.72 15.2    16.76247
```

B

Table 5.10 Random forest

The Root Mean Squared Error is calculated by SquareRoot (mean ((Actual – predicted) ^2)) = 2.6

What is the contribution of each tree to the overall prediction? It is as simple as this. Each observation goes through each of the 1000 trees for prediction. Let's say we are dealing with a binary classification model. For observation number 1, out of 1000 trees, 800 predict YES, and 200 predict NO. As per the principle of voting, the final prediction reported by the random forest model for observation 1 is YES. While working on a regression problem, the average of 1000 predictions is the final prediction by the random forest model for observation number 1.

Variable Importance

There are four frequently used criteria based on which a variable is decided for splitting a node. As mentioned earlier, they are Gini index, chi-square, information gain and reduction in variance. The earlier a variable is chosen for split, the more important the feature is. This translates to the fact that the variable which splits the root node into two child nodes is the most important independent feature for the model. This behavior of splitting nodes recursively enables us to list out the variables with decreasing order of importance, as shown in figure 5.9 below.

R Functions Used for Generating the Output

- *Importance ()*
- *varImpPlot()*

	%IncMSE	IncNodePurity
crim	21.542115	2001.39599
zn	3.854204	60.38415
indus	15.493618	1558.50106
chas	4.402436	131.68203
nox	18.775490	1925.69943
rm	49.279050	8523.86358
age	18.906217	809.40349
dis	25.747635	2240.26127
rad	6.645534	200.73403
tax	13.622905	636.41214
ptratio	15.917803	720.38463
black	10.610932	487.07063
lstat	44.733777	10078.18835

Table 5.11 Variable importance representation 1

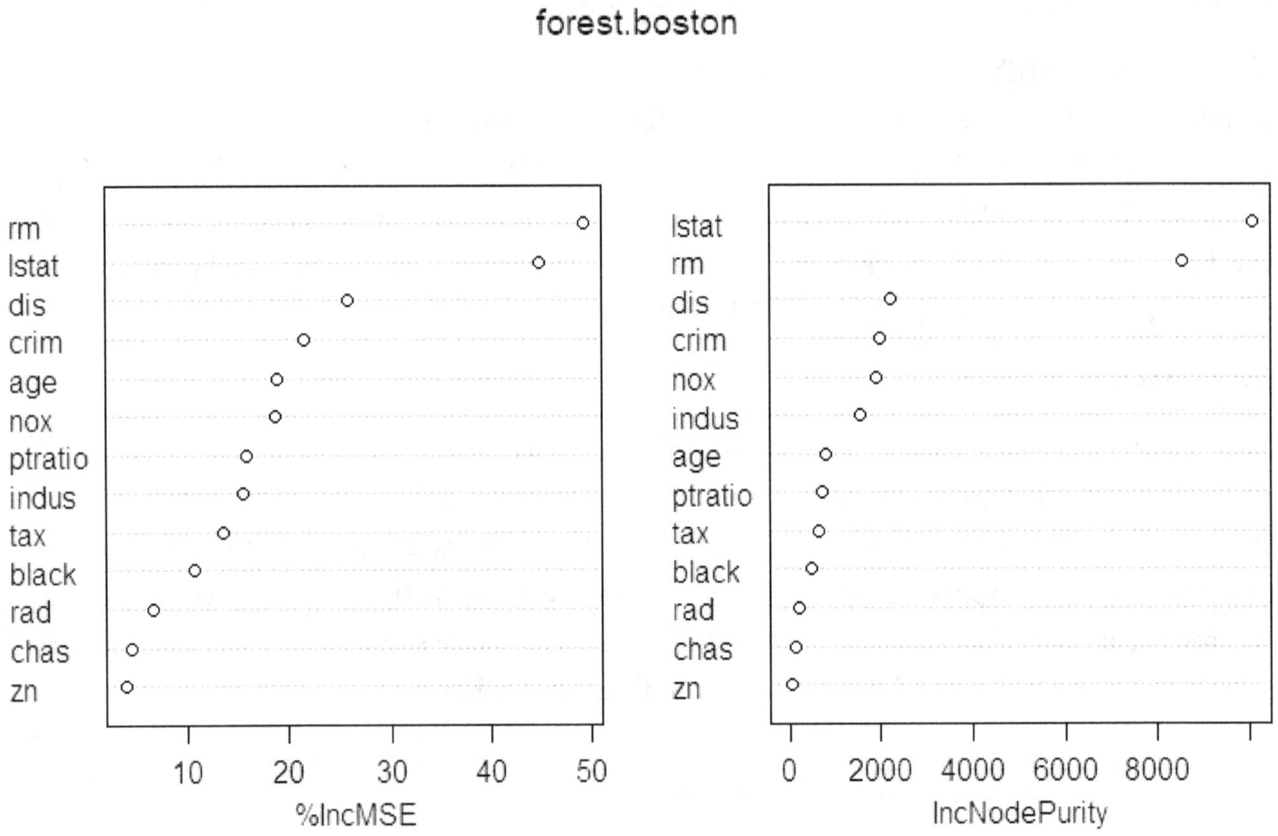

Figure 5.9 Variable importance representation 2

Mean Decrease Accuracy (%IncMSE) and Mean Decrease Gini (IncNodePurity) are two measures that random forest considers while deciding the rank of variables. Considering both the parameters, we see from figure 5.9 that *rm* and *lstat* are the two most important features for predicting house prices (*medv*) among all features.

Chapter 6

Association Mining

We will discuss the following items in this chapter:

- A transaction dataset
- Item, item set, support, confidence, lift
- Rule, antecedent, consequent
- Generation of association rules

Package: arules

Dataset: Groceries (of type transactions)

The *Groceries* dataset contains one month (30 days) of real-world point-of-sale transaction data from a typical local grocery outlet. The dataset includes 9835 transactions, and the items are aggregated to 169 categories.

Association Mining is also known as Market Basket Analysis. Let's define the terminologies relevant to the association mining technique.

Item: This is an individual object that was purchased by at least one customer during the period of data collection and analysis.

Item set: This is a set of objects bought together by a customer in one visit to the store.

Frequent item set: This is an item set that occurs very frequently in the dataset.

Support of an item set: This is the fraction of transactions that contains the item set. High support indicates that the combination of items in the item set is very popular

Confidence: Confidence of a rule is the conditional probability of RHS (Right Hand Side) given LHS (Left Hand Side)

Antecedent item set: The item set on the LHS of a rule

Consequent item set: The item set on the RHS of a rule

In terms of formulas:

Confidence = (Number of transactions with both antecedent and consequent item sets)/(Number of transactions with antecedent item set)

Benchmark confidence = (Number of transactions with consequent item set)/(Total number of transactions)

Lift = (Confidence)/(Benchmark confidence)

Ten different item sets from the data are shown in Table 6.1

R Functions Used for Generating the Output

- *Head()*
- *inspect()*

```
     items
[1]  {citrus fruit,semi-finished bread,margarine,ready soups}
[2]  {tropical fruit,yogurt,coffee}
[3]  {whole milk}
[4]  {pip fruit,yogurt,cream cheese ,meat spreads}
[5]  {other vegetables,whole milk,condensed milk,long life bakery product}
[6]  {whole milk,butter,yogurt,rice,abrasive cleaner}
[7]  {rolls/buns}
[8]  {other vegetables,UHT-milk,rolls/buns,bottled beer,liquor (appetizer)}
[9]  {pot plants}
[10] {whole milk,cereals}
```

Table 6.1 Transactions

The corresponding size of the ten item sets is as follows:

R Functions Used for Generating the Output

- *Head()*
- *size()*

```
4 3 1 4 4 5 1 5 1 2
```

All frequent item sets with minimum support of 0.07 and a maximum length of 4 are shown in Table 6.2 below. The length of an item set is the number of items in an item set.

R Function Used for Generating the Output

- *eclat()*

	items	support	count
[1]	{other vegetables,whole milk}	0.07483477	736
[2]	{whole milk}	0.25551601	2513
[3]	{other vegetables}	0.19349263	1903
[4]	{rolls/buns}	0.18393493	1809
[5]	{yogurt}	0.13950178	1372
[6]	{soda}	0.17437722	1715
[7]	{root vegetables}	0.10899847	1072
[8]	{tropical fruit}	0.10493137	1032
[9]	{bottled water}	0.11052364	1087
[10]	{sausage}	0.09395018	924
[11]	{shopping bags}	0.09852567	969
[12]	{citrus fruit}	0.08276563	814
[13]	{pastry}	0.08896797	875
[14]	{pip fruit}	0.07564820	744
[15]	{whipped/sour cream}	0.07168277	705
[16]	{fruit/vegetable juice}	0.07229283	711
[17]	{newspapers}	0.07981698	785
[18]	{bottled beer}	0.08052872	792
[19]	{canned beer}	0.07768175	764

Table 6.2 Frequent item sets

The length of the above-resulting set is the number of transactions included in the result set, which is 19, satisfying the conditions of minimum support and maximum length, as mentioned earlier. The length of the dataset as a whole is the number of transactions contained in the dataset, which is 9835 for *Groceries*.

The top ten frequently occurring items in the dataset are shown in figure 6.1 below.

R Function Used for Generating the Output

- *ItemFrequencyPlot()*

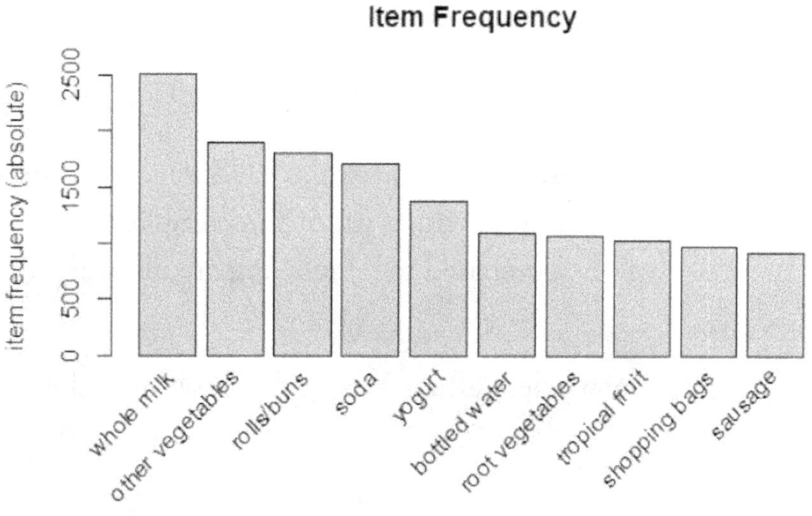

Figure 6.1 Items with high frequency

Rules are generated using the *apriori* algorithm with minimum support of 0.001 and minimum confidence of 0.5. Rules are sorted by decreasing order of confidence, as shown in Table 6.3 below.

R Functions Used for Generating the Output

- *apriori()*
- *sort()*

	lhs		rhs	support	confidence	lift	count
[1]	{rice,sugar}	=>	{whole milk}	0.001220132	1	3.913649	12
[2]	{canned fish,hygiene articles}	=>	{whole milk}	0.001118454	1	3.913649	11
[3]	{root vegetables,butter,rice}	=>	{whole milk}	0.001016777	1	3.913649	10
[4]	{root vegetables,whipped/sour cream,flour}	=>	{whole milk}	0.001728521	1	3.913649	17
[5]	{butter,soft cheese,domestic eggs}	=>	{whole milk}	0.001016777	1	3.913649	10
[6]	{citrus fruit,root vegetables,soft cheese}	=>	{other vegetables}	0.001016777	1	5.168156	10
[7]	{pip fruit,butter,hygiene articles}	=>	{whole milk}	0.001016777	1	3.913649	10
[8]	{root vegetables,whipped/sour cream,hygiene articles}	=>	{whole milk}	0.001016777	1	3.913649	10
[9]	{pip fruit,root vegetables,hygiene articles}	=>	{whole milk}	0.001016777	1	3.913649	10
[10]	{cream cheese ,domestic eggs,sugar}	=>	{whole milk}	0.001118454	1	3.913649	11

Table 6.3 Rules as the output of the apriori algorithm

We can again sort the rules by decreasing the order of lift, as shown in Table 6.4 below.

R Functions Used for Generating the Output

- *Apriori()*
- *sort()*
- *head()*

	lhs		rhs	support	confidence	lift	count
[1]	{Instant food products,soda}	=>	{hamburger meat}	0.001220132	0.6315789	18.99565	12
[2]	{soda,popcorn}	=>	{salty snack}	0.001220132	0.6315789	16.69779	12
[3]	{flour,baking powder}	=>	{sugar}	0.001016777	0.5555556	16.40807	10
[4]	{ham,processed cheese}	=>	{white bread}	0.001931876	0.6333333	15.04549	19
[5]	{whole milk,Instant food products}	=>	{hamburger meat}	0.001525165	0.5000000	15.03823	15
[6]	{other vegetables,curd,yogurt,whipped/sour cream}	=>	{cream cheese }	0.001016777	0.5882353	14.83409	10
[7]	{processed cheese,domestic eggs}	=>	{white bread}	0.001118454	0.5238095	12.44364	11
[8]	{tropical fruit,other vegetables,yogurt,white bread}	=>	{butter}	0.001016777	0.6666667	12.03058	10
[9]	{hamburger meat,yogurt,whipped/sour cream}	=>	{butter}	0.001016777	0.6250000	11.27867	10
[10]	{tropical fruit,other vegetables,whole milk,yogurt,domestic eggs}	=>	{butter}	0.001016777	0.6250000	11.27867	10

Table 6.4 Rules by decreasing order of lift

The rules with a confidence of one imply that whenever the LHS item was purchased, the RHS item was also purchased 100% of the time. A rule with a lift of three implies that the items in LHS and RHS are three times more likely to be purchased together compared to the purchases when they are assumed to be unrelated.

Rules that lead to the purchase of whole milk are displayed in Table 6.5 below, ordered by decreasing order of lift.

R Functions Used for Generating the Output

- *Apriori()*
- *sort()*
- *head()*

```
     lhs                                                    rhs          support     confidence lift     count
[1]  {rice,sugar}                                        => {whole milk} 0.001220132 1          3.913649 12
[2]  {canned fish,hygiene articles}                      => {whole milk} 0.001118454 1          3.913649 11
[3]  {root vegetables,butter,rice}                       => {whole milk} 0.001016777 1          3.913649 10
[4]  {root vegetables,whipped/sour cream,flour}          => {whole milk} 0.001728521 1          3.913649 17
[5]  {butter,soft cheese,domestic eggs}                  => {whole milk} 0.001016777 1          3.913649 10
[6]  {pip fruit,butter,hygiene articles}                 => {whole milk} 0.001016777 1          3.913649 10
[7]  {root vegetables,whipped/sour cream,hygiene articles} => {whole milk} 0.001016777 1          3.913649 10
[8]  {pip fruit,root vegetables,hygiene articles}        => {whole milk} 0.001016777 1          3.913649 10
[9]  {cream cheese ,domestic eggs,sugar}                 => {whole milk} 0.001118454 1          3.913649 11
[10] {curd,domestic eggs,sugar}                          => {whole milk} 0.001016777 1          3.913649 10
```

Table 6.5 Rules leading to *whole milk*

Customers who bought milk also bought the following item sets shown under the RHS in Table 6.6 below and are ordered by decreasing order of confidence.

```
    lhs             rhs                support    confidence lift      count
[1] {whole milk} => {other vegetables} 0.07483477 0.2928770  1.5136341 736
[2] {whole milk} => {rolls/buns}       0.05663447 0.2216474  1.2050318 557
[3] {whole milk} => {yogurt}           0.05602440 0.2192598  1.5717351 551
[4] {whole milk} => {root vegetables}  0.04890696 0.1914047  1.7560310 481
[5] {whole milk} => {tropical fruit}   0.04229792 0.1655392  1.5775950 416
[6] {whole milk} => {soda}             0.04006101 0.1567847  0.8991124 394
```

Table 6.6 Rules with *whole milk* leading to purchase of other items

Market Basket Analysis can be used for cross-selling. We will easily be able to identify the top-ranked rules. Whenever a customer purchases the LHS items, he can be suggested to take a look at the RHS items too.

Chapter 7

Clustering

We will discuss the following items in this chapter:

- Understand the *iris* dataset
- Scaling
- K-means clustering
- Elbow curve (determining the ideal number of clusters)
- Understand the cluster output summary
- Visualization of clusters
- Profiling clusters

Consider the *iris* dataset. Given below is the list of columns contained in the dataset. A short description of each variable is also presented.

Sepal.Length Length of the sepal

Sepal.Width Width of the sepal

Petal.Length Length of the petal

Petal.Width Width of the petal

Species Species name of the flower

Let's see how the observations look like.

R Function Used for Generating the Output

- *Head()*

```
  Sepal.Length Sepal.Width Petal.Length Petal.Width Species
1          5.1         3.5          1.4         0.2  setosa
2          4.9         3.0          1.4         0.2  setosa
3          4.7         3.2          1.3         0.2  setosa
4          4.6         3.1          1.5         0.2  setosa
5          5.0         3.6          1.4         0.2  setosa
6          5.4         3.9          1.7         0.4  setosa
```

Table 7.1 View *iris* dataset

Check the structure of the dataset.

R Function Used for Generating the Output

- *Str()*

```
'data.frame':   150 obs. of  5 variables:
 $ Sepal.Length: num  5.1 4.9 4.7 4.6 5 5.4 4.6 5 4.4 4.9 ...
 $ Sepal.Width : num  3.5 3 3.2 3.1 3.6 3.9 3.4 3.4 2.9 3.1 ...
 $ Petal.Length: num  1.4 1.4 1.3 1.5 1.4 1.7 1.4 1.5 1.4 1.5 ...
 $ Petal.Width : num  0.2 0.2 0.2 0.2 0.2 0.4 0.3 0.2 0.2 0.1 ...
 $ Species     : Factor w/ 3 levels "setosa","versicolor",..: 1 1 1 1 1 1 1 1 1 1 ...
```

Table 7.2 Structure of the *iris* dataset

Take a look at the summary.

R Function Used for Generating the Output

- *Summary()*

```
  Sepal.Length    Sepal.Width     Petal.Length    Petal.Width          Species
 Min.   :4.300   Min.   :2.000   Min.   :1.000   Min.   :0.100   setosa    :50
 1st Qu.:5.100   1st Qu.:2.800   1st Qu.:1.600   1st Qu.:0.300   versicolor:50
 Median :5.800   Median :3.000   Median :4.350   Median :1.300   virginica :50
 Mean   :5.843   Mean   :3.057   Mean   :3.758   Mean   :1.199
 3rd Qu.:6.400   3rd Qu.:3.300   3rd Qu.:5.100   3rd Qu.:1.800
 Max.   :7.900   Max.   :4.400   Max.   :6.900   Max.   :2.500
```

Table 7.3 Summary of the *iris* dataset

We will use K-means clustering here. It requires to take datasets with numeric variables only as input. Hence, we have kept the *Species* column aside.

R Function Used for Generating the Output

- *Head()*

```
  Sepal.Length Sepal.Width Petal.Length Petal.Width
1          5.1         3.5          1.4         0.2
2          4.9         3.0          1.4         0.2
3          4.7         3.2          1.3         0.2
4          4.6         3.1          1.5         0.2
5          5.0         3.6          1.4         0.2
6          5.4         3.9          1.7         0.4
```

Table 7.4 View iris dataset with *Species* removed

Next, we scale the values. Why is scaling necessary? Let's assume that among many variables, we have included two variables named *age* (years) and *salary* (rupees) in our K-means clustering input. Age would usually vary between 20 and 60. On the other hand, the salary will range from 10,000 to 40,000. The clustering algorithm should treat age and salary on the same ground. In the scenario of scaled values, both age and salary come within similar ranges.

R Function Used for Generating the Output

- *Scale()*

```
     Sepal.Length Sepal.Width Petal.Length Petal.Width
[1,]   -0.8976739  1.01560199    -1.335752   -1.311052
[2,]   -1.1392005 -0.13153881    -1.335752   -1.311052
[3,]   -1.3807271  0.32731751    -1.392399   -1.311052
[4,]   -1.5014904  0.09788935    -1.279104   -1.311052
[5,]   -1.0184372  1.24503015    -1.335752   -1.311052
[6,]   -0.5353840  1.93331463    -1.165809   -1.048667
```

Table 7.5 Scaled *iris* numeric-only dataset

Take a look at the summary of the scaled dataset. Especially, check the minimum and maximum values. Why is the mean zero for each variable?

R Function Used for Generating the Output

- *Summary()*

```
  Sepal.Length       Sepal.Width       Petal.Length       Petal.Width
 Min.   :-1.86378   Min.   :-2.4258   Min.   :-1.5623   Min.   :-1.4422
 1st Qu.:-0.89767   1st Qu.:-0.5904   1st Qu.:-1.2225   1st Qu.:-1.1799
 Median :-0.05233   Median :-0.1315   Median : 0.3354   Median : 0.1321
 Mean   : 0.00000   Mean   : 0.0000   Mean   : 0.0000   Mean   : 0.0000
 3rd Qu.: 0.67225   3rd Qu.: 0.5567   3rd Qu.: 0.7602   3rd Qu.: 0.7880
 Max.   : 2.48370   Max.   : 3.0805   Max.   : 1.7799   Max.   : 1.7064
```

Table 7.6 Summary of the scaled *iris* dataset

Identify the ideal number of clusters to be created. Take the unscaled values for this. K-means requires the number of clusters to be provided as an input parameter. We make use of the *elbow curve*, as shown in figure 7.1 below. We pick a point beyond which there is no significant decrease in *within sum squares (WSS)*. A high WSS would indicate a loose coupling among the elements of a cluster.

R Functions Used for Generating the Output

- *Kmeans()*
- *sum()*
- *apply()*
- *plot()*

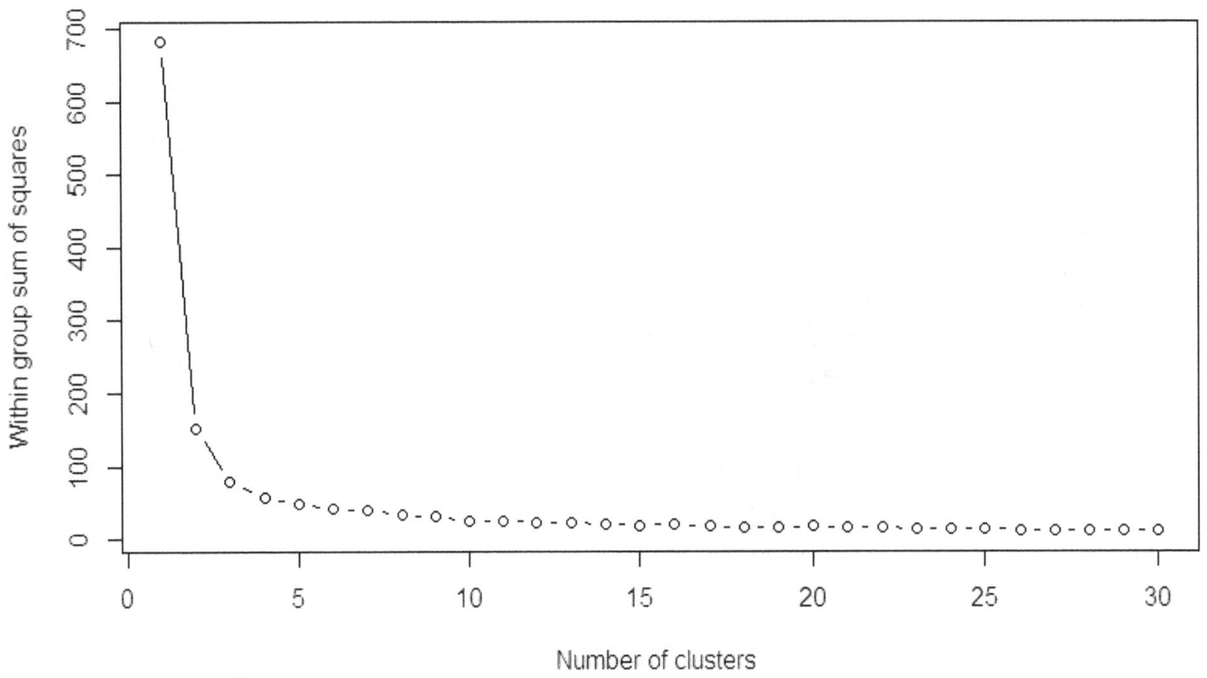

Figure 7.1 Elbow curve (determining the ideal number of clusters using WSS)

WSS should be as low as possible. WSS considers the distances between two elements within the same cluster. There is another measure called Between Sum Squares (BSS), which considers the distances between two clusters. This means that BSS should be as high as possible. Intuitively, this makes sense because we would like our cluster elements within a cluster tightly packed. In contrast, we would like two clusters to be highly distinct from each other.

Figure 7.2, displayed below, shows the BSS with a different number of clusters between 2 to 30. Here is a little task for you. Similar to the elbow curve, can we use this BSS curve to give us an indication of an ideal number of clusters our observations should be divided into?

R Functions Used for Generating the Output

- *Kmeans()*
- *sum()*
- *apply()*
- *plot()*

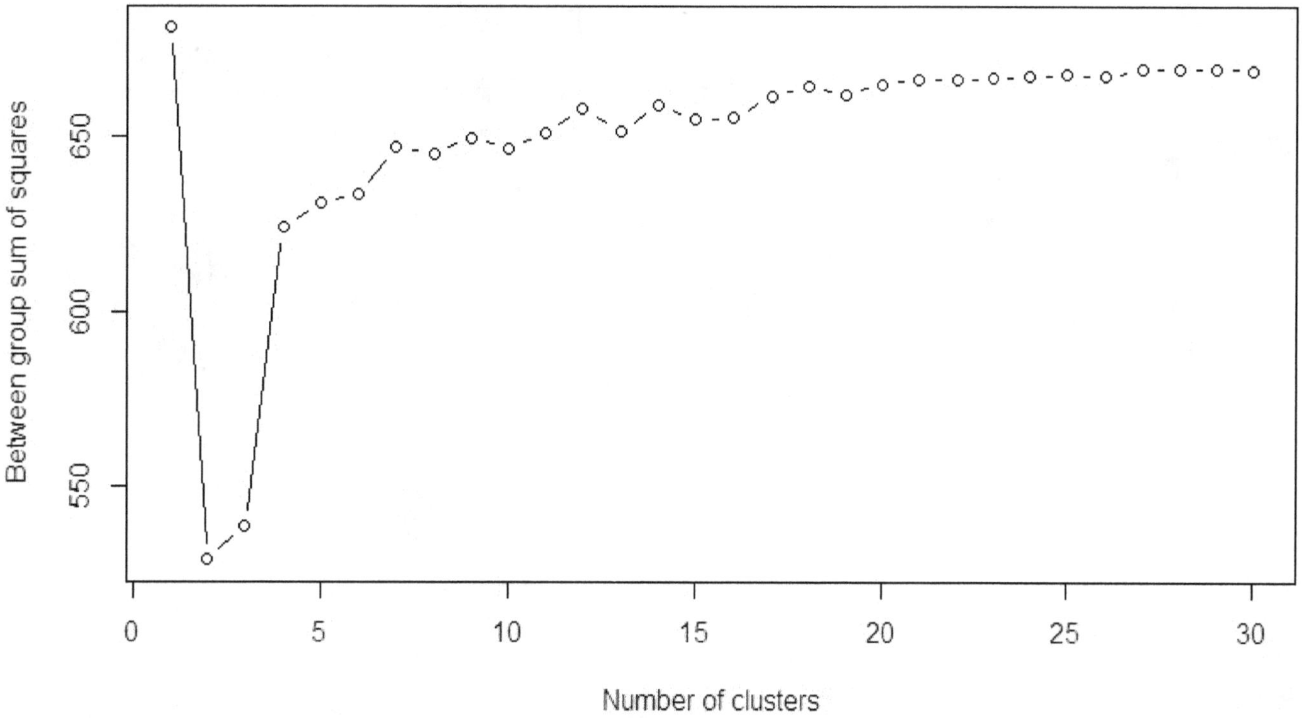

Figure 7.2 Determining the ideal number of clusters using BSS

Build the clusters. Build five of them. The output, as shown in Table 7.7 below, summarizes the clustering exercise.

R Function Used for Generating the Output

- *Kmeans()*

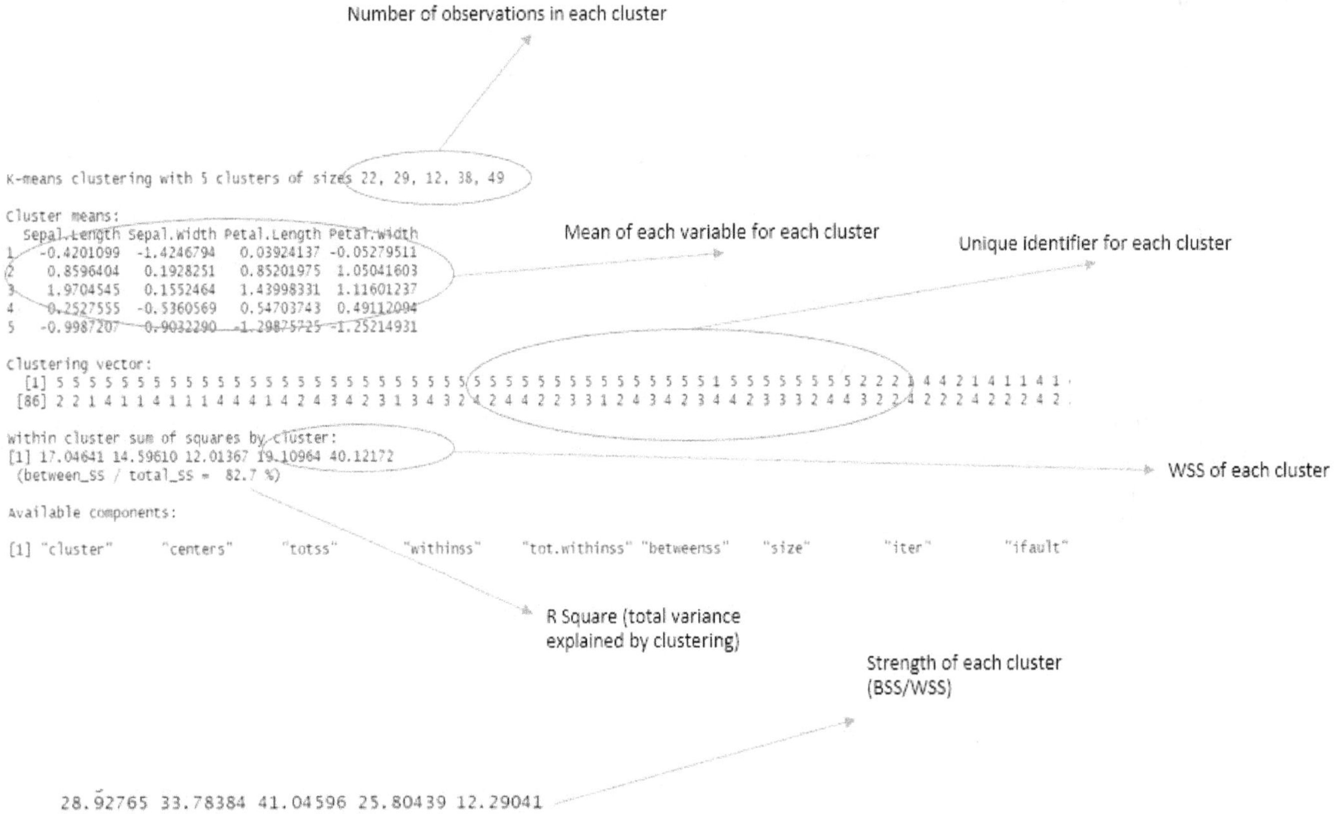

Table 7.7 Clustering output summary

We should attach back the cluster numbers to the original dataset to identify which observation goes with which cluster. Check the last column added for cluster number, as shown in Table 7.8 below.

R Function Used for Generating the Output

- *Head()*

	Sepal.Length	Sepal.Width	Petal.Length	Petal.Width	Species	cluster
1	5.1	3.5	1.4	0.2	setosa	1
2	4.9	3.0	1.4	0.2	setosa	3
3	4.7	3.2	1.3	0.2	setosa	3
4	4.6	3.1	1.5	0.2	setosa	3
5	5.0	3.6	1.4	0.2	setosa	1
6	5.4	3.9	1.7	0.4	setosa	1

Table 7.8 Cluster number attached

R Function Used for Generating the Output

- *Clusplot()*

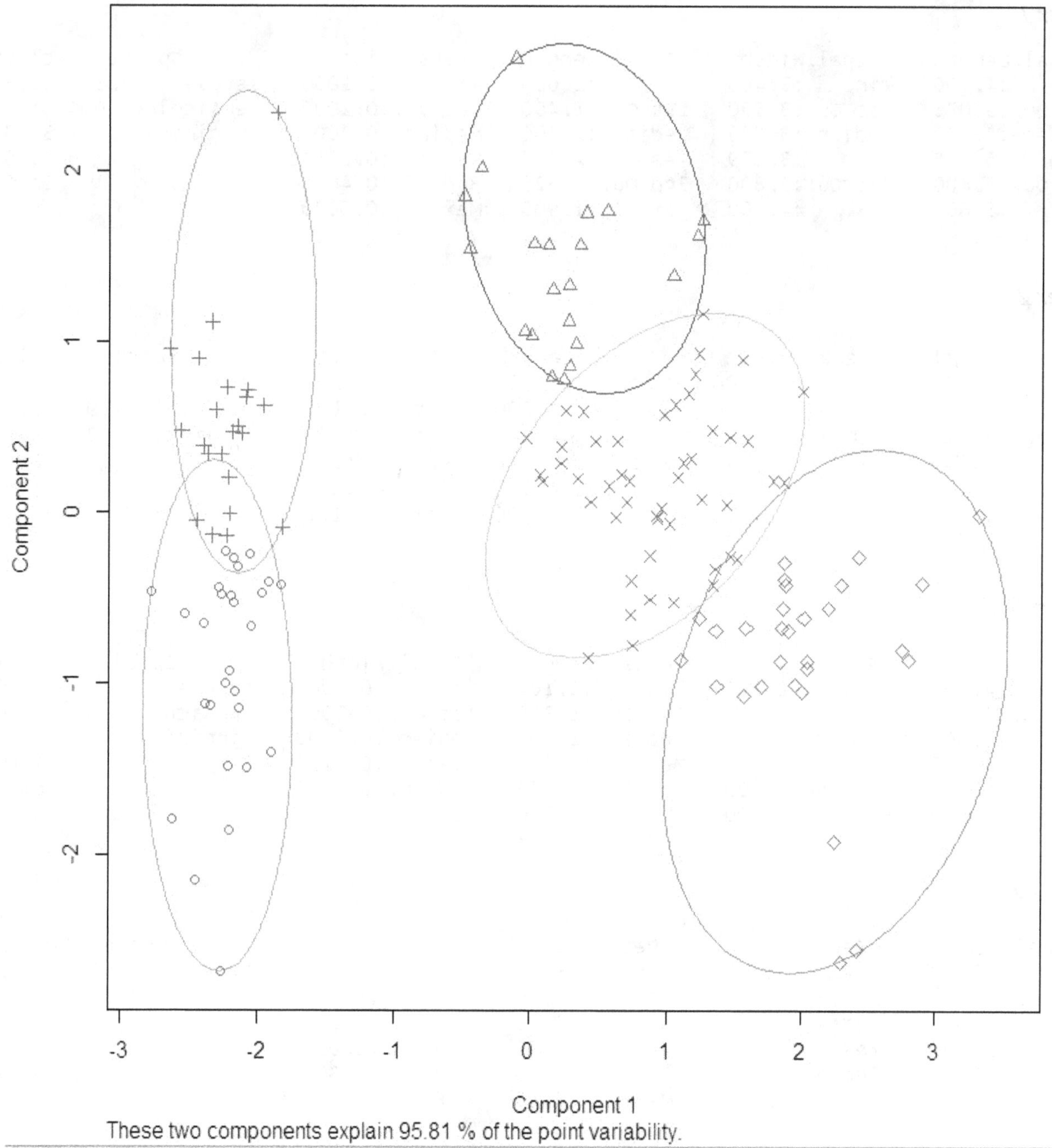

Figure 7.3 Visual representations of clusters

Provided above in figure 7.3 is a plot of the clusters by considering the top two components, which explains 95.81% of the point variability. Next, let's profile each cluster. Compare the summaries of the five clusters, as shown in Table 7.9 below.

R Function Used for Generating the Output

- *Summary()*

Cluster 1

```
 Sepal.Length    Sepal.Width     Petal.Length    Petal.Width            Species    cluster
Min.   :4.600   Min.   :3.400   Min.   :1.000   Min.   :0.1000   setosa    :28   1:28
1st Qu.:5.075   1st Qu.:3.500   1st Qu.:1.400   1st Qu.:0.2000   versicolor: 0   2: 0
Median :5.150   Median :3.600   Median :1.500   Median :0.2000   virginica : 0   3: 0
Mean   :5.225   Mean   :3.679   Mean   :1.475   Mean   :0.2714                   4: 0
3rd Qu.:5.400   3rd Qu.:3.800   3rd Qu.:1.525   3rd Qu.:0.4000                   5: 0
Max.   :5.800   Max.   :4.400   Max.   :1.900   Max.   :0.6000
```

Cluster 2

```
 Sepal.Length    Sepal.Width     Petal.Length    Petal.Width       Species    cluster
Min.   :4.900   Min.   :2.000   Min.   :3.000   Min.   :1.0   setosa    : 0   1: 0
1st Qu.:5.200   1st Qu.:2.300   1st Qu.:3.700   1st Qu.:1.0   versicolor:19   2:21
Median :5.500   Median :2.500   Median :4.000   Median :1.2   virginica : 2   3: 0
Mean   :5.543   Mean   :2.443   Mean   :3.948   Mean   :1.2                   4: 0
3rd Qu.:5.800   3rd Qu.:2.600   3rd Qu.:4.200   3rd Qu.:1.3                   5: 0
Max.   :6.300   Max.   :2.700   Max.   :5.000   Max.   :1.7
```

Cluster 3

```
 Sepal.Length    Sepal.Width     Petal.Length    Petal.Width            Species    cluster
Min.   :4.300   Min.   :2.300   Min.   :1.100   Min.   :0.1000   setosa    :22   1: 0
1st Qu.:4.600   1st Qu.:3.000   1st Qu.:1.325   1st Qu.:0.2000   versicolor: 0   2: 0
Median :4.800   Median :3.100   Median :1.400   Median :0.2000   virginica : 0   3:22
Mean   :4.727   Mean   :3.109   Mean   :1.445   Mean   :0.2136                   4: 0
3rd Qu.:4.900   3rd Qu.:3.200   3rd Qu.:1.575   3rd Qu.:0.2000                   5: 0
Max.   :5.100   Max.   :3.400   Max.   :1.900   Max.   :0.5000
```

Cluster 4

```
 Sepal.Length    Sepal.Width     Petal.Length    Petal.Width           Species    cluster
Min.   :5.400   Min.   :2.500   Min.   :3.60   Min.   :1.200   setosa    : 0   1: 0
1st Qu.:5.825   1st Qu.:2.800   1st Qu.:4.50   1st Qu.:1.400   versicolor:29   2: 0
Median :6.100   Median :2.900   Median :4.80   Median :1.500   virginica :21   3: 0
Mean   :6.138   Mean   :2.886   Mean   :4.79   Mean   :1.616                   4:50
3rd Qu.:6.400   3rd Qu.:3.000   3rd Qu.:5.10   3rd Qu.:1.800                   5: 0
Max.   :6.800   Max.   :3.400   Max.   :5.80   Max.   :2.400
```

Cluster 5

```
 Sepal.Length    Sepal.Width     Petal.Length  Petal.Width          Species    cluster
Min.   :6.200   Min.   :2.600   Min.   :4.7   Min.   :1.400   setosa    : 0   1: 0
1st Qu.:6.700   1st Qu.:3.000   1st Qu.:5.4   1st Qu.:2.000   versicolor: 2   2: 0
Median :6.900   Median :3.100   Median :5.8   Median :2.200   virginica :27   3: 0
Mean   :6.997   Mean   :3.159   Mean   :5.8   Mean   :2.124                   4: 0
3rd Qu.:7.300   3rd Qu.:3.300   3rd Qu.:6.1   3rd Qu.:2.300                   5:29
Max.   :7.900   Max.   :3.800   Max.   :6.9   Max.   :2.500
```

Table 7.9 Profile of five clusters

## Chapter 8

Frequently Used Data Science Terms

This is an informal chapter on the frequently used language in data science. The phrase emerging out of a box is a phrase related to the term inside the box. Sometimes, it is a short description. Sometimes, it is just an expansion. Some other times, it merely tells where the term fits on the data science map. But every time, it is related to the term inside the box.

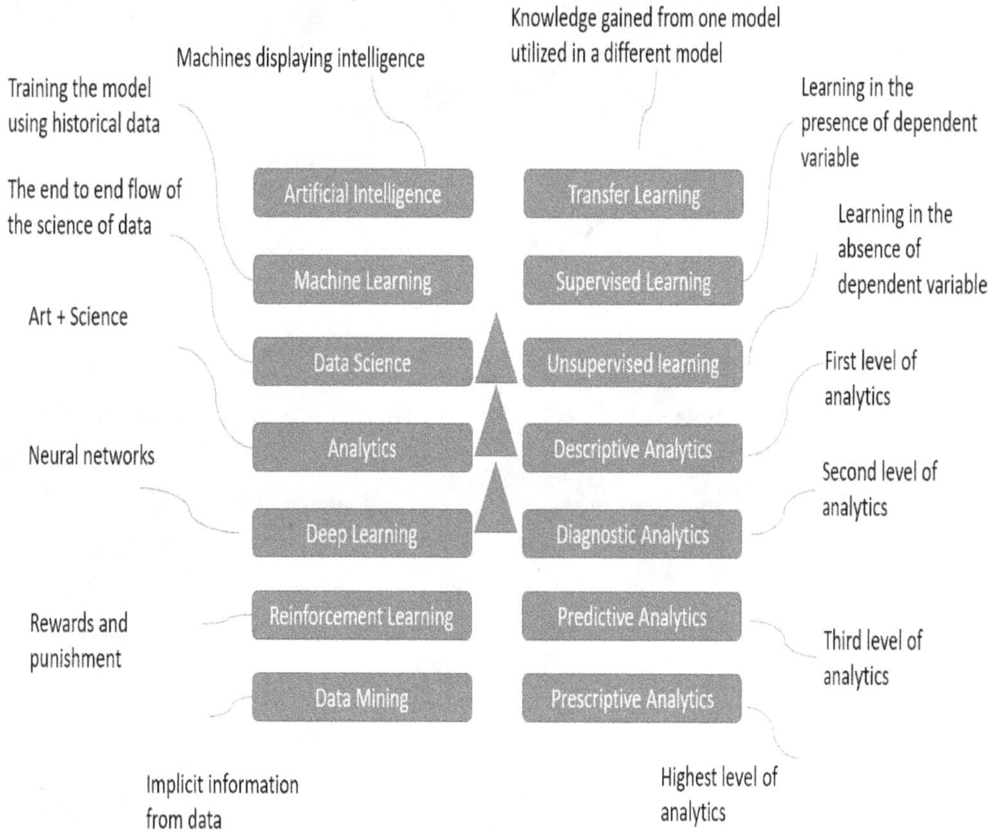

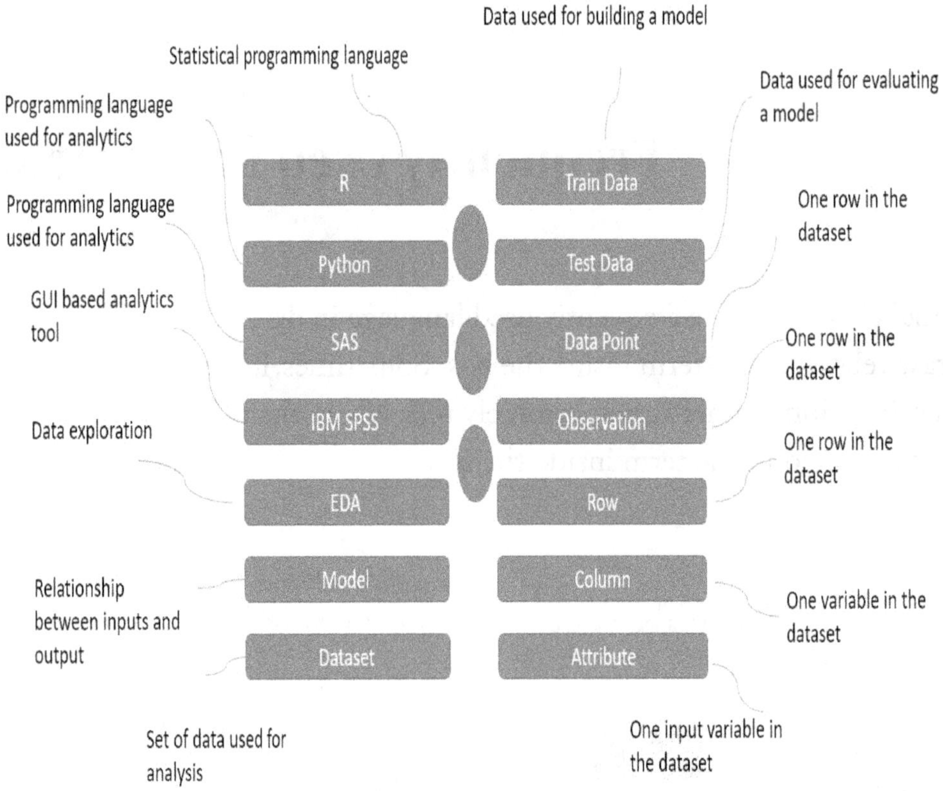
Data used for building a model
Statistical programming language
Data used for evaluating a model
Programming language used for analytics
R
Train Data
Programming language used for analytics
One row in the dataset
Python
Test Data
GUI based analytics tool
SAS
Data Point
One row in the dataset
IBM SPSS
Observation
Data exploration
One row in the dataset
EDA
Row
Model
Column
Relationship between inputs and output
One variable in the dataset
Dataset
Attribute
Set of data used for analysis
One input variable in the dataset

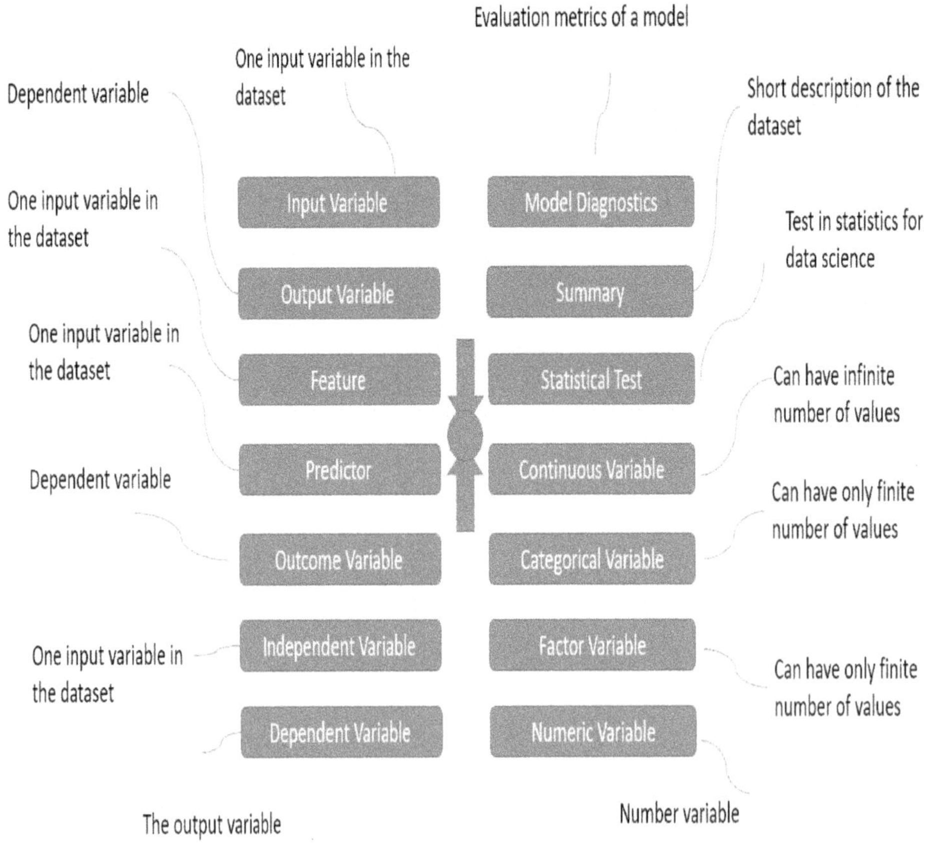
Evaluation metrics of a model
One input variable in the dataset
Dependent variable
Short description of the dataset
Input Variable
Model Diagnostics
One input variable in the dataset
Test in statistics for data science
Output Variable
Summary
One input variable in the dataset
Feature
Statistical Test
Can have infinite number of values
Predictor
Continuous Variable
Dependent variable
Can have only finite number of values
Outcome Variable
Categorical Variable
One input variable in the dataset
Independent Variable
Factor Variable
Can have only finite number of values
Dependent Variable
Numeric Variable
The output variable
Number variable

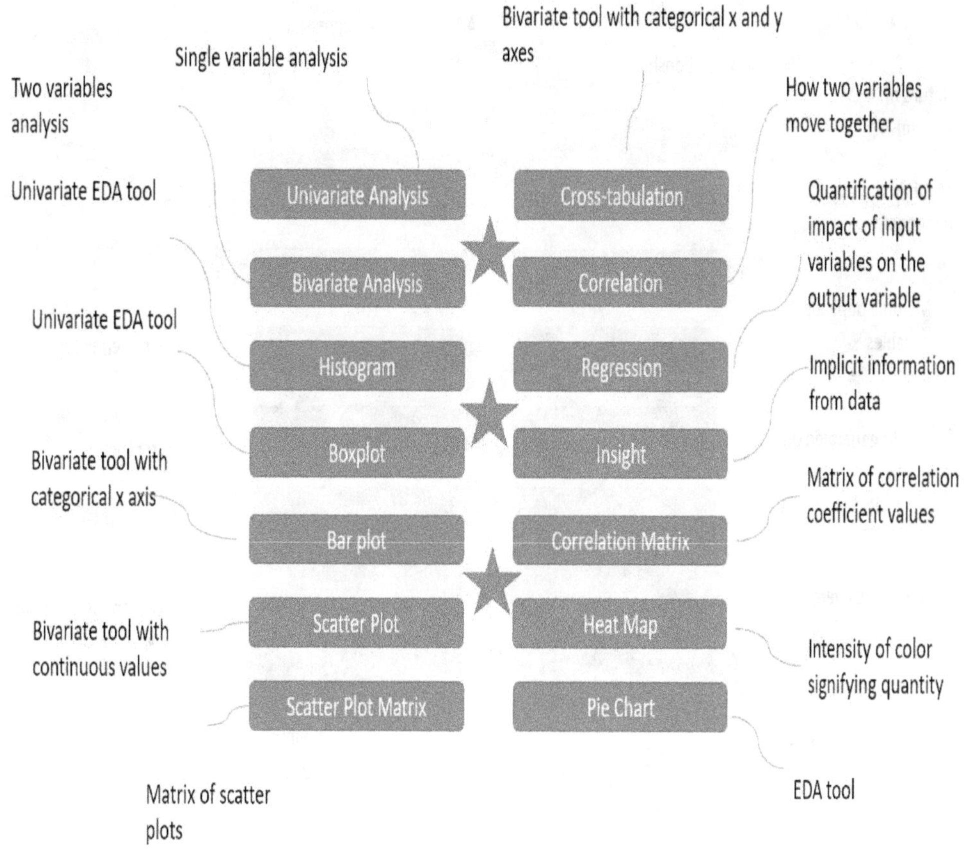
Single variable analysis
Bivariate tool with categorical x and y axes
Two variables analysis
How two variables move together
Univariate EDA tool
Univariate Analysis
Cross-tabulation
Quantification of impact of input variables on the output variable
Bivariate Analysis
Correlation
Univariate EDA tool
Histogram
Regression
Implicit information from data
Boxplot
Insight
Bivariate tool with categorical x axis
Matrix of correlation coefficient values
Bar plot
Correlation Matrix
Bivariate tool with continuous values
Scatter Plot
Heat Map
Intensity of color signifying quantity
Scatter Plot Matrix
Pie Chart
Matrix of scatter plots
EDA tool

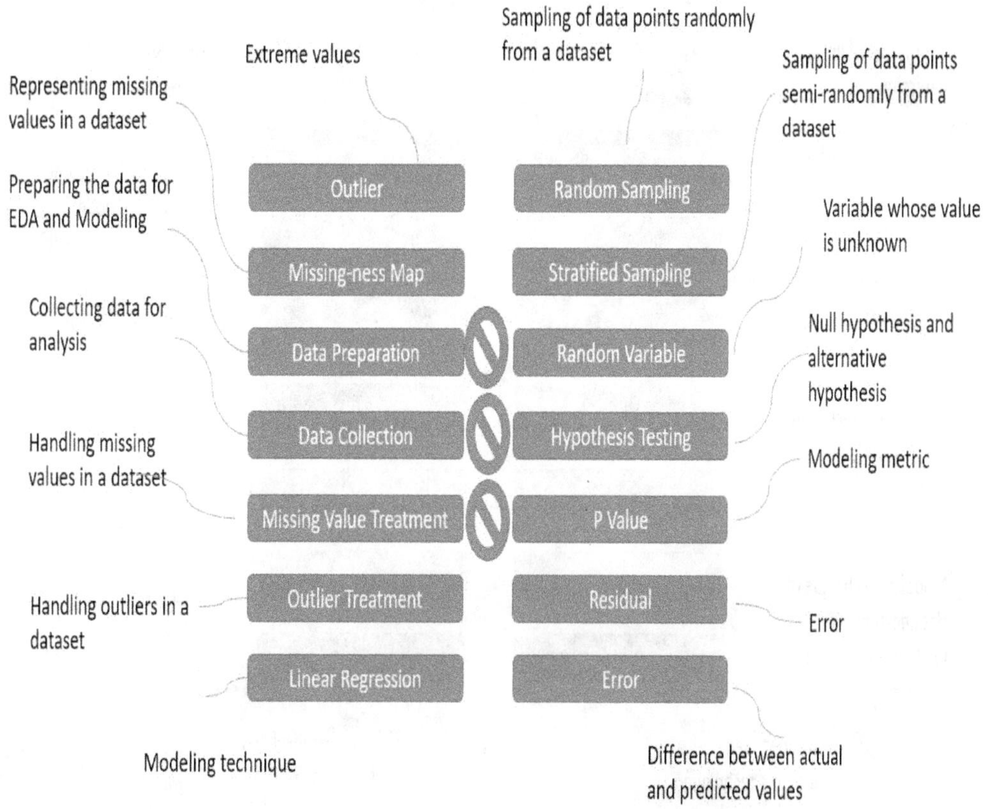
Sampling of data points randomly from a dataset
Extreme values
Representing missing values in a dataset
Sampling of data points semi-randomly from a dataset
Preparing the data for EDA and Modeling
Outlier
Random Sampling
Variable whose value is unknown
Missing-ness Map
Stratified Sampling
Collecting data for analysis
Null hypothesis and alternative hypothesis
Data Preparation
Random Variable
Handling missing values in a dataset
Data Collection
Hypothesis Testing
Modeling metric
Missing Value Treatment
P Value
Handling outliers in a dataset
Outlier Treatment
Residual
Error
Linear Regression
Error
Modeling technique
Difference between actual and predicted values

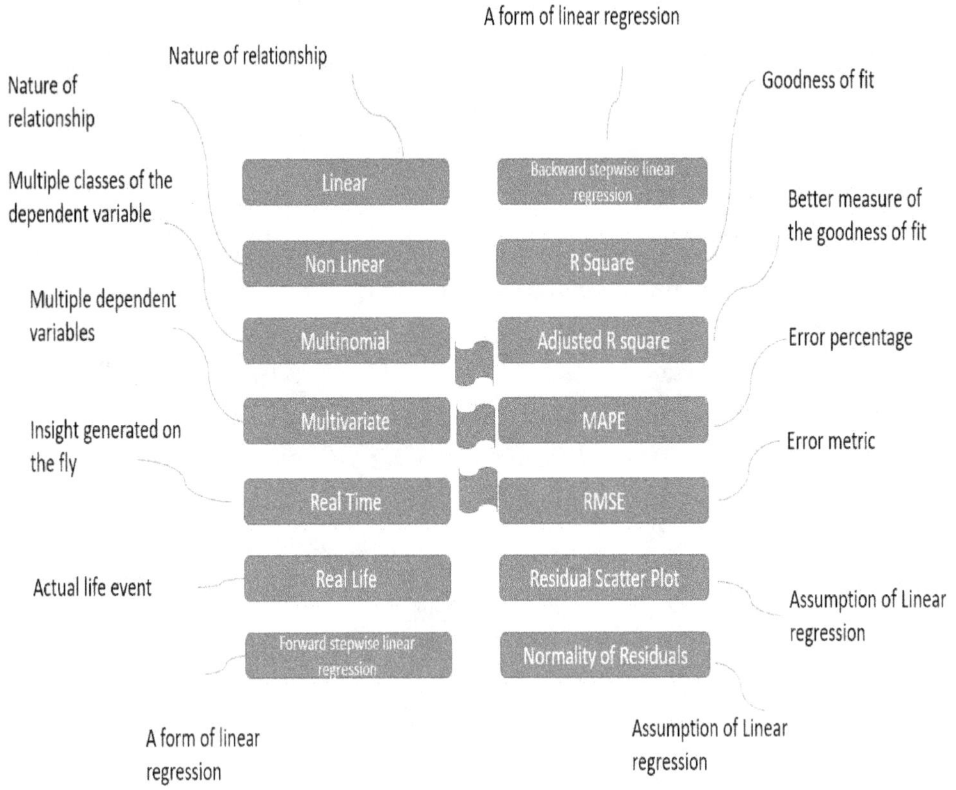
A form of linear regression
Nature of relationship
Nature of relationship
Goodness of fit
Linear
Backward stepwise linear regression
Multiple classes of the dependent variable
Better measure of the goodness of fit
Non Linear
R Square
Multiple dependent variables
Multinomial
Adjusted R square
Error percentage
Multivariate
MAPE
Insight generated on the fly
Error metric
Real Time
RMSE
Actual life event
Real Life
Residual Scatter Plot
Assumption of Linear regression
Forward stepwise linear regression
Normality of Residuals
A form of linear regression
Assumption of Linear regression

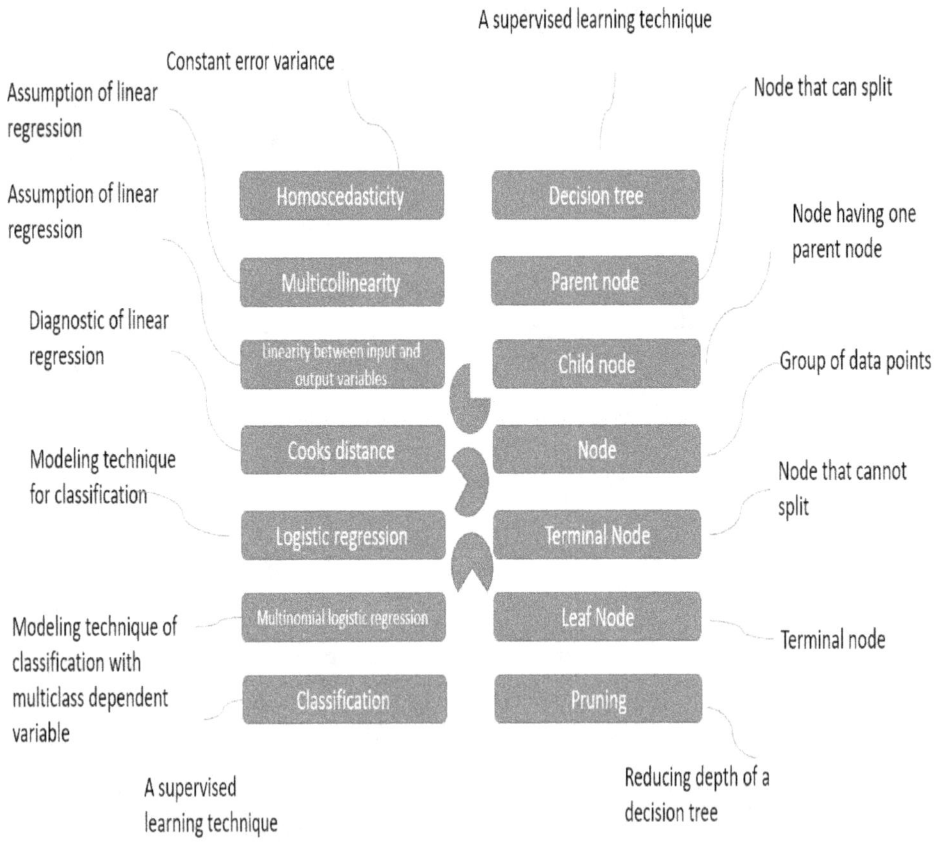
A supervised learning technique
Constant error variance
Assumption of linear regression
Node that can split
Homoscedasticity
Decision tree
Assumption of linear regression
Node having one parent node
Multicollinearity
Parent node
Diagnostic of linear regression
Linearity between input and output variables
Child node
Group of data points
Cooks distance
Node
Modeling technique for classification
Node that cannot split
Logistic regression
Terminal Node
Modeling technique of classification with multiclass dependent variable
Multinomial logistic regression
Leaf Node
Terminal node
Classification
Pruning
A supervised learning technique
Reducing depth of a decision tree

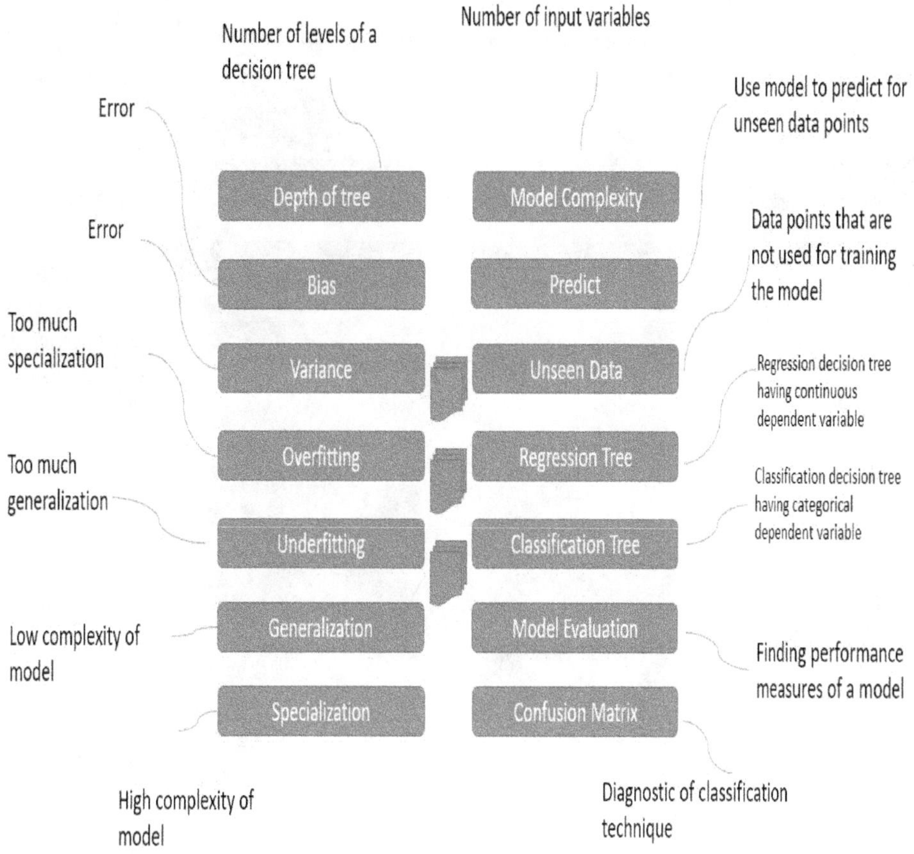
Number of levels of a decision tree
Number of input variables
Error
Use model to predict for unseen data points
Depth of tree
Model Complexity
Error
Data points that are not used for training the model
Bias
Predict
Too much specialization
Variance
Unseen Data
Regression decision tree having continuous dependent variable
Overfitting
Regression Tree
Too much generalization
Classification decision tree having categorical dependent variable
Underfitting
Classification Tree
Low complexity of model
Generalization
Model Evaluation
Finding performance measures of a model
Specialization
Confusion Matrix
High complexity of model
Diagnostic of classification technique

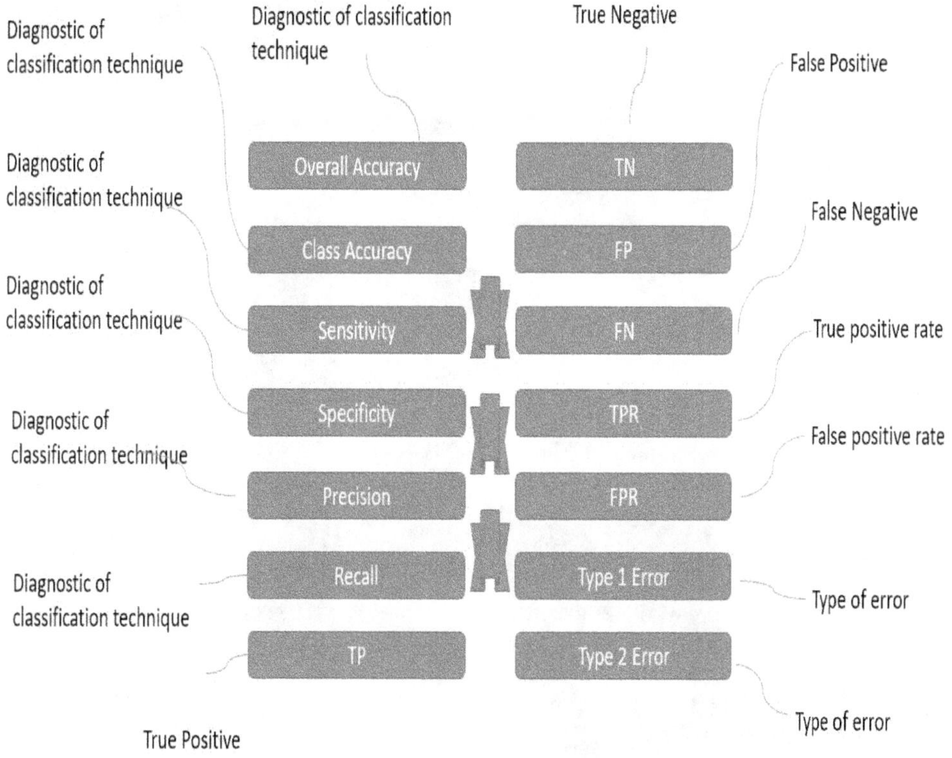
Diagnostic of classification technique
Diagnostic of classification technique
True Negative
False Positive
Overall Accuracy
TN
Diagnostic of classification technique
False Negative
Class Accuracy
FP
Diagnostic of classification technique
Sensitivity
FN
True positive rate
Specificity
TPR
Diagnostic of classification technique
False positive rate
Precision
FPR
Diagnostic of classification technique
Recall
Type 1 Error
Type of error
TP
Type 2 Error
Type of error
True Positive

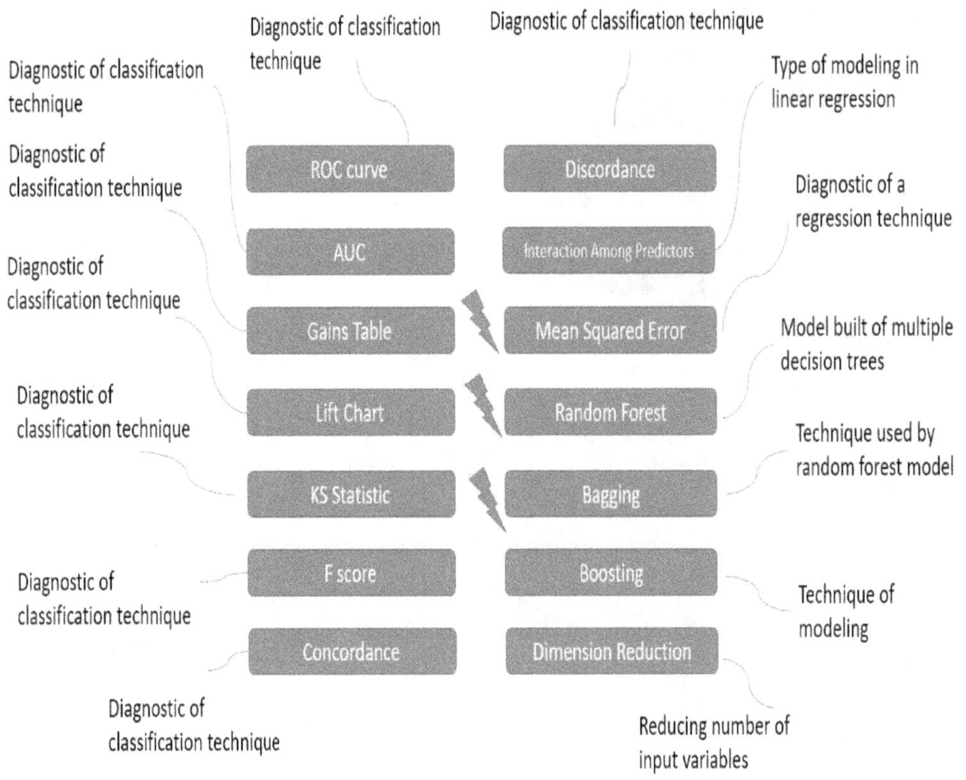
Diagnostic of classification technique
Diagnostic of classification technique
Type of modeling in linear regression
Diagnostic of classification technique
Diagnostic of classification technique
ROC curve
Discordance
Diagnostic of a regression technique
AUC
Interaction Among Predictors
Diagnostic of classification technique
Gains Table
Mean Squared Error
Model built of multiple decision trees
Diagnostic of classification technique
Lift Chart
Random Forest
Technique used by random forest model
KS Statistic
Bagging
F score
Boosting
Diagnostic of classification technique
Technique of modeling
Concordance
Dimension Reduction
Diagnostic of classification technique
Reducing number of input variables

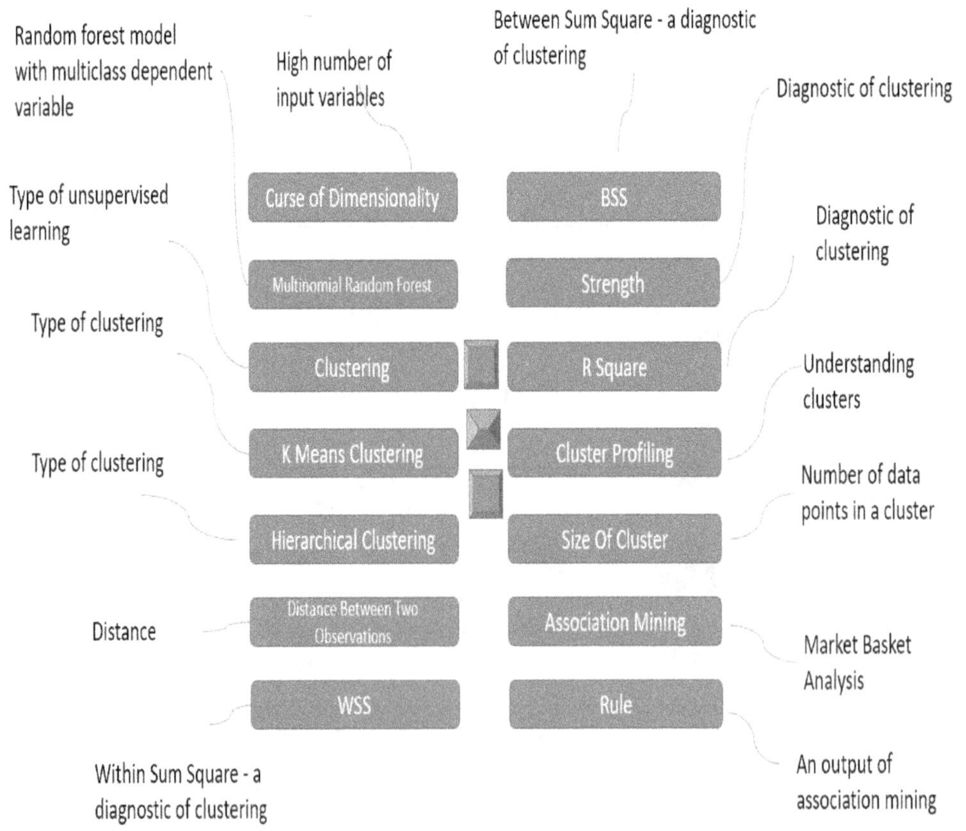
Between Sum Square - a diagnostic of clustering
Random forest model with multiclass dependent variable
High number of input variables
Diagnostic of clustering
Type of unsupervised learning
Curse of Dimensionality
BSS
Diagnostic of clustering
Multinomial Random Forest
Strength
Type of clustering
Clustering
R Square
Understanding clusters
K Means Clustering
Cluster Profiling
Type of clustering
Number of data points in a cluster
Hierarchical Clustering
Size Of Cluster
Distance
Distance Between Two Observations
Association Mining
Market Basket Analysis
WSS
Rule
Within Sum Square - a diagnostic of clustering
An output of association mining

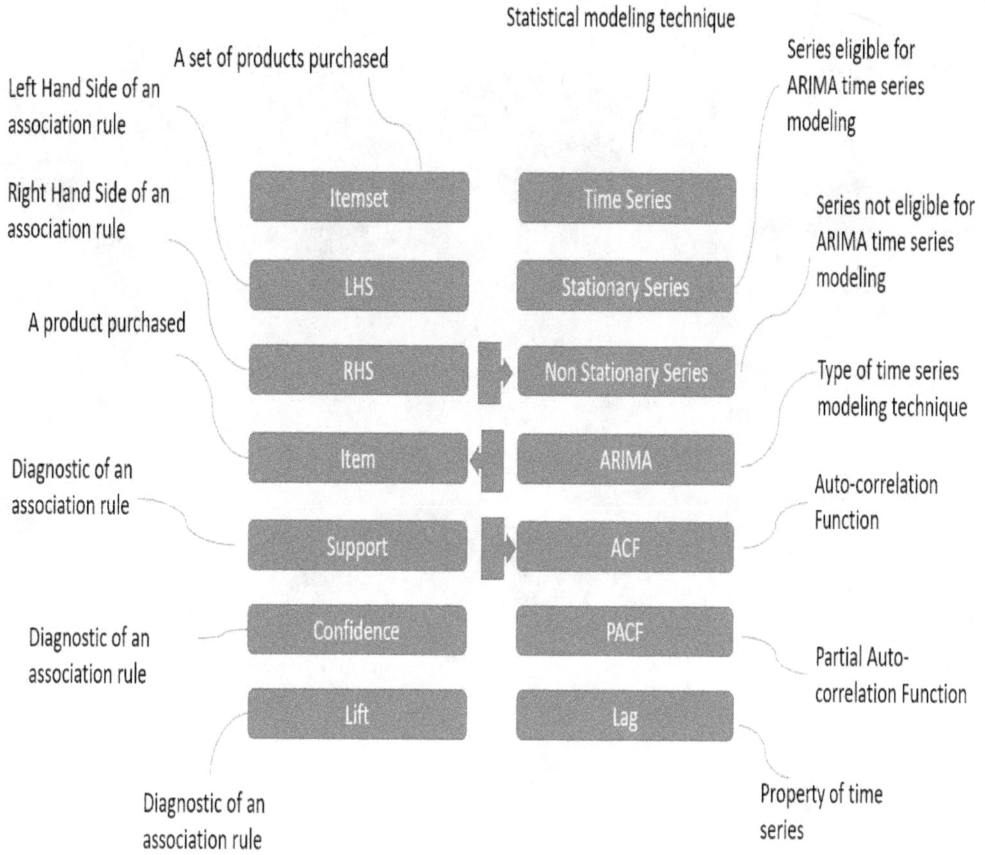
Statistical modeling technique
A set of products purchased
Series eligible for ARIMA time series modeling
Left Hand Side of an association rule
Right Hand Side of an association rule
Itemset
Time Series
Series not eligible for ARIMA time series modeling
LHS
Stationary Series
A product purchased
RHS
Non Stationary Series
Type of time series modeling technique
Item
ARIMA
Diagnostic of an association rule
Auto-correlation Function
Support
ACF
Confidence
PACF
Diagnostic of an association rule
Partial Auto-correlation Function
Lift
Lag
Diagnostic of an association rule
Property of time series

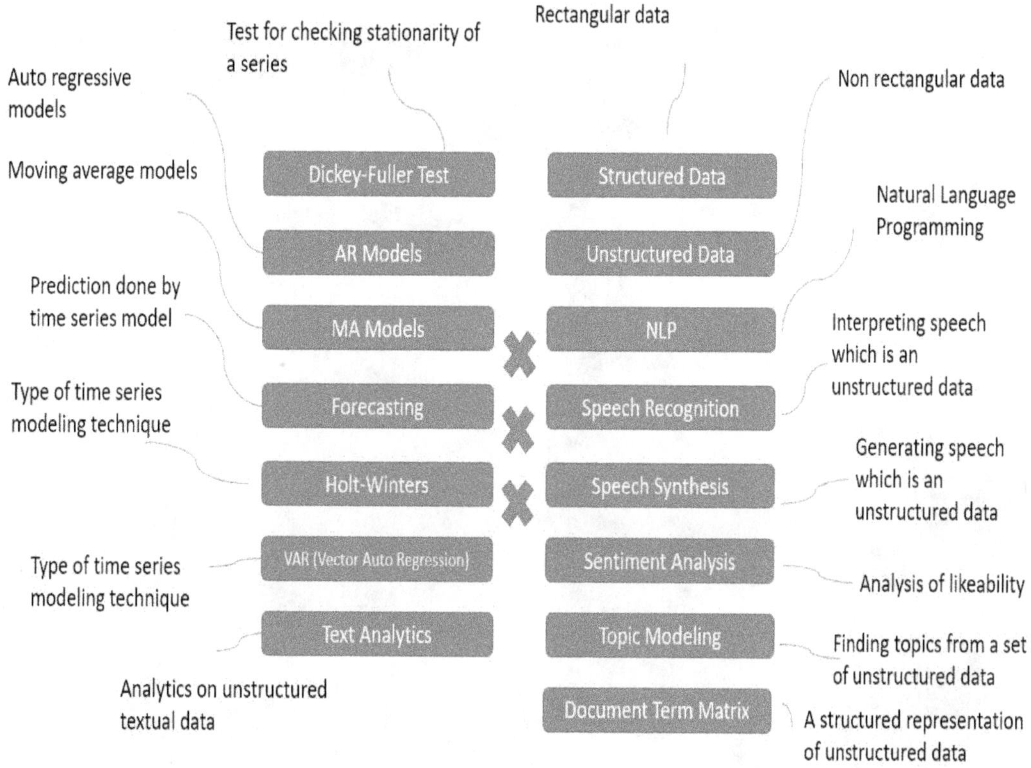
Rectangular data
Test for checking stationarity of a series
Auto regressive models
Non rectangular data
Moving average models
Dickey-Fuller Test
Structured Data
Natural Language Programming
AR Models
Unstructured Data
Prediction done by time series model
MA Models
NLP
Interpreting speech which is an unstructured data
Type of time series modeling technique
Forecasting
Speech Recognition
Generating speech which is an unstructured data
Holt-Winters
Speech Synthesis
Type of time series modeling technique
VAR (Vector Auto Regression)
Sentiment Analysis
Analysis of likeability
Text Analytics
Topic Modeling
Finding topics from a set of unstructured data
Analytics on unstructured textual data
Document Term Matrix
A structured representation of unstructured data

Chapter 9

Dimension Reduction

What are dimensions?

In terms of data science, dimensions are nothing but the columns in the dataset. They are also referred to as variables or features or attributes.

The curse of dimensionality

When more features are available in the data set, the chances of high sparsity of data increases as well. This decreases the statistical significance of the data. The increase in dimensions creates an exponential need for data scientists to handle them. High dimensionality decreases the performance of the model by creating overfitting models. Such models perform poorly with new unseen data. This phenomenon is called "the curse of dimensionality".

Why dimension reduction?

A dataset with a high number of dimensions

- Impacts the performance of the model negatively
- Needs more computing power
- Needs large storage space
- Is hard to understand

There are many techniques to reduce dimensions.

Feature selection

Feature selection is the process in which we select a subset of the features from a large number of features based on statistical analysis. For example, features with low variance can be removed. Features can also be removed if there is a lot of missing values in the variable. In addition, only certain required features can be chosen based on business domain knowledge of the data scientist.

Correlation

Correlation coefficient values range between –1 and 1. A value of 1 is a perfect positive correlation, and that of –1 is a perfect negative correlation. If two independent variables are highly correlated, either positive or negative, only one of them should be used as an input variable during the model building process.

Removing features with low variance

A variable with low or zero variance should be removed from the dataset. Both numeric and non-numeric data have to be checked for variance.

Multicollinearity

Multicollinearity is a phenomenon in which correlation among a few independent variables is high. For example, if the distance traveled in kilometers and distance traveled in miles are both available in the training data as independent variables, then one of them should be discarded.

Feature extraction

Feature extraction is the process in which a new feature is derived using multiple existing features. In the process, the number of features is reduced. The generated feature has a combination of parts of data from multiple features. Hence, it produces better results.

Principal Component Analysis (PCA) and random forest variable importance analysis can also be used for reducing the number of dimensions in the training dataset. A detailed description of each of these methods is out of the scope of the current book. Hence, we will leave it here.

Chapter 10

Machine Learning Using Python

For the examples that we just saw using R and for the examples that we are going to study in Python in the following pages, we have used the same data sets. A brief description of the columns is given below.

Auto dataset

mpg	Miles per gallon
cylinders	Number of cylinders between 4 and 8
displacement	Engine displacement (cu. inches)
horsepower	Engine horsepower
weight	Vehicle weight (lbs.)
acceleration	Time to accelerate from 0 to 60 mph (sec.)
year	Model year (modulo 100)
origin	Origin of car (1. American, 2. European, 3. Japanese)
name	Vehicle name

Iris dataset

Sepal.Length	Length of the sepal
Sepal.Width	Width of the sepal
Petal.Length	Length of the petal
Petal.Width	Width of the petal
Species	Species name of the flower

Salaries dataset

rank	A factor with levels AssocProf, AsstProf and Prof
discipline	A factor with levels A ("theoretical" departments) or B ("applied" departments)
yrs.since.phd	Years since PhD
yrs.service	Years of service
sex	A factor with levels Female Male
salary	Nine-month salary, in dollars

Titanic dataset

PassengerId	Unique identifier for a passenger
Survived	Survival indicator
Pclass	Passenger class
Name	Name of passenger
Sex	Gender of passenger
Age	Age of passenger
SibSp	Number of siblings/spouses aboard
Parch	Number of parents/children aboard
Ticket	Ticket number
Fare	Passenger fare
Cabin	Cabin of passenger
Embarked	Port of embarking (C = Cherbourg; Q = Queenstown; S = Southampton)

Carseats dataset

Sales	Unit sales (in thousands) at each location
CompPrice	Price charged by competitor at each location
Income	Community income level (in thousands of dollars)
Advertising	Local advertising budget for company at each location (in thousands of dollars)
Population	Population size in region (in thousands)

Price	Price the company charges for car seats at each site
ShelveLoc	A factor with levels Bad, Good and Medium indicating the quality of the shelving location for the car seats at each site
Age	Average age of the local population
Education	Education level at each location
Urban	A factor with levels No and Yes to indicate whether the store is in an urban or rural location
US	A factor with levels No and Yes to indicate whether the store is in the US or not

Exploratory Data Analysis

Python code snippet

```
# Import python's os module
import os

# Print current working directory
print(os.getcwd())
```

Output

```
C:\Users\Malaya
```

Python code snippet

```
# Change current working directory
os.chdir("D:\DS Training\Python_2020")

# Print current working directory
print(os.getcwd())
```

Output

```
D:\DS Training\Python_2020
```

Python code snippet

```
# Print a string
print("Hello. How are you doing? By the time you read this, COVID-19 scare would have gone. Stay blessed with a healthy life!")
Hello. How are you doing? By the time you read this, COVID-19 scare would have gone. Stay blessed with a healthy life!
```

Python code snippet

```
# Add two numbers
print(5 + 6)

# This is how a comment line is written
```

Output

```
11
```

Python code snippet

```
# Boolean variables
a = True
b = False

print(type(a))
print(type(b))
```

Output

```
<class 'bool'>
<class 'bool'>
```

Python code snippet

```
# String variables
c = "This is Python"
d = 'This is Python in play'
```

```
print(type(c))
print(type(d))
```

Output

```
<class 'str'>
<class 'str'>
```

Python code snippet

```
# Numeric variables
x = 20
y = 30.2
z = 10 + 3j

print(type(x))
print(type(y))
print(type(z))
```

Output

```
<class 'int'>
<class 'float'>
<class 'complex'>
```

Python code snippet

```
# Sequence variables – list, tuple, range
e = [2, 5.5, 10 + 10j, "Hello"]
f = (2, 5.5, 10 + 10j, "Hello")
g = range(20)

# Access elements of the list
print(e[0])
print(e[1])
print(e[2])
print(e[3])
```

```
print(type(e))
print(type(f))
```

Output

```
2
5.5
(10+10j)
Hello
<class 'list'>
<class 'tuple'>
```

Python code snippet

```
# Print data type
print(type(g))

# Print value
print(g)
```

Output

```
<class 'range'>
range(0, 20)
```

Python code snippet

```
# Mutable list
e[1] = 100
print(e)

# Immutable tuple
# f[1] = 200
print(f)
```

Output

```
[2, 100, (10+10j), 'Hello']
(2, 5.5, (10+10j), 'Hello')
```

Python code snippet

```
# Reassignment of an integer variable
print(x)
x = 30
print(x)
```

Output

```
20
30
```

Python code snippet

```
# Dictionary variable
h = {"name": "Malaya", "age": 37, "qualification": "MBA", "role": ["data science", "analytics", "data mining", 260] }

print(type(h))
print(h)

# Print an element of dictionary
print(h["name"])
print(h["role"])

# Print data type of an element of dictionary
print(type(h["name"]))
print(type(h["age"]))
print(type(h["role"]))
```

Output

```
<class 'dict'>
{'name': 'Malaya', 'age': 37, 'qualification': 'MBA', 'role': ['data science', 'analytics', 'data mining', 260]}
Malaya
['data science', 'analytics', 'data mining', 260]
<class 'str'>
<class 'int'>
<class 'list'>
```

Python code snippet

```
import pandas as pd

# Read CSV file from working directory
Auto_from_R_to_Python = pd.read_csv("Auto_from_R_to_Python.csv")

# Print the data frame
print(Auto_from_R_to_Python)

# Get the data type of Auto_from_R_to_Python
print(type(Auto_from_R_to_Python))
```

Output

```
      mpg  cylinders  displacement  horsepower  weight
acceleration  year  \
0    18.0          8         307.0         130    3504
12.0     70
1    15.0          8         350.0         165    3693
11.5     70
2    18.0          8         318.0         150    3436
11.0     70
3    16.0          8         304.0         150    3433
12.0     70
4    17.0          8         302.0         140    3449
10.5     70
..    ...        ...           ...         ...     ...
...    ...
387  27.0          4         140.0          86    2790
15.6     82
388  44.0          4          97.0          52    2130
24.6     82
389  32.0          4         135.0          84    2295
11.6     82
390  28.0          4         120.0          79    2625
18.6     82
391  31.0          4         119.0          82    2720
19.4     82

     origin                       name
0         1  chevrolet chevelle malibu
1         1          buick skylark 320
2         1         plymouth satellite
3         1              amc rebel sst
4         1                ford torino
..      ...                        ...
387       1            ford mustang gl
388       2                  vw pickup
389       1              dodge rampage
390       1                ford ranger
391       1                 chevy s-10

[392 rows x 9 columns]
<class 'pandas.core.frame.DataFrame'>
```

Python code snippet

```
# Display first 15 rows of the data frame
print(Auto_from_R_to_Python.head(15))

# Display last 15 rows of the data frame
print(Auto_from_R_to_Python.tail(15))

# Print one column of the data frame
print(Auto_from_R_to_Python[["mpg"]])

print(type(Auto_from_R_to_Python))
```

Output

```
      mpg  cylinders  displacement  horsepower  weight
acceleration  year  \
0   18.0          8         307.0         130    3504
12.0     70
1   15.0          8         350.0         165    3693
11.5     70
2   18.0          8         318.0         150    3436
11.0     70
3   16.0          8         304.0         150    3433
12.0     70
4   17.0          8         302.0         140    3449
10.5     70
5   15.0          8         429.0         198    4341
10.0     70
6   14.0          8         454.0         220    4354
9.0     70
7   14.0          8         440.0         215    4312
8.5     70
8   14.0          8         455.0         225    4425
10.0     70
9   15.0          8         390.0         190    3850
8.5     70
10  15.0          8         383.0         170    3563
10.0     70
11  14.0          8         340.0         160    3609
8.0     70
12  15.0          8         400.0         150    3761
9.5     70
13  14.0          8         455.0         225    3086
10.0     70
14  24.0          4         113.0          95    2372
15.0     70
```

```
    origin                       name
0        1  chevrolet chevelle malibu
1        1          buick skylark 320
2        1         plymouth satellite
3        1              amc rebel sst
4        1                ford torino
5        1           ford galaxie 500
6        1           chevrolet impala
7        1          plymouth fury iii
8        1           pontiac catalina
9        1         amc ambassador dpl
10       1        dodge challenger se
11       1         plymouth 'cuda 340
12       1      chevrolet monte carlo
13       1    buick estate wagon (sw)
14       3      toyota corona mark ii


      mpg  cylinders  displacement  horsepower  weight
acceleration  year  \
377  38.0          4          91.0          67    1965
15.0    82
378  32.0          4          91.0          67    1965
15.7    82
379  38.0          4          91.0          67    1995
16.2    82
380  25.0          6         181.0         110    2945
16.4    82
381  38.0          6         262.0          85    3015
17.0    82
382  26.0          4         156.0          92    2585
14.5    82
383  22.0          6         232.0         112    2835
14.7    82
384  32.0          4         144.0          96    2665
13.9    82
385  36.0          4         135.0          84    2370
13.0    82
386  27.0          4         151.0          90    2950
17.3    82
387  27.0          4         140.0          86    2790
15.6    82
388  44.0          4          97.0          52    2130
24.6    82
389  32.0          4         135.0          84    2295
11.6    82
390  28.0          4         120.0          79    2625
18.6    82
391  31.0          4         119.0          82    2720
19.4    82
```

```
     origin                               name
377       3                        honda civic
378       3                 honda civic (auto)
379       3                      datsun 310 gx
380       1              buick century limited
381       1  oldsmobile cutlass ciera (diesel)
382       1         chrysler lebaron medallion
383       1                     ford granada l
384       3                   toyota celica gt
385       1                  dodge charger 2.2
386       1                   chevrolet camaro
387       1                    ford mustang gl
388       2                          vw pickup
389       1                      dodge rampage
390       1                        ford ranger
391       1                         chevy s-10
      mpg
0    18.0
1    15.0
2    18.0
3    16.0
4    17.0
..    ...
387  27.0
388  44.0
389  32.0
390  28.0
391  31.0

[392 rows x 1 columns]
<class 'pandas.core.frame.DataFrame'>
```

Python code snippet

```
# Create an empty data frame
df_empty = pd.DataFrame()
print(df_empty)

# Create data frame from a list
list_1 = [2, 5.5, 10 + 10j, "Hello"]
df_1 = pd.DataFrame(list_1)
print(df_1)
print(type(df_1))
```

Output

```
Empty DataFrame
Columns: []
Index: []
           0
0          2
1        5.5
2  (10+10j)
3      Hello
<class 'pandas.core.frame.DataFrame'>
```

Python code snippet

```
# Create a data frame from a list of lists
data_1 = [['Starbucks',65],['Amadora',70],['Mamagoto',40],['Nandos',90],['Little Italy',55],['Jonahs Bistro', 95]]
df_restaurants = pd.DataFrame(data_1, columns = ['Restaurant_Name', 'Score'])
print(df_restaurants)
print(type(df_restaurants))

# Create a data frame from a list of lists with score of type floating point
data_1 = [['Starbucks',65],['Amadora',70],['Mamagoto',40],['Nandos',90],['Little Italy',55],['Jonahs Bistro', 95]]
df_restaurants = pd.DataFrame(data_1, columns = ['Restaurant_Name', 'Score'], dtype = float)
print(df_restaurants)
print(type(df_restaurants))
```

Output

```
  Restaurant_Name  Score
0       Starbucks     65
1         Amadora     70
2        Mamagoto     40
3          Nandos     90
4    Little Italy     55
5   Jonahs Bistro     95
<class 'pandas.core.frame.DataFrame'>
  Restaurant_Name  Score
0       Starbucks   65.0
1         Amadora   70.0
2        Mamagoto   40.0
3          Nandos   90.0
4    Little Italy   55.0
5   Jonahs Bistro   95.0
<class 'pandas.core.frame.DataFrame'>
```

Python code snippet

```
# Create a data frame from a dictionary of lists
data_1 = {'Restaurant_Name' : ['Starbucks', 'Amadora', 'Mamagoto', 'Nandos', 'Little Italy', 'Jonahs
Bistro'], 'Score' : [65, 70, 40, 90, 55, 95]}
df_restaurants = pd.DataFrame(data_1)
print(df_restaurants)

# Create a data frame from a dictionary of lists with index
data_1 = {'Restaurant_Name' : ['Starbucks', 'Amadora', 'Mamagoto', 'Nandos', 'Little Italy', 'Jonahs
Bistro'], 'Score' : [65, 70, 40, 90, 55, 95]}
df_restaurants = pd.DataFrame(data_1, index = ['A', 'B', 'C', 'D', 'E', 'F'])
print(df_restaurants)
```

Output

```
  Restaurant_Name  Score
0       Starbucks     65
1         Amadora     70
2        Mamagoto     40
3          Nandos     90
4    Little Italy     55
5   Jonahs Bistro     95
  Restaurant_Name  Score
A       Starbucks     65
B         Amadora     70
C        Mamagoto     40
D          Nandos     90
E    Little Italy     55
F   Jonahs Bistro     95
```

Python code snippet

```
# Create a data frame from a list of dictionaries
data_1 = [{'Starbucks': 65}, {'Amadora' : 70}, {'Mamagoto': 40}, {'Nandos': 90}, {'Little Italy': 55},
{'Jonahs Bistro': 95}]
df_restaurants = pd.DataFrame(data_1)
print(df_restaurants)

# Create a data frame from a list of dictionaries with row names
data_1 = [{'Starbucks': 65}, {'Amadora' : 70}, {'Mamagoto': 40}, {'Nandos': 90}, {'Little Italy': 55},
{'Jonahs Bistro': 95}]
df_restaurants = pd.DataFrame(data_1, index = ['A', 'B', 'C', 'D', 'E', 'F'])
print(df_restaurants)
```

Output

```
   Starbucks  Amadora  Mamagoto  Nandos  Little Italy  Jonahs
Bistro
0       65.0      NaN       NaN     NaN           NaN
NaN
1        NaN     70.0       NaN     NaN           NaN
NaN
2        NaN      NaN      40.0     NaN           NaN
NaN
3        NaN      NaN       NaN    90.0           NaN
NaN
4        NaN      NaN       NaN     NaN          55.0
NaN
5        NaN      NaN       NaN     NaN           NaN
95.0
   Starbucks  Amadora  Mamagoto  Nandos  Little Italy  Jonahs
Bistro
A       65.0      NaN       NaN     NaN           NaN
NaN
B        NaN     70.0       NaN     NaN           NaN
NaN
C        NaN      NaN      40.0     NaN           NaN
NaN
D        NaN      NaN       NaN    90.0           NaN
NaN
E        NaN      NaN       NaN     NaN          55.0
NaN
F        NaN      NaN       NaN     NaN           NaN
95.0
```

Python code snippet

```
# Create a data frame from a dictionary of series
data_1 = {'Restaurant Name': pd.Series(['Starbucks', 'Amadora', 'Mamagoto', 'Nandos', 'Little Italy',
'Jonahs Bistro'], index = ['A', 'B', 'C', 'D', 'E', 'F'] ),
'Score': pd.Series([65, 70, 40, 90, 55, 95], index = ['A', 'B', 'C', 'D', 'E', 'F'] )}
df_restaurants = pd.DataFrame(data_1)
print(df_restaurants)
```

Output

```
   Restaurant Name  Score
A        Starbucks     65
B          Amadora     70
C         Mamagoto     40
D           Nandos     90
E     Little Italy     55
F    Jonahs Bistro     95
```

Python code snippet

```
# Display a column
print(df_restaurants['Score'])

# Add a new column to the existing data frame
data_1 = {'Restaurant Name': pd.Series(['Starbucks', 'Amadora', 'Mamagoto', 'Nandos', 'Little Italy', 'Jonahs Bistro'], index = ['A', 'B', 'C', 'D', 'E', 'F'] ),
'Score': pd.Series([65, 70, 40, 90, 55, 95], index = ['A', 'B', 'C', 'D', 'E', 'F'] )}
df_restaurants = pd.DataFrame(data_1)

df_restaurants['Number of Employees'] = pd.Series([30, 42, 18, 100, 250, 19], index = ['A', 'B', 'C', 'D', 'E', 'F'])
print(df_restaurants)
```

Output

```
A    65
B    70
C    40
D    90
E    55
F    95
Name: Score, dtype: int64
   Restaurant Name  Score  Number of Employees
A        Starbucks     65                   30
B          Amadora     70                   42
C         Mamagoto     40                   18
D           Nandos     90                  100
E     Little Italy     55                  250
F    Jonahs Bistro     95                   19
```

Python code snippet

```
# Create a new column for sum and add to the data frame
df_restaurants['Sum'] = df_restaurants['Score'] + df_restaurants['Number of Employees']
print(df_restaurants)

print(type(df_restaurants))

# Delete a column from a data frame
df_restaurants.pop('Score')
print(df_restaurants)

print(type(df_restaurants))
```

Output

```
  Restaurant Name  Score  Number of Employees  Sum
A       Starbucks     65                   30   95
B         Amadora     70                   42  112
C        Mamagoto     40                   18   58
D          Nandos     90                  100  190
E    Little Italy     55                  250  305
F   Jonahs Bistro     95                   19  114
<class 'pandas.core.frame.DataFrame'>
  Restaurant Name  Number of Employees  Sum
A       Starbucks                   30   95
B         Amadora                   42  112
C        Mamagoto                   18   58
D          Nandos                  100  190
E    Little Italy                  250  305
F   Jonahs Bistro                   19  114
<class 'pandas.core.frame.DataFrame'>
```

Python code snippet

```
# Select a row from data frame
df_nandos = df_restaurants.loc['D']
print(df_nandos)
```

 # Select a row from data frame
print(df_restaurants.loc['A'])

 # Select a set of rows from data frame
print(df_restaurants.iloc[1])
print(df_restaurants.iloc[2:4])

Output

```
Restaurant Name          Nandos
Number of Employees         100
Sum                         190
Name: D, dtype: object
Restaurant Name          Starbucks
Number of Employees             30
Sum                             95
Name: A, dtype: object
Restaurant Name          Amadora
Number of Employees           42
Sum                          112
Name: B, dtype: object
  Restaurant Name  Number of Employees  Sum
C        Mamagoto                   18   58
D          Nandos                  100  190
```

Python code snippet

 # Add a new row to the data frame
df_Sea_Shell = pd.DataFrame([['Sea Shell', 18, 34]], columns = ['Restaurant Name', 'Number of Employees', 'Sum'], index = ['G'])
df_restaurants = df_restaurants.append(df_Sea_Shell)
print(df_restaurants)

 # Delete rows from the data frame
df_restaurants = df_restaurants.drop(['C', 'E'])
print(df_restaurants)

Output

```
  Restaurant Name  Number of Employees  Sum
A       Starbucks                   30   95
B         Amadora                   42  112
C        Mamagoto                   18   58
D          Nandos                  100  190
E    Little Italy                  250  305
F   Jonahs Bistro                   19  114
G       Sea Shell                   18   34
  Restaurant Name  Number of Employees  Sum
A       Starbucks                   30   95
B         Amadora                   42  112
D          Nandos                  100  190
F   Jonahs Bistro                   19  114
G       Sea Shell                   18   34
```

Python code snippet

```
# Scatter plot
import matplotlib.pyplot as plot

x = Auto_from_R_to_Python['mpg']
y = Auto_from_R_to_Python['displacement']
plot.scatter(x, y, alpha=0.5)
plot.title('Scatter plot')
plot.xlabel('mpg')
plot.ylabel('displacement')
plot.show()
```

Output

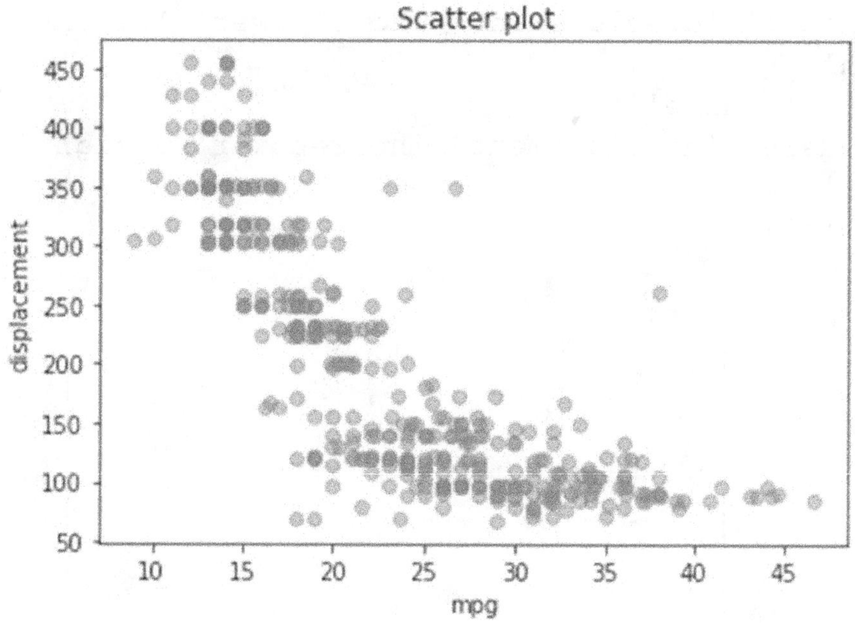

Python code snippet

```
# Pairwise scatter plot
import seaborn as sb

Auto_100 = Auto_from_R_to_Python

# Display column names of the data frame before deleting name
print(Auto_100.columns.values)

# Delete name. It is too granular
del Auto_100['name']

# Display column names of the data frame after deleting name
print(Auto_100.columns.values)

sb.pairplot(Auto_100)
plot.show()
```

Output

```
['mpg' 'cylinders' 'displacement' 'horsepower' 'weight'
'acceleration'
 'year' 'origin' 'name']
['mpg' 'cylinders' 'displacement' 'horsepower' 'weight'
'acceleration'
 'year' 'origin']
```

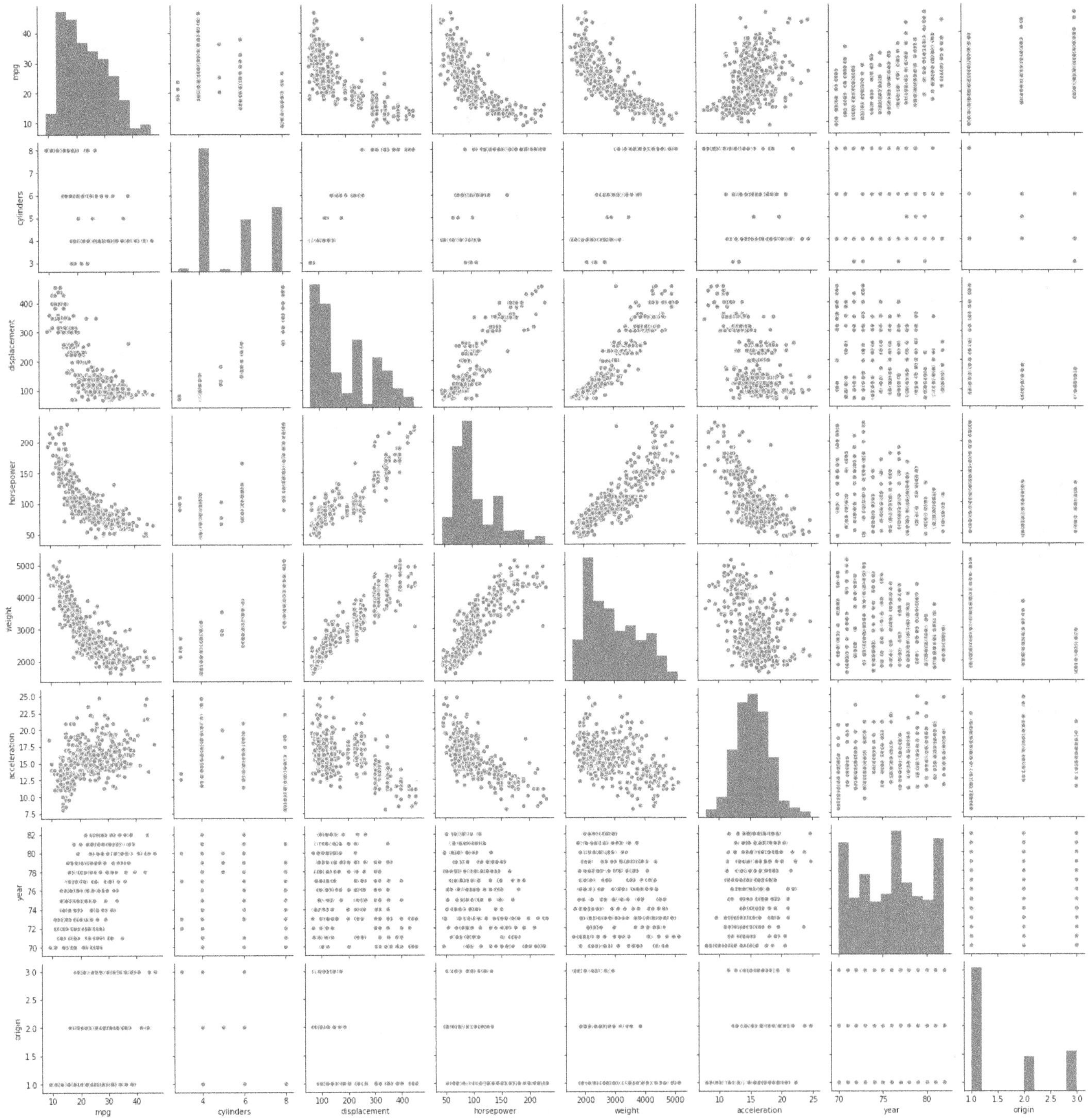

Linear Regression

Python code snippet

```
# Read CSV file from working directory
Salaries_from_R_to_Python = pd.read_csv("Salaries_from_R_to_Python.csv")

# Print the data frame
print(Salaries_from_R_to_Python)

# Get the data type of Salaries_from_R_to_Python
print(type(Salaries_from_R_to_Python))
```

Output

```
          rank discipline  yrs.since.phd  yrs.service   sex
salary
0         Prof          B             19           18  Male
139750
1         Prof          B             20           16  Male
173200
2     AsstProf          B              4            3  Male
79750
3         Prof          B             45           39  Male
115000
4         Prof          B             40           41  Male
141500
..         ...        ...            ...          ...   ...
...
392       Prof          A             33           30  Male
103106
393       Prof          A             31           19  Male
150564
394       Prof          A             42           25  Male
101738
395       Prof          A             25           15  Male
95329
396   AsstProf          A              8            4  Male
81035

[397 rows x 6 columns]
<class 'pandas.core.frame.DataFrame'>
```

Python code snippet

```
# View the column names and their data types from a data frame
print(Salaries_from_R_to_Python.dtypes)

# Check information related to columns of the data frame
print(Salaries_from_R_to_Python.info())
```

Output

```
rank              object
discipline        object
yrs.since.phd      int64
yrs.service        int64
sex               object
salary             int64
dtype: object
<class 'pandas.core.frame.DataFrame'>
RangeIndex: 397 entries, 0 to 396
Data columns (total 6 columns):
 #   Column         Non-Null Count  Dtype
---  ------         --------------  -----
 0   rank           397 non-null    object
 1   discipline     397 non-null    object
 2   yrs.since.phd  397 non-null    int64
 3   yrs.service    397 non-null    int64
 4   sex            397 non-null    object
 5   salary         397 non-null    int64
dtypes: int64(3), object(3)
memory usage: 18.7+ KB
None
```

Python code snippet

```
# Scatter plot between years since phd and salary
x1 = Salaries_from_R_to_Python['yrs.since.phd']
y1 = Salaries_from_R_to_Python['salary']
plot.scatter(x1, y1, alpha=0.5)
plot.title('Scatter plot')
```

```
plot.xlabel('yrs.since.phd')
plot.ylabel('salary')
plot.show()
```

Output

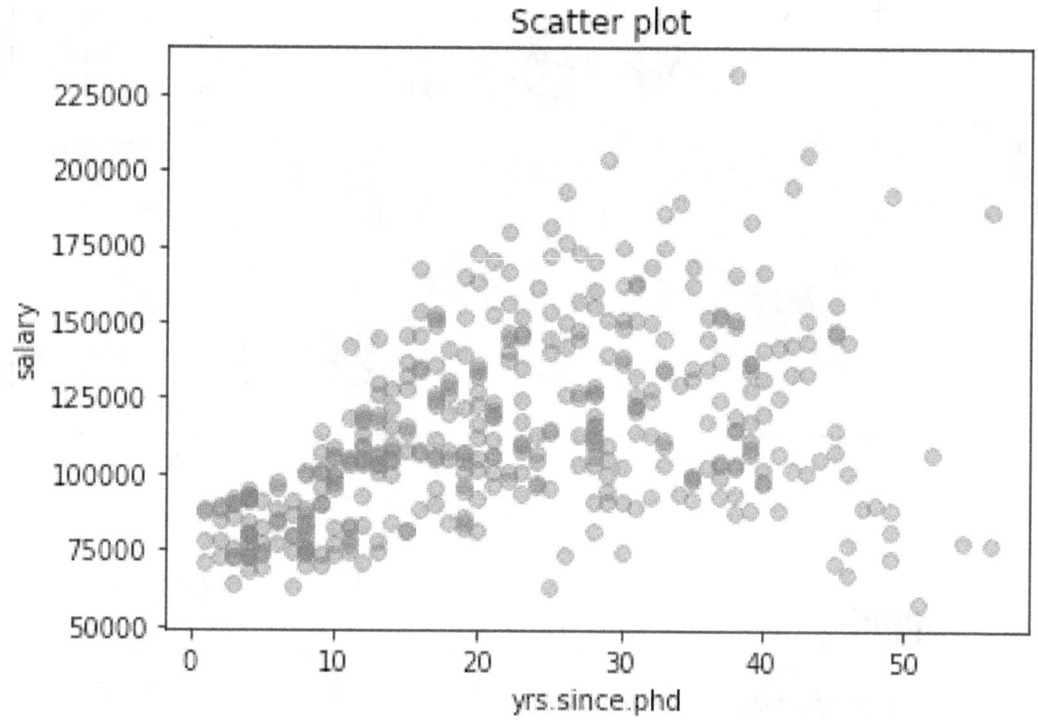

Python code snippet

```
# Scatter plot between years of service and salary
x2 = Salaries_from_R_to_Python['yrs.service']
y2 = Salaries_from_R_to_Python['salary']
plot.scatter(x2, y2, alpha=0.5)
plot.title('Scatter plot')
plot.xlabel('yrs.service')
plot.ylabel('salary')
plot.show()
```

Output

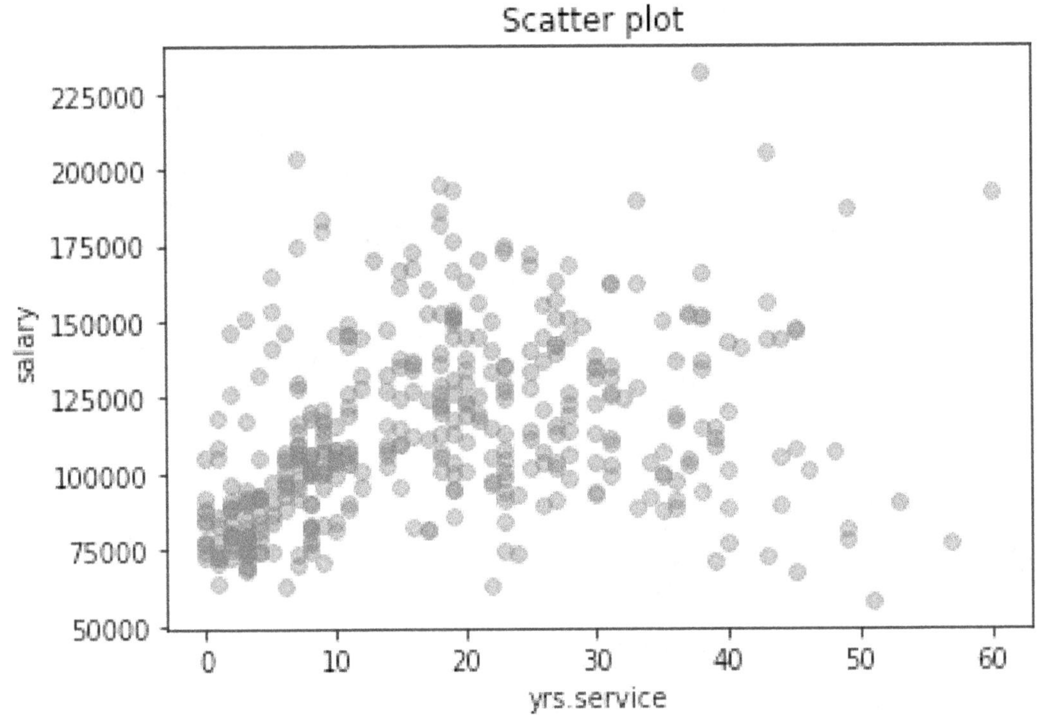

Python code snippet

```
# Scatter plot between years of service and years since phd
x3 = Salaries_from_R_to_Python['yrs.service']
y3 = Salaries_from_R_to_Python['yrs.since.phd']
plot.scatter(x3, y3, alpha=0.5)
plot.title('Scatter plot')
plot.xlabel('yrs.service')
plot.ylabel('yrs.since.phd')
plot.show()
```

Output

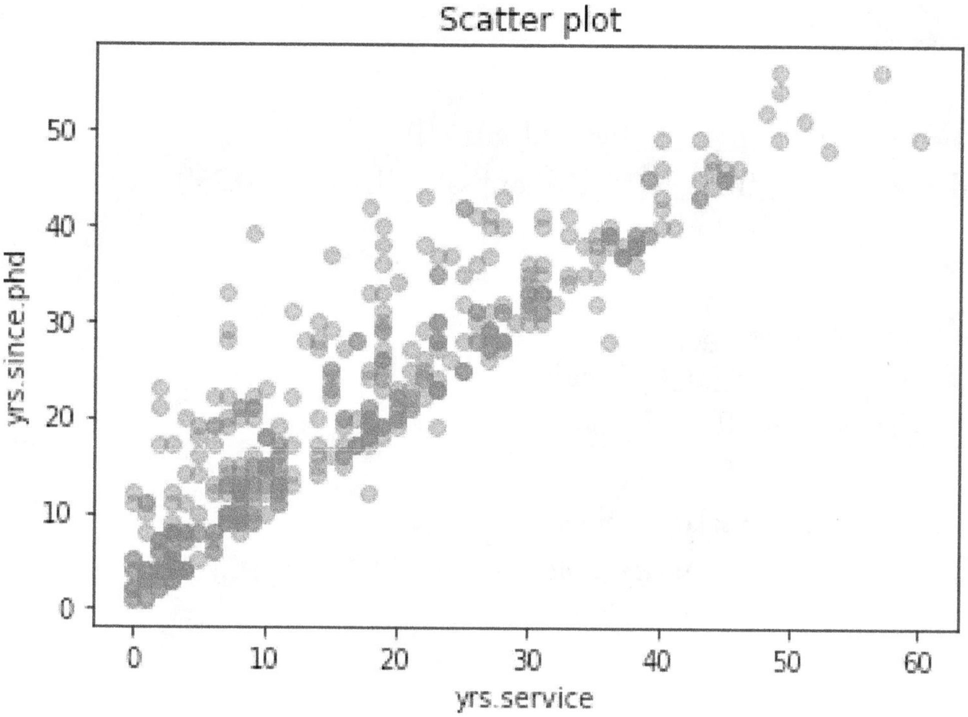

Python code snippet

```
# Pearson's correlation
print(x3.corr(y3))

# Spearman's correlation
print(x3.corr(y3, method = 'spearman'))

# Kendall's correlation
print(x3.corr(y3, method = 'kendall'))
```

Output

```
0.9096491483396811
0.9062777271240507
0.764323830197049
```

Python code snippet

```
# Box plot of salary
import seaborn as sb

sb.boxplot(data = Salaries_from_R_to_Python['salary'])
sb.swarmplot(data = Salaries_from_R_to_Python['salary'], color = '0.25')
plot.show()

# Box plot of salary for each rank
rank_holder = Salaries_from_R_to_Python['rank']
salary_holder = Salaries_from_R_to_Python['salary']

sb.boxplot(x = rank_holder, y = salary_holder)
sb.swarmplot(x = rank_holder, y = salary_holder, color = '0.25')
plot.show()
```

Output

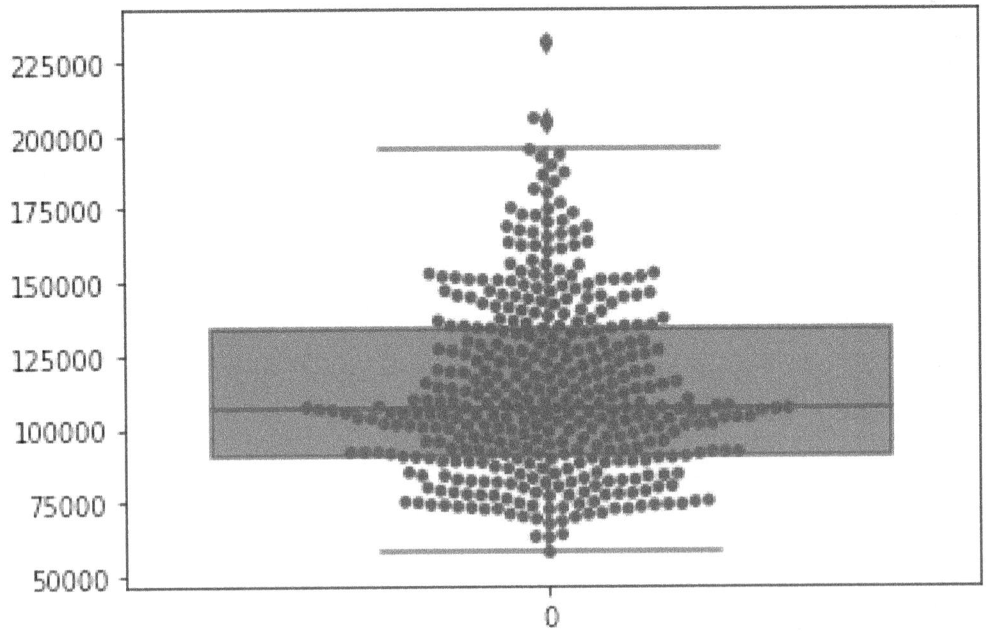

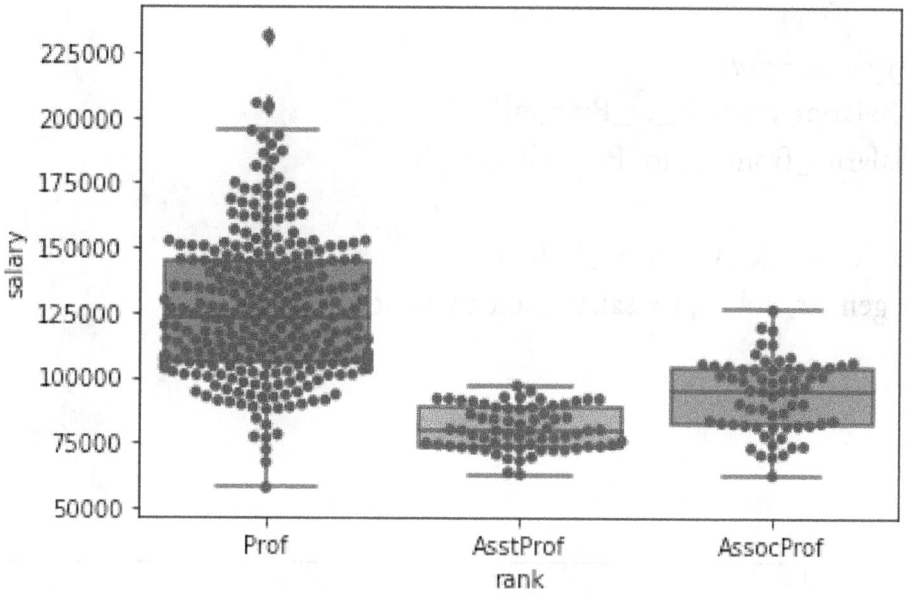

Python code snippet

```
# Box plot of salary for each discipline
discipline_holder = Salaries_from_R_to_Python['discipline']
salary_holder = Salaries_from_R_to_Python['salary']

sb.boxplot(x = discipline_holder, y = salary_holder)
sb.swarmplot(x = discipline_holder, y = salary_holder, color = '0.25')
plot.show()
```

Output

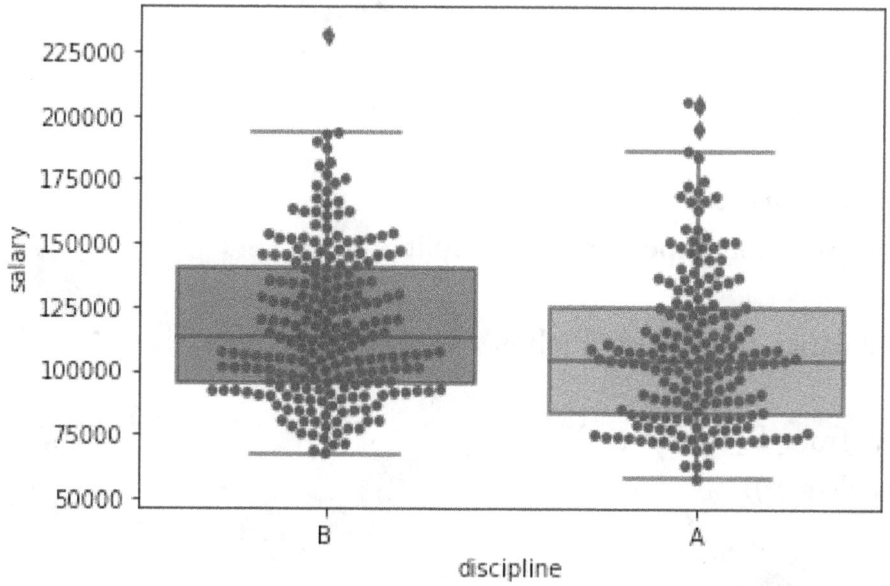

Python code snippet

```
# Box plot of salary for each gender
gender_holder = Salaries_from_R_to_Python['sex']
salary_holder = Salaries_from_R_to_Python['salary']

sb.boxplot(x = gender_holder, y = salary_holder)
sb.swarmplot(x = gender_holder, y = salary_holder, color = '0.25')
plot.show()
```

Output

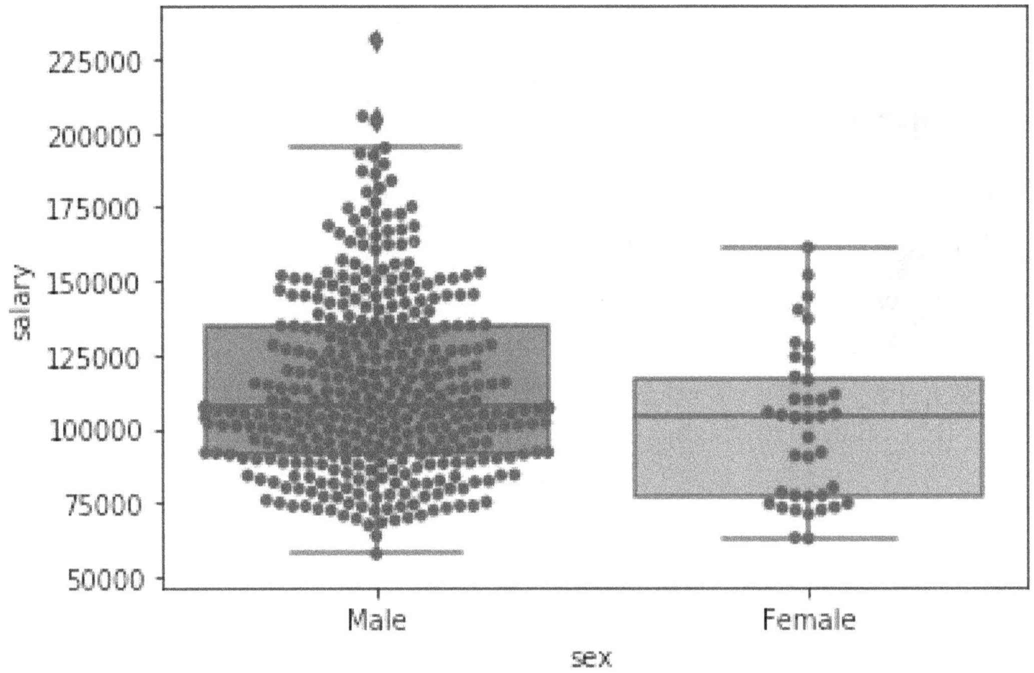

Python code snippet

```
# Divide the data into train and test sets
from sklearn.model_selection import train_test_split

salaries_dataset = Salaries_from_R_to_Python

print(type(Salaries_from_R_to_Python))
print(type(salaries_dataset))
```

print('Independent variables dataset before deleting target is ' , salaries_dataset.columns.values)

salaries_dataset = salaries_dataset.drop('salary' , axis='columns')

print('Independent variables dataset after deleting target is ' , salaries_dataset.columns.values)

x = salaries_dataset
print('Information about x is as follows: ' , x.head(10))
print('datatype of x is ' , type(x))

print('remark 100 is ' , Salaries_from_R_to_Python.columns.values)

Output

```
<class 'pandas.core.frame.DataFrame'>
<class 'pandas.core.frame.DataFrame'>
Independent variables dataset before deleting target is
['rank' 'discipline' 'yrs.since.phd' 'yrs.service' 'sex'
'salary']
Independent variables dataset after deleting target is
['rank' 'discipline' 'yrs.since.phd' 'yrs.service' 'sex']
Information about x is as follows:           rank discipline
yrs.since.phd  yrs.service     sex
0        Prof          B          19          18     Male
1        Prof          B          20          16     Male
2    AsstProf          B           4           3     Male
3        Prof          B          45          39     Male
4        Prof          B          40          41     Male
5   AssocProf          B           6           6     Male
6        Prof          B          30          23     Male
7        Prof          B          45          45     Male
8        Prof          B          21          20     Male
9        Prof          B          18          18   Female
datatype of x is  <class 'pandas.core.frame.DataFrame'>
remark 100 is  ['rank' 'discipline' 'yrs.since.phd'
'yrs.service' 'sex' 'salary']
```

Python code snippet

```
y = Salaries_from_R_to_Python['salary']
print('Information about y is as follows: ' , y.head(10))
print('datatype of y before conversion is ' , type(y))
y = y.to_frame()
print('datatype of y after conversion is ' , type(y))
```

Output

```
Information about y is as follows:  0    139750
1    173200
2     79750
3    115000
4    141500
5     97000
6    175000
7    147765
8    119250
9    129000
Name: salary, dtype: int64
datatype of y before conversion is  <class
'pandas.core.series.Series'>
datatype of y after conversion is  <class
'pandas.core.frame.DataFrame'>
```

Python code snippet

```
# One hot encoding
for i in x.columns:
if x[i].dtype==object:
dummy_columns = pd.get_dummies(x[i])
x = x.join(dummy_columns)
del x[i]

x_train, x_test, y_train, y_test = train_test_split(x, y, test_size=0.30, random_state = 200)
```

```
row_count_train, col_count_train = x_train.shape
print('Number of rows in train ' , row_count_train)
print('Number of columns in train ' , col_count_train)

row_count_test, col_count_test = x_test.shape
print('Number of rows in test ' , row_count_test)
print('Number of columns in test ' , col_count_test)

print('List of column names are: ' , x_train.columns.values)
```

Output

```
Number of rows in train  277
Number of columns in train  9
Number of rows in test  120
Number of columns in test  9
List of column names are:  ['yrs.since.phd' 'yrs.service'
'AssocProf' 'AsstProf' 'Prof' 'A' 'B'
 'Female' 'Male']
```

Python code snippet

```
from sklearn import linear_model

lm = linear_model.LinearRegression()
model = lm.fit(x_train, y_train)

print('COEFFICIENTS: ' , model.coef_)
print('INTERCEPT: ' , model.intercept_)
```

Output

```
COEFFICIENTS:  [[   360.3295689    -436.19123352
6999.73105487 -19608.81910005
   26608.55015493  -6664.21083832   6664.21083832
2927.8370075
    2927.8370075 ]]
INTERCEPT:  [96809.74113764]
```

Python code snippet

```
import sklearn.metrics as metrics
import numpy as np


def mape(y_true, y_pred):

y_true, y_pred = np.array(y_true), np.array(y_pred)
return np.mean(np.abs((y_true - y_pred) / y_true)) * 100

# User defined function for calculating linear regression performance metrics
def linear_regression_performance_metrics(y_true, y_pred):

r_square = metrics.r2_score(y_true, y_pred)
mean_absolute_percentage_error = mape(y_true, y_pred)
mean_squared_error = metrics.mean_squared_error(y_true, y_pred)
mean_squared_log_error = metrics.mean_squared_log_error(y_true, y_pred)

print('R Square: ', round(r_square, 4))
print('Mean Absolute Percentage Error: ', round(mean_absolute_percentage_error, 4))
print('Mean Squared Error: ', round(mean_squared_error, 4))
print('Root Mean Square Error: ', round(np.sqrt(mean_squared_error), 4))
print('Mean Squared Log Error: ', round(mean_squared_log_error, 4))

# Get the predicted values of y from train data
y_pred_train = model.predict(x_train)

# Get the train performance metrics
print('TRAIN PERFORMANCE')
linear_regression_performance_metrics(y_train, y_pred_train)

# Get the predicted values of y from test data
y_pred_test = model.predict(x_test)

print('TEST PERFORMANCE')
# Get the test performance metrics
linear_regression_performance_metrics(y_test, y_pred_test)
```

Output

```
TRAIN PERFORMANCE
R Square:  0.4541
Mean Absolute Percentage Error:  14.3042
Mean Squared Error:  485682530.5644
Root Mean Square Error:  22038.2062
Mean Squared Log Error:  0.0323
TEST PERFORMANCE
R Square:  0.4493
Mean Absolute Percentage Error:  14.0443
Mean Squared Error:  535867098.7999
Root Mean Square Error:  23148.8034
Mean Squared Log Error:  0.0322
```

Logistic Regression

Python code snippet

```
# Read CSV file from working directory
Titanic_from_R_to_Python = pd.read_csv("Titanic_from_R_to_Python.csv")

# Print the data frame
print(Titanic_from_R_to_Python)

# Get the data type of Titanic_from_R_to_Python
print(type(Titanic_from_R_to_Python))

# View the column names and their data types from a data frame
print(Titanic_from_R_to_Python.dtypes)

# Check information related to columns of the data frame
print(Titanic_from_R_to_Python.info())
```

Output

```
     PassengerId  Survived  Pclass  \
0              1         0       3
1              2         1       1
2              3         1       3
3              4         1       1
4              5         0       3
..           ...       ...     ...
886          887         0       2
887          888         1       1
888          889         0       3
889          890         1       1
890          891         0       3
```

```
                                                    Name     Sex
Age  SibSp  \
0                              Braund, Mr. Owen Harris    male
22.0      1
1    Cumings, Mrs. John Bradley (Florence Briggs Th...  female
38.0      1
2                               Heikkinen, Miss. Laina  female
26.0      0
3         Futrelle, Mrs. Jacques Heath (Lily May Peel)  female
35.0      1
4                             Allen, Mr. William Henry    male
35.0      0
..                                                 ...     ...
...     ...
886                              Montvila, Rev. Juozas    male
27.0      0
887                       Graham, Miss. Margaret Edith  female
19.0      0
888           Johnston, Miss. Catherine Helen "Carrie"  female
NaN      1
889                              Behr, Mr. Karl Howell    male
26.0      0
890                                Dooley, Mr. Patrick    male
32.0      0


     Parch            Ticket     Fare Cabin Embarked
0        0         A/5 21171   7.2500   NaN        S
1        0          PC 17599  71.2833   C85        C
2        0  STON/O2. 3101282   7.9250   NaN        S
3        0            113803  53.1000  C123        S
4        0            373450   8.0500   NaN        S
..     ...               ...      ...   ...      ...
886      0            211536  13.0000   NaN        S
887      0            112053  30.0000   B42        S
888      2        W./C. 6607  23.4500   NaN        S
889      0            111369  30.0000  C148        C
890      0            370376   7.7500   NaN        Q
```

```
[891 rows x 12 columns]
<class 'pandas.core.frame.DataFrame'>
PassengerId      int64
Survived         int64
Pclass           int64
Name            object
Sex             object
Age            float64
SibSp            int64
Parch            int64
Ticket          object
Fare           float64
Cabin           object
Embarked        object
dtype: object
<class 'pandas.core.frame.DataFrame'>
RangeIndex: 891 entries, 0 to 890
Data columns (total 12 columns):
 #   Column       Non-Null Count  Dtype
---  ------       --------------  -----
 0   PassengerId  891 non-null    int64
 1   Survived     891 non-null    int64
 2   Pclass       891 non-null    int64
 3   Name         891 non-null    object
 4   Sex          891 non-null    object
 5   Age          714 non-null    float64
 6   SibSp        891 non-null    int64
 7   Parch        891 non-null    int64
 8   Ticket       891 non-null    object
 9   Fare         891 non-null    float64
 10  Cabin        204 non-null    object
 11  Embarked     889 non-null    object
dtypes: float64(2), int64(5), object(5)
memory usage: 83.7+ KB
None
```

Python code snippet

 # Change PassengerId, Survived and Pclass to categorical variables

Titanic_from_R_to_Python['PassengerId'] = pd.Categorical(Titanic_from_R_to_Python.PassengerId)

Titanic_from_R_to_Python['Survived'] = pd.Categorical(Titanic_from_R_to_Python.Survived)

Titanic_from_R_to_Python['Pclass'] = pd.Categorical(Titanic_from_R_to_Python.Pclass)

 # Check data types after conversion

print(Titanic_from_R_to_Python.info())

Output

```
<class 'pandas.core.frame.DataFrame'>
RangeIndex: 891 entries, 0 to 890
Data columns (total 12 columns):
 #   Column       Non-Null Count  Dtype
---  ------       --------------  -----
 0   PassengerId  891 non-null    category
 1   Survived     891 non-null    category
 2   Pclass       891 non-null    category
 3   Name         891 non-null    object
 4   Sex          891 non-null    object
 5   Age          714 non-null    float64
 6   SibSp        891 non-null    int64
 7   Parch        891 non-null    int64
 8   Ticket       891 non-null    object
 9   Fare         891 non-null    float64
 10  Cabin        204 non-null    object
 11  Embarked     889 non-null    object
dtypes: category(3), float64(2), int64(2), object(5)
memory usage: 113.4+ KB
None
```

Python code snippet

```
# Data exploration
# Check unique values of few variables
print('Unique values of Survived are ' ,Titanic_from_R_to_Python['Survived'].unique())
print('Unique values of Passenger Class are ' ,Titanic_from_R_to_Python['Pclass'].unique())
print('Unique values of Sibling Spouse are ' ,Titanic_from_R_to_Python['SibSp'].unique())
print('Unique values of Parent Child are ' ,Titanic_from_R_to_Python['Parch'].unique())
```

Output

```
Unique values of Survived are  [0, 1]
Categories (2, int64): [0, 1]
Unique values of Passenger Class are  [3, 1, 2]
Categories (3, int64): [3, 1, 2]
Unique values of Sibling Spouse are  [1 0 3 4 2 5 8]
Unique values of Parent Child are  [0 1 2 5 3 4 6]
```

Python code snippet

```
# Relationship between Survived and Gender
print(pd.crosstab(Titanic_from_R_to_Python.Sex, Titanic_from_R_to_Python.Survived))
```

Output

```
Survived    0    1
Sex
female     81  233
male      468  109
```

Python code snippet

```
# Relationship between Survived and Age
import seaborn as sb
import matplotlib.pyplot as plot

Survived_holder = Titanic_from_R_to_Python['Survived']
Age_holder = Titanic_from_R_to_Python['Age']

sb.boxplot(x = Survived_holder, y = Age_holder)
sb.swarmplot(x = Survived_holder, y = Age_holder, color = '0.25')
plot.show()
```

Output

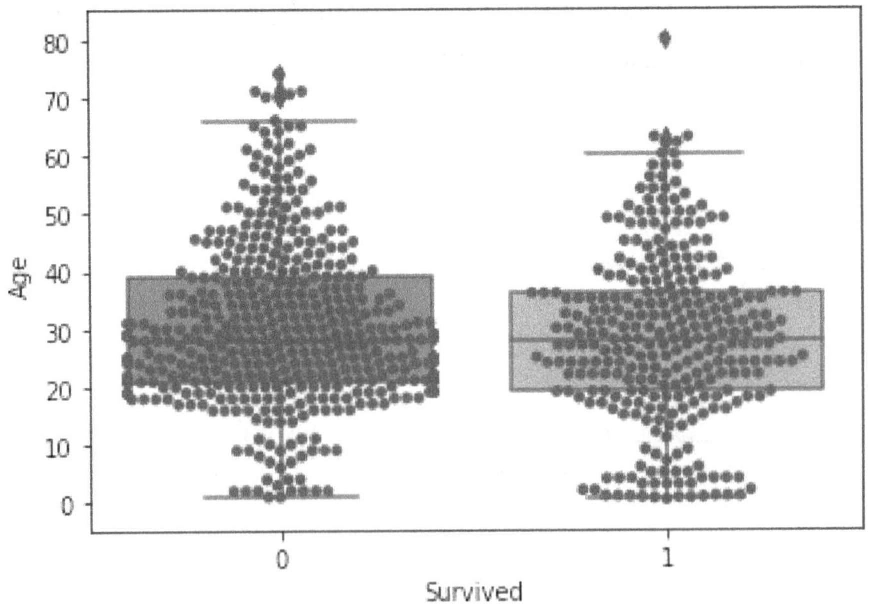

Python code snippet

```
# Relationship between Survived and passenger class
print(pd.crosstab(Titanic_from_R_to_Python.Pclass, Titanic_from_R_to_Python.Survived))
```

Output

```
Survived    0    1
Pclass
1          80  136
2          97   87
3         372  119
```

Python code snippet

```
# Divide the data into train and test sets
from sklearn.model_selection import train_test_split

titanic_dataset = Titanic_from_R_to_Python

print(type(Titanic_from_R_to_Python))
print(type(titanic_dataset))

print('Before deleting target and variables is ' , titanic_dataset.columns.values)

# Drop target and other non relevant variables
titanic_dataset = titanic_dataset.drop('Survived' , axis='columns')
titanic_dataset = titanic_dataset.drop('PassengerId' , axis='columns')
titanic_dataset = titanic_dataset.drop('Name' , axis='columns')
titanic_dataset = titanic_dataset.drop('Ticket' , axis='columns')
titanic_dataset = titanic_dataset.drop('Cabin' , axis='columns')

print('After deleting target and variables is ' , titanic_dataset.columns.values)
```

Output

```
<class 'pandas.core.frame.DataFrame'>
<class 'pandas.core.frame.DataFrame'>
Before deleting target and variables is  ['PassengerId'
'Survived' 'Pclass' 'Name' 'Sex' 'Age' 'SibSp' 'Parch'
 'Ticket' 'Fare' 'Cabin' 'Embarked']
After deleting target and variables is  ['Pclass' 'Sex' 'Age'
'SibSp' 'Parch' 'Fare' 'Embarked']
```

Python code snippet

```
x = titanic_dataset
print('Information about x is as follows: \n' , x.head(3))
print('datatype of x is ' , type(x))

print('Remark 100 is ' , Titanic_from_R_to_Python.columns.values)
```

Output

```
Information about x is as follows:
   Pclass     Sex   Age  SibSp  Parch     Fare Embarked
0       3    male  22.0      1      0   7.2500        S
1       1  female  38.0      1      0  71.2833        C
2       3  female  26.0      0      0   7.9250        S
datatype of x is  <class 'pandas.core.frame.DataFrame'>
Remark 100 is  ['PassengerId' 'Survived' 'Pclass' 'Name' 'Sex'
'Age' 'SibSp' 'Parch'
 'Ticket' 'Fare' 'Cabin' 'Embarked']
```

Python code snippet

```
# Replace Pclass 1, 2, 3 with Pclass1, Pclass2 and Pclass3
x['Pclass'].replace(1, 'Pclass1',inplace=True)
x['Pclass'].replace(2, 'Pclass2',inplace=True)
x['Pclass'].replace(3, 'Pclass3',inplace=True)

# Find out if there is any missing value in the data frame
print('The following is missing value summary of the data frame column wise \n' , x.isnull().sum())
```

```
# Replace missing age values with mean age
x['Age'].fillna((x['Age'].mean()), inplace=True)

# Replace missing embarked values with the most frequent embarked value
x = x.apply(lambda x: x.fillna(x.value_counts().index[0]))

# Find out if there is any missing value in the data frame
print('The following is missing value summary of the data frame column wise after dropping \n' ,
x.isnull().sum())
```

Output

```
The following is missing value summary of the data frame
column wise
 Pclass        0
Sex           0
Age         177
SibSp         0
Parch         0
Fare          0
Embarked      2
dtype: int64
The following is missing value summary of the data frame
column wise after dropping
 Pclass      0
Sex         0
Age         0
SibSp       0
Parch       0
Fare        0
Embarked    0
dtype: int64
```

Python code snippet

```
y = Titanic_from_R_to_Python['Survived']

print('Information about y is as follows: \n' , y.head(3))

# Convert data type of target variable from series to data frame
print('datatype of y before conversion is ' , type(y))
y = y.to_frame()
print('datatype of y after conversion is ' , type(y))
```

Output

```
Information about y is as follows:
 0    0
1    1
2    1
Name: Survived, dtype: category
Categories (2, int64): [0, 1]
datatype of y before conversion is  <class
'pandas.core.series.Series'>
datatype of y after conversion is  <class
'pandas.core.frame.DataFrame'>
```

Python code snippet

```
# Carry out one hot encoding for categorical variables
for j in x.columns:

print('x[j].dtype is ' , x[j].dtype)
if (x[j].dtype == object or str(x[j].dtype) == 'category'):
dummy_columns = pd.get_dummies(x[j])
x = x.join(dummy_columns)
print('I am deleting column' , j, 'from the data set. ' , 'Value of j is ' , j)
del x[j]

x_train, x_test, y_train, y_test = train_test_split(x, y, test_size=0.30, random_state = 200)

# Find out the dimensions of train and test sets
```

```
row_count_train, col_count_train = x_train.shape
print('Number of rows in train ' , row_count_train)
print('Number of columns in train ' , col_count_train)

row_count_test, col_count_test = x_test.shape
print('Number of rows in test ' , row_count_test)
print('Number of columns in test ' , col_count_test)

print('List of column names are: ' , x_train.columns.values)
```

Output

```
x[j].dtype is  category
I am deleting column Pclass from the data set.  Value of j is
Pclass
x[j].dtype is  object
I am deleting column Sex from the data set.  Value of j is
Sex
x[j].dtype is  float64
x[j].dtype is  int64
x[j].dtype is  int64
x[j].dtype is  float64
x[j].dtype is  object
I am deleting column Embarked from the data set.  Value of j
is  Embarked
Number of rows in train  623
Number of columns in train  12
Number of rows in test  268
Number of columns in test  12
List of column names are:  ['Age' 'SibSp' 'Parch' 'Fare'
'Pclass1' 'Pclass2' 'Pclass3' 'female'
 'male' 'C' 'Q' 'S']
```

Python code snippet

```
print(x_train.head(10))

print(x_train.shape)
print(list(x_train.columns))
print(y_train['Survived'].value_counts())
```

Output

```
           Age  SibSp  Parch     Fare  Pclass1  Pclass2
Pclass3  female  \
46   29.699118      1      0  15.5000        0        0
1        0
245  44.000000      2      0  90.0000        1        0
0        0
86   16.000000      1      3  34.3750        0        0
1        0
176  29.699118      3      1  25.4667        0        0
1        0
183   1.000000      2      1  39.0000        0        1
0        0
402  21.000000      1      0   9.8250        0        0
1        1
361  29.000000      1      0  27.7208        0        1
0        0
851  74.000000      0      0   7.7750        0        0
1        0
428  29.699118      0      0   7.7500        0        0
1        0
196  29.699118      0      0   7.7500        0        0
1        0

     male  C  Q  S
46      1  0  1  0
245     1  0  1  0
86      1  0  0  1
176     1  0  0  1
183     1  0  0  1
402     0  0  0  1
361     1  1  0  0
851     1  0  0  1
428     1  0  1  0
196     1  0  1  0
(623, 12)
['Age', 'SibSp', 'Parch', 'Fare', 'Pclass1', 'Pclass2',
'Pclass3', 'female', 'male', 'C', 'Q', 'S']
0    384
1    239
Name: Survived, dtype: int64
```

Python code snippet

```
# Build the logistic regression model
from sklearn.linear_model import LogisticRegression
from sklearn import metrics

model = LogisticRegression(max_iter = 1000)
model.fit(x_train, y_train)

# Following are the performance measures on the test set
# Accuracy of test set
print(model.score(x_test, y_test))
```

Output

```
0.7723880597014925
```

Python code snippet

```
# Get the confusion matrix
from sklearn.metrics import confusion_matrix

# Predict on the test data
y_pred_test = model.predict(x_test)
confusion_matrix_test = confusion_matrix(y_test, y_pred_test)
print('The confusion matrix is as follows \n' , confusion_matrix_test)


# Get the classification report
from sklearn.metrics import classification_report

print(classification_report(y_test, y_pred_test))
```

Output

```
The confusion matrix is as follows
 [[139  26]
 [ 35  68]]
              precision    recall  f1-score   support

           0       0.80      0.84      0.82       165
           1       0.72      0.66      0.69       103

    accuracy                           0.77       268
   macro avg       0.76      0.75      0.76       268
weighted avg       0.77      0.77      0.77       268
```

Python code snippet

```
# Plot the ROC curve and get the AUC value
from sklearn.metrics import roc_auc_score
from sklearn.metrics import roc_curve
import matplotlib.pyplot as plot

roc_auc_test = roc_auc_score(y_test, model.predict(x_test))
fpr, tpr, thresholds = roc_curve(y_test, model.predict_proba(x_test)[:,1])
plot.figure()
plot.plot(fpr, tpr, label='Logistic Regression (area = %0.2f)' % roc_auc_test)
plot.plot([0, 1], [0, 1],'r--')
plot.xlim([0.0, 1.0])
plot.ylim([0.0, 1.05])
plot.xlabel('FPR')
plot.ylabel('TPR')
plot.title('Test ROC')
plot.legend(loc="lower right")
plot.show()
```

Output

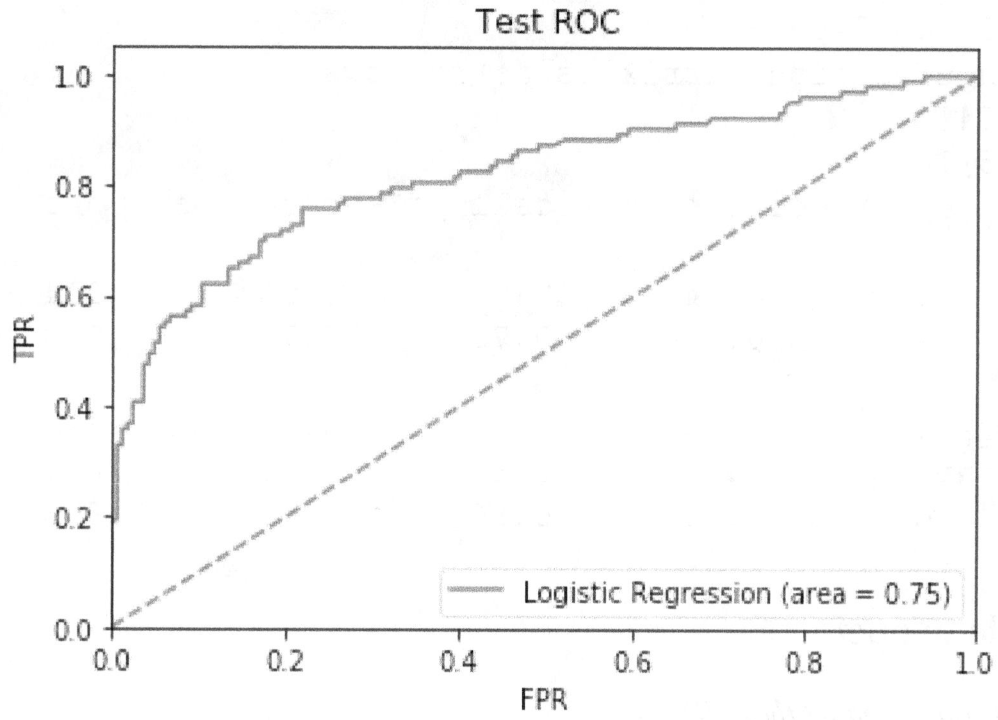

Python code snippet

```
# Following are the performance measures on the train set

# Accuracy of train set
print(model.score(x_train, y_train))

# Get the confusion matrix
from sklearn.metrics import confusion_matrix

# Predict on the train data
y_pred_train = model.predict(x_train)
confusion_matrix_train = confusion_matrix(y_train, y_pred_train)
print('The train confusion matrix is as follows \n' , confusion_matrix_train)

# Get the classification report
print(classification_report(y_train, y_pred_train))
```

Output

```
0.8105939004815409
The train confusion matrix is as follows
 [[330  54]
 [ 64 175]]
              precision    recall  f1-score   support

           0       0.84      0.86      0.85       384
           1       0.76      0.73      0.75       239

    accuracy                           0.81       623
   macro avg       0.80      0.80      0.80       623
weighted avg       0.81      0.81      0.81       623
```

Python code snippet

```
# Plot the ROC curve and get the AUC value
roc_auc_train = roc_auc_score(y_train, model.predict(x_train))
fpr, tpr, thresholds = roc_curve(y_train, model.predict_proba(x_train)[:,1])
plot.figure()
plot.plot(fpr, tpr, label='Logistic Regression (area = %0.2f)' % roc_auc_train)
plot.plot([0, 1], [0, 1],'r--')
plot.xlim([0.0, 1.0])
plot.ylim([0.0, 1.05])
plot.xlabel('FPR')
plot.ylabel('TPR')
plot.title('Train ROC')
plot.legend(loc="lower right")
plot.show()
```

Output

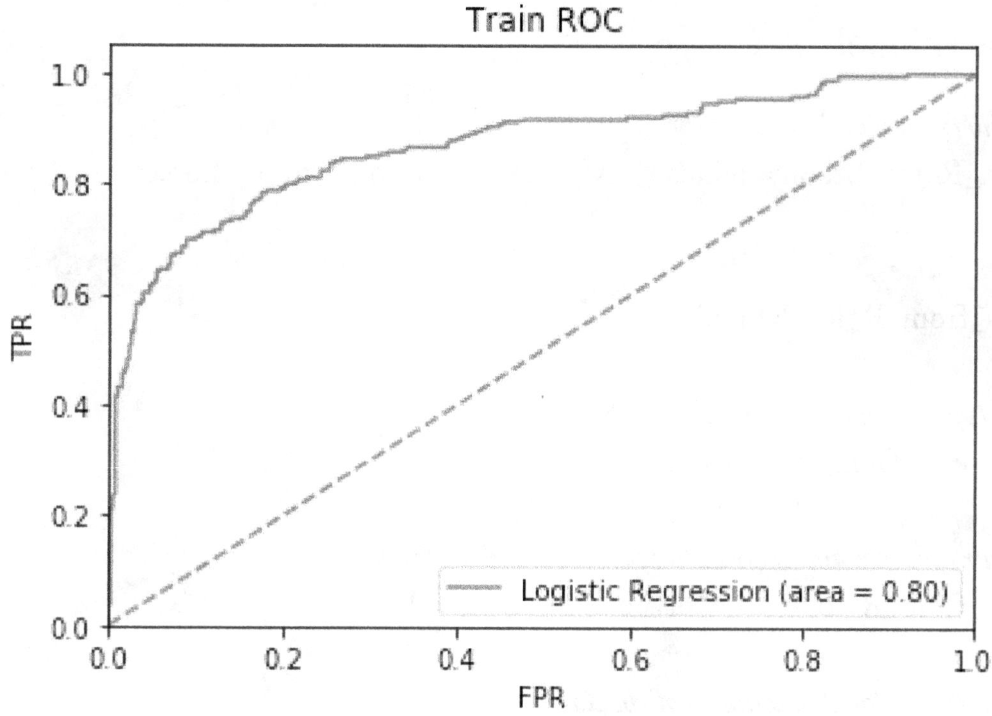
Train ROC
TPR
FPR
1.0
0.8
0.6
0.4
0.2
0.0
0.0
0.2
0.4
0.6
0.8
1.0
Logistic Regression (area = 0.80)

Decision Trees

Python code snippet

```
# Read CSV file from working directory
Carseats_from_R_to_Python = pd.read_csv("Carseats_from_R_to_Python.csv")

# Print the data frame
print(Carseats_from_R_to_Python)

# Get the data type of Titanic_from_R_to_Python
print(type(Carseats_from_R_to_Python))

# View the column names and their data types from a data frame
print(Carseats_from_R_to_Python.dtypes)

# Check information related to columns of the data frame
print(Carseats_from_R_to_Python.info())
```

Output

```
     Sales  CompPrice  Income  Advertising  Population  Price
ShelveLoc  Age  \
0     9.50        138      73           11         276    120
Bad    42
1    11.22        111      48           16         260     83
Good    65
2    10.06        113      35           10         269     80
Medium    59
3     7.40        117     100            4         466     97
Medium    55
4     4.15        141      64            3         340    128
Bad    38
..     ...        ...     ...          ...         ...    ...
...   ...
395  12.57        138     108           17         203    128
Good    33
396   6.14        139      23            3          37    120
Medium    55
397   7.41        162      26           12         368    159
Medium    40
398   5.94        100      79            7         284     95
Bad    50
399   9.71        134      37            0          27    120
Good    49
```

```
     Education Urban   US
0           17   Yes  Yes
1           10   Yes  Yes
2           12   Yes  Yes
3           14   Yes  Yes
4           13   Yes   No
..         ...   ...  ...
395         14   Yes  Yes
396         11    No  Yes
397         18   Yes  Yes
398         12   Yes  Yes
399         16   Yes  Yes

[400 rows x 11 columns]
<class 'pandas.core.frame.DataFrame'>
Sales          float64
CompPrice        int64
Income           int64
Advertising      int64
Population       int64
Price            int64
ShelveLoc       object
Age              int64
Education        int64
Urban           object
US              object
dtype: object
<class 'pandas.core.frame.DataFrame'>
RangeIndex: 400 entries, 0 to 399
Data columns (total 11 columns):
 #   Column       Non-Null Count  Dtype
---  ------       --------------  -----
 0   Sales        400 non-null    float64
 1   CompPrice    400 non-null    int64
 2   Income       400 non-null    int64
 3   Advertising  400 non-null    int64
 4   Population   400 non-null    int64
 5   Price        400 non-null    int64
 6   ShelveLoc    400 non-null    object
 7   Age          400 non-null    int64
 8   Education    400 non-null    int64
 9   Urban        400 non-null    object
 10  US           400 non-null    object
dtypes: float64(1), int64(7), object(3)
memory usage: 34.5+ KB
None
```

Python code snippet

```
# Plot histogram of sales
import matplotlib.pyplot as plot

plot.hist(Carseats_from_R_to_Python['Sales'], bins=10)
plot.show()
```

Output

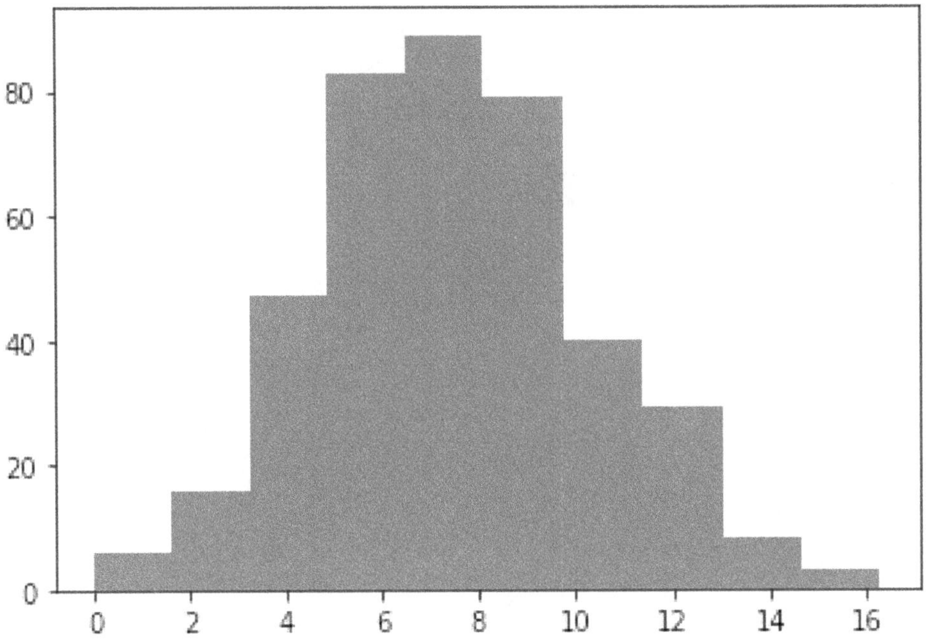

Python code snippet

```
import numpy as np

# Create a new column called High. Assign yes if Sales is >= 8. Assign no otherwise
Carseats_from_R_to_Python['High'] = np.where(Carseats_from_R_to_Python['Sales'] >= 8, 'yes',
'no')
print(Carseats_from_R_to_Python)

# Check if the new column High is created correctly
# Relationship between High and Sales
import seaborn as sb
```

```
High_holder = Carseats_from_R_to_Python['High']
Sales_holder = Carseats_from_R_to_Python['Sales']

sb.boxplot(x = High_holder, y = Sales_holder)
sb.swarmplot(x = High_holder, y = Sales_holder, color = '0.25')
plot.show()
```

Output

```
     Sales  CompPrice  Income  Advertising  Population  Price
ShelveLoc  Age  \
0     9.50        138      73           11         276    120
Bad   42
1    11.22        111      48           16         260     83
Good   65
2    10.06        113      35           10         269     80
Medium   59
3     7.40        117     100            4         466     97
Medium   55
4     4.15        141      64            3         340    128
Bad   38
..     ...        ...     ...          ...         ...    ...
...  ...
395  12.57        138     108           17         203    128
Good   33
396   6.14        139      23            3          37    120
Medium   55
397   7.41        162      26           12         368    159
Medium   40
398   5.94        100      79            7         284     95
Bad   50
399   9.71        134      37            0          27    120
Good   49

     Education Urban   US High
0           17   Yes  Yes  yes
1           10   Yes  Yes  yes
2           12   Yes  Yes  yes
3           14   Yes  Yes   no
4           13   Yes   No   no
..         ...   ...  ...  ...
395         14   Yes  Yes  yes
396         11    No  Yes   no
397         18   Yes  Yes   no
398         12   Yes  Yes   no
399         16   Yes  Yes  yes

[400 rows x 12 columns]
```

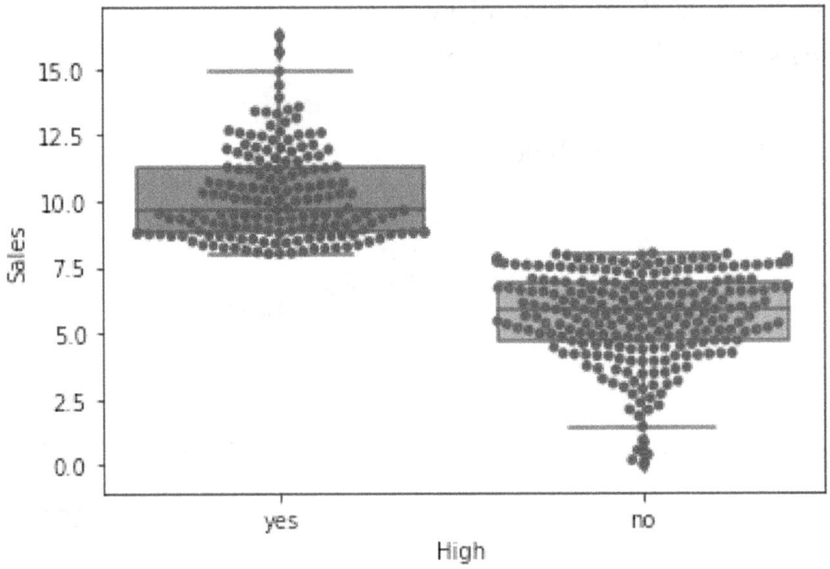

Python code snippet

```
# Carry out some data exploration

# Relationship between High and competitor price
High_holder = Carseats_from_R_to_Python['High']
CompPrice_holder = Carseats_from_R_to_Python['CompPrice']

sb.boxplot(x = High_holder, y = CompPrice_holder)
sb.swarmplot(x = High_holder, y = CompPrice_holder, color = '0.25')
plot.show()
```

Output

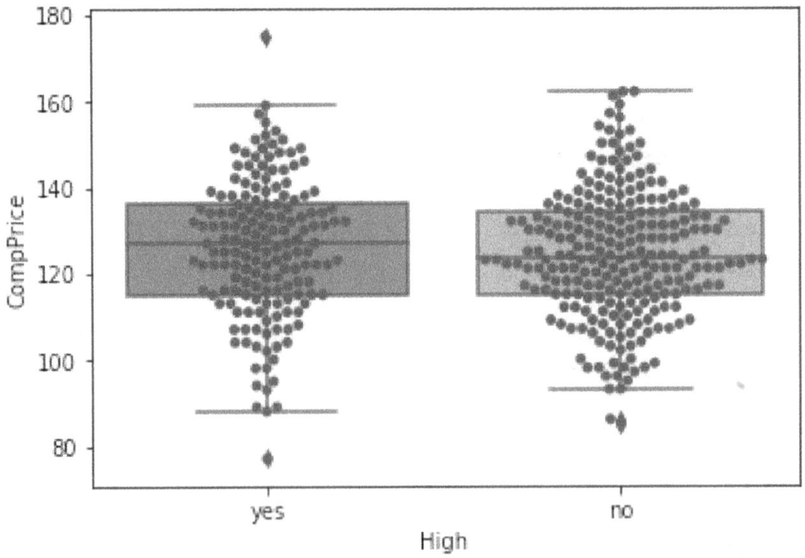

Python code snippet

```
# Relationship between High and income
High_holder = Carseats_from_R_to_Python['High']
Income_holder = Carseats_from_R_to_Python['Income']

sb.boxplot(x = High_holder, y = Income_holder)
sb.swarmplot(x = High_holder, y = Income_holder, color = '0.25')
plot.show()
```

Output

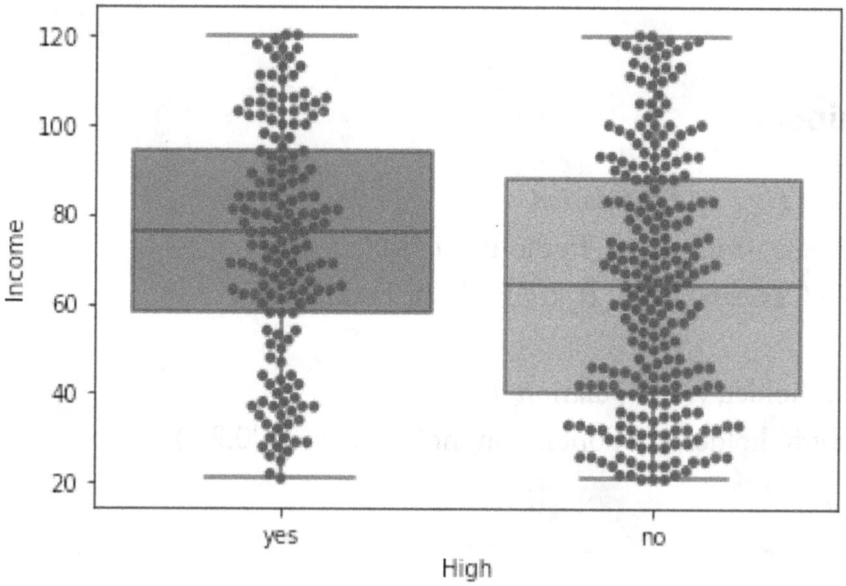

Python code snippet

```
# Relationship between High and advertising
High_holder = Carseats_from_R_to_Python['High']
Advertising_holder = Carseats_from_R_to_Python['Advertising']

sb.boxplot(x = High_holder, y = Advertising_holder)
sb.swarmplot(x = High_holder, y = Advertising_holder, color = '0.25')
plot.show()
```

Output

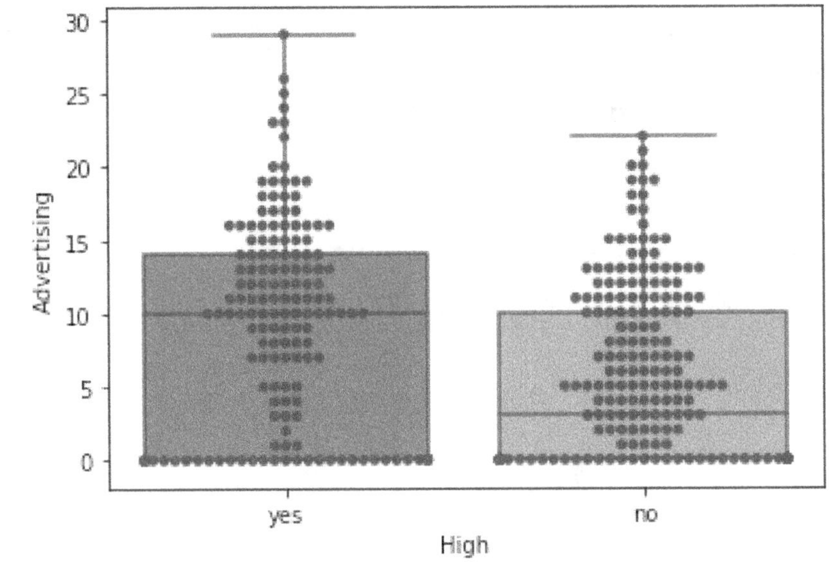

Python code snippet

```
# Relationship between High and population
High_holder = Carseats_from_R_to_Python['High']
Population_holder = Carseats_from_R_to_Python['Population']

sb.boxplot(x = High_holder, y = Population_holder)
sb.swarmplot(x = High_holder, y = Population_holder, color = '0.25')
plot.show()
```

Output

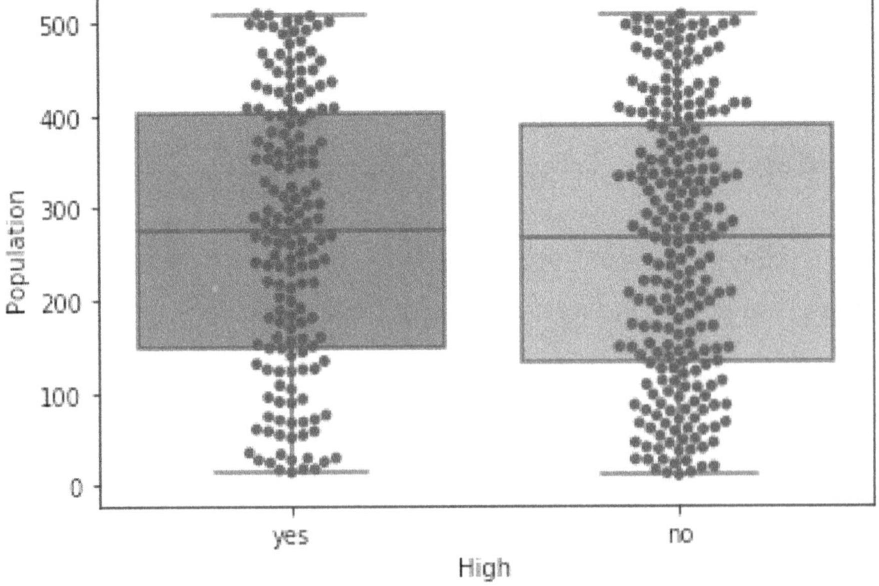

Python code snippet

```
# Relationship between High and price
High_holder = Carseats_from_R_to_Python['High']
Price_holder = Carseats_from_R_to_Python['Price']

sb.boxplot(x = High_holder, y = Price_holder)
sb.swarmplot(x = High_holder, y = Price_holder, color = '0.25')
plot.show()
```

Output

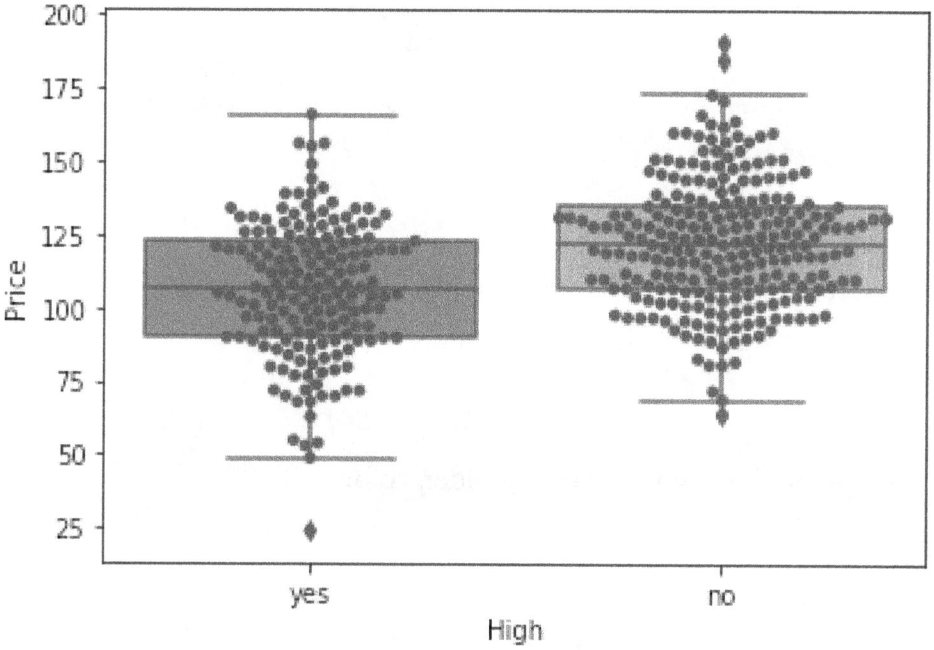

Python code snippet

```
# Relationship between High and Age
High_holder = Carseats_from_R_to_Python['High']
Age_holder = Carseats_from_R_to_Python['Age']

sb.boxplot(x = High_holder, y = Age_holder)
sb.swarmplot(x = High_holder, y = Age_holder, color = '0.25')
plot.show()
```

Output

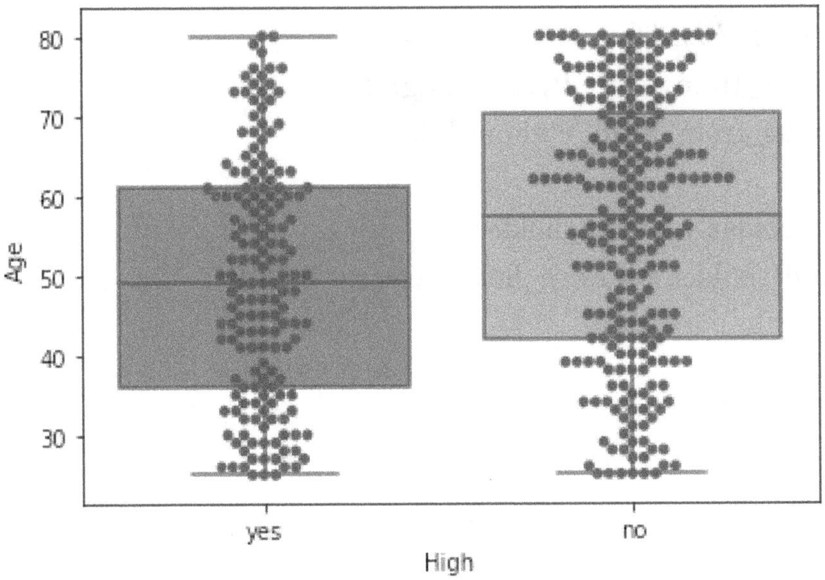

Python code snippet

```
# Relationship between High and Education
High_holder = Carseats_from_R_to_Python['High']
Education_holder = Carseats_from_R_to_Python['Education']

sb.boxplot(x = High_holder, y = Education_holder)
sb.swarmplot(x = High_holder, y = Education_holder, color = '0.25')
plot.show()
```

Output

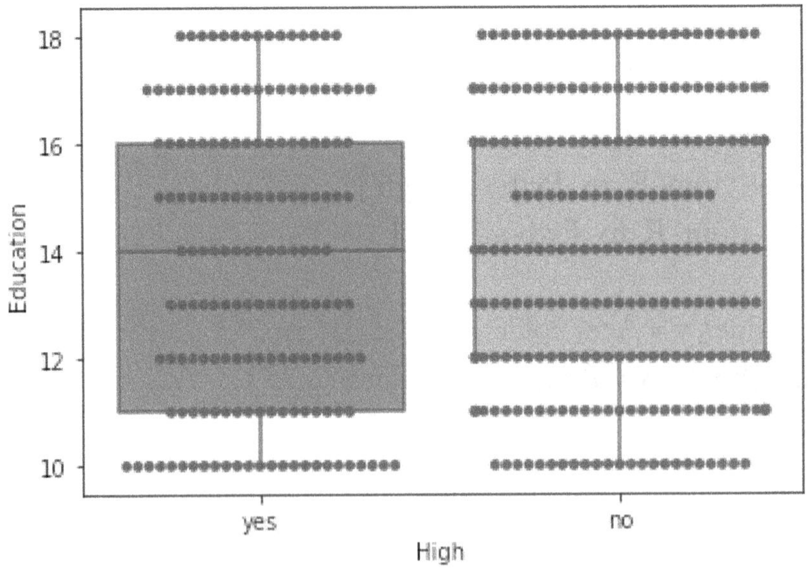

Python code snippet

```
# Three ways of looking at the distribution of Education
print(Carseats_from_R_to_Python['Education'].describe())
print(Carseats_from_R_to_Python['Education'])
print(Carseats_from_R_to_Python['Education'].unique())
```

Output

```
count    400.000000
mean      13.900000
std        2.620528
min       10.000000
25%       12.000000
50%       14.000000
75%       16.000000
max       18.000000
Name: Education, dtype: float64
0      17
1      10
2      12
3      14
4      13
       ..
395    14
396    11
397    18
398    12
399    16
Name: Education, Length: 400, dtype: int64
[17 10 12 14 13 16 15 18 11]
```

Python code snippet

```
# Relationship between High and ShelveLoc
print(pd.crosstab(Carseats_from_R_to_Python.ShelveLoc, Carseats_from_R_to_Python.High))
print('\n')

# Relationship between High and Urban
print(pd.crosstab(Carseats_from_R_to_Python.Urban, Carseats_from_R_to_Python.High))
print('\n')
```

```
# Relationship between High and US
print(pd.crosstab(Carseats_from_R_to_Python.US, Carseats_from_R_to_Python.High))
```

Output

```
High          no  yes
ShelveLoc
Bad           82   14
Good          19   66
Medium       135   84


High     no  yes
Urban
No       64   54
Yes     172  110


High    no  yes
US
No     101   41
Yes    135  123
```

Python code snippet

```
# Divide the data into train and test sets
from sklearn.model_selection import train_test_split

carseats_dataset = Carseats_from_R_to_Python

print(type(Carseats_from_R_to_Python))
print(type(carseats_dataset))

print('Before deleting target and variables is ', carseats_dataset.columns.values)

# Drop target and Sales
carseats_dataset = carseats_dataset.drop('High', axis='columns')
carseats_dataset = carseats_dataset.drop('Sales', axis='columns')

print('After deleting target and variables is ', carseats_dataset.columns.values)
```

Output

```
<class 'pandas.core.frame.DataFrame'>
<class 'pandas.core.frame.DataFrame'>
Before deleting target and variables is  ['Sales' 'CompPrice'
'Income' 'Advertising' 'Population' 'Price'
 'ShelveLoc' 'Age' 'Education' 'Urban' 'US' 'High']
After deleting target and variables is  ['CompPrice' 'Income'
'Advertising' 'Population' 'Price' 'ShelveLoc' 'Age'
 'Education' 'Urban' 'US']
```

Python code snippet

```
x = carseats_dataset
print('Information about x is as follows: \n', x.head(3))
print('datatype of x is ', type(x))

print('Remark 100 is ', Carseats_from_R_to_Python.columns.values)
```

Output

```
Information about x is as follows:
    CompPrice  Income  Advertising  Population  Price
ShelveLoc  Age  \
0        138      73           11         276    120        Bad
42
1        111      48           16         260     83       Good
65
2        113      35           10         269     80     Medium
59

   Education Urban   US
0         17   Yes  Yes
1         10   Yes  Yes
2         12   Yes  Yes
datatype of x is  <class 'pandas.core.frame.DataFrame'>
Remark 100 is  ['Sales' 'CompPrice' 'Income' 'Advertising'
'Population' 'Price'
 'ShelveLoc' 'Age' 'Education' 'Urban' 'US' 'High']
```

Python code snippet

```
# Find out if there is any missing value in the data frame
print('The following is missing value summary of the data frame column wise \n', x.isnull().sum())
```

Output

```
The following is missing value summary of the data frame
column wise
 CompPrice      0
Income         0
Advertising    0
Population     0
Price          0
ShelveLoc      0
Age            0
Education      0
Urban          0
US             0
dtype: int64
```

Python code snippet

```
y = Carseats_from_R_to_Python['High']

print('Information about y is as follows: \n', y.head(3))

# Replace Urban Yes, No with Urban_Yes, Urban_No
x['Urban'].replace('Yes', 'Urban_Yes',inplace=True)
x['Urban'].replace('No', 'Urban_No',inplace=True)

# Replace US Yes, No with US_Yes, US_No
x['US'].replace('Yes', 'US_Yes',inplace=True)
x['US'].replace('No', 'US_No',inplace=True)

# Convert data type of target variable from series to data frame
print('datatype of y before conversion is ', type(y))
y = y.to_frame()
print('datatype of y after conversion is ', type(y))
```

Output

```
Information about y is as follows:
 0    yes
1    yes
2    yes
Name: High, dtype: object
datatype of y before conversion is  <class
'pandas.core.series.Series'>
datatype of y after conversion is  <class
'pandas.core.frame.DataFrame'>
```

Python code snippet

```
# Carry out one hot encoding for categorical variables
for j in x.columns:

print('x[j].dtype is ', x[j].dtype)
if (x[j].dtype == object or str(x[j].dtype) == 'category'):
dummy_columns = pd.get_dummies(x[j])
x = x.join(dummy_columns)
print('I am deleting column', j, 'from the data set. ', 'Value of j is ', j)
del x[j]

x_train, x_test, y_train, y_test = train_test_split(x, y, test_size=0.30, random_state=200)

# Find out the dimensions of train and test sets
row_count_train, col_count_train = x_train.shape
print('Number of rows in train ', row_count_train)
print('Number of columns in train ', col_count_train)

row_count_test, col_count_test = x_test.shape
print('Number of rows in test ', row_count_test)
print('Number of columns in test ', col_count_test)

print('List of column names are: ', x_train.columns.values)
```

Output

```
x[j].dtype is  int64
x[j].dtype is  int64
x[j].dtype is  int64
x[j].dtype is  int64
x[j].dtype is  int64
x[j].dtype is  object
I am deleting column ShelveLoc from the data set.  Value of j
is  ShelveLoc
x[j].dtype is  int64
x[j].dtype is  int64
x[j].dtype is  object
I am deleting column Urban from the data set.  Value of j is
Urban
x[j].dtype is  object
I am deleting column US from the data set.  Value of j is  US
Number of rows in train  280
Number of columns in train  14
Number of rows in test  120
Number of columns in test  14
List of column names are:  ['CompPrice' 'Income' 'Advertising'
'Population' 'Price' 'Age' 'Education'
 'Bad' 'Good' 'Medium' 'Urban_No' 'Urban_Yes' 'US_No'
'US_Yes']
```

Python code snippet

```
print(x_train.head(10))
print(x_train.shape)
print(list(x_train.columns))
print(y_train['High'].value_counts())
```

Output

```
     CompPrice  Income  Advertising  Population  Price  Age
Education  Bad  \
206        162      67            0          27    160   77
17     0
59         118      71            4         148    114   80
13     0
122        119     100            5          45    108   75
10     0
172        104     102           13         123    110   35
16     0
321        123      39            5         499     98   34
15     0
374        131      47            7          90    118   47
12     0
361        131      25           10         183    104   56
15     0
359        130      62           11         396    130   66
14     1
257        125      62           14         477    112   80
13     0
284        106      46           11         414     96   79
17     1

     Good  Medium  Urban_No  Urban_Yes  US_No  US_Yes
206     0       1         0          1      0       1
59      0       1         0          1      1       0
122     0       1         0          1      0       1
172     1       0         0          1      0       1
321     0       1         0          1      1       0
374     0       1         0          1      0       1
361     0       1         1          0      0       1
359     0       0         0          1      0       1
257     0       1         0          1      0       1
284     0       0         1          0      1       0
(280, 14)
['CompPrice', 'Income', 'Advertising', 'Population', 'Price',
'Age', 'Education', 'Bad', 'Good', 'Medium', 'Urban_No',
'Urban_Yes', 'US_No', 'US_Yes']
no     162
yes    118
Name: High, dtype: int64
```

Python code snippet

```
# Build an individual classification decision tree
from sklearn.tree import DecisionTreeClassifier
from sklearn import tree

model = DecisionTreeClassifier(random_state = 100, max_leaf_nodes = 7, min_samples_leaf = 5,
max_depth= 5)
model.fit(x_train, y_train)

from sklearn.tree import export_graphviz
import pydotplus
from IPython.display import Image

# Create DOT data
dot_data = tree.export_graphviz(model)

# Draw graph
graph = pydotplus.graph_from_dot_data(dot_data)

# Create PDF
graph.write_pdf("Carseats_1.pdf")

# Create PNG
graph.write_png("Carseats_1.png")
```

Output

```
True
```

Python code snippet

```
# Decision tree performance measures on the test data

# Accuracy of test set
print(model.score(x_test, y_test))
```

```
# Get the confusion matrix
from sklearn.metrics import confusion_matrix

# Predict on the test data
y_pred_test = model.predict(x_test)
confusion_matrix_test = confusion_matrix(y_test, y_pred_test)
print('The confusion matrix is as follows \n' , confusion_matrix_test)

# Get the classification report
from sklearn import metrics
from sklearn.metrics import classification_report

print(classification_report(y_test, y_pred_test))
```

Output

```
0.75
The confusion matrix is as follows
 [[62 12]
 [18 28]]
              precision    recall  f1-score   support

          no       0.78      0.84      0.81        74
         yes       0.70      0.61      0.65        46

    accuracy                           0.75       120
   macro avg       0.74      0.72      0.73       120
weighted avg       0.75      0.75      0.75       120
```

Python code snippet

```
# Decision tree regression

# Read CSV file from working directory
Boston_from_R_to_Python = pd.read_csv("Boston_from_R_to_Python.csv")

# Print the data frame
print(Boston_from_R_to_Python)
```

```
# Get the data type of Boston_from_R_to_Python
print(type(Boston_from_R_to_Python))

# View the column names and their data types from a data frame
print(Boston_from_R_to_Python.dtypes)

# Check information related to columns of the data frame
print(Boston_from_R_to_Python.info())
```

Output

```
           crim    zn  indus  chas    nox     rm   age     dis
rad  tax  \
0     0.00632  18.0   2.31     0  0.538  6.575  65.2  4.0900
1  296
1     0.02731   0.0   7.07     0  0.469  6.421  78.9  4.9671
2  242
2     0.02729   0.0   7.07     0  0.469  7.185  61.1  4.9671
2  242
3     0.03237   0.0   2.18     0  0.458  6.998  45.8  6.0622
3  222
4     0.06905   0.0   2.18     0  0.458  7.147  54.2  6.0622
3  222
..        ...   ...    ...   ...    ...    ...   ...     ...
...   ...
501   0.06263   0.0  11.93     0  0.573  6.593  69.1  2.4786
1  273
502   0.04527   0.0  11.93     0  0.573  6.120  76.7  2.2875
1  273
503   0.06076   0.0  11.93     0  0.573  6.976  91.0  2.1675
1  273
504   0.10959   0.0  11.93     0  0.573  6.794  89.3  2.3889
1  273
505   0.04741   0.0  11.93     0  0.573  6.030  80.8  2.5050
1  273
```

```
     ptratio   black  lstat  medv
0       15.3  396.90   4.98  24.0
1       17.8  396.90   9.14  21.6
2       17.8  392.83   4.03  34.7
3       18.7  394.63   2.94  33.4
4       18.7  396.90   5.33  36.2
..       ...     ...    ...   ...
501     21.0  391.99   9.67  22.4
502     21.0  396.90   9.08  20.6
503     21.0  396.90   5.64  23.9
504     21.0  393.45   6.48  22.0
505     21.0  396.90   7.88  11.9

[506 rows x 14 columns]
<class 'pandas.core.frame.DataFrame'>
crim       float64
zn         float64
indus      float64
chas         int64
nox        float64
rm         float64
age        float64
dis        float64
rad          int64
tax          int64
ptratio    float64
black      float64
lstat      float64
medv       float64
dtype: object
<class 'pandas.core.frame.DataFrame'>
RangeIndex: 506 entries, 0 to 505
```

```
Data columns (total 14 columns):
 #   Column   Non-Null Count  Dtype
---  ------   --------------  -----
 0   crim     506 non-null    float64
 1   zn       506 non-null    float64
 2   indus    506 non-null    float64
 3   chas     506 non-null    int64
 4   nox      506 non-null    float64
 5   rm       506 non-null    float64
 6   age      506 non-null    float64
 7   dis      506 non-null    float64
 8   rad      506 non-null    int64
 9   tax      506 non-null    int64
 10  ptratio  506 non-null    float64
 11  black    506 non-null    float64
 12  lstat    506 non-null    float64
 13  medv     506 non-null    float64
dtypes: float64(11), int64(3)
memory usage: 55.5 KB
None
```

Python code snippet

```
# Check few rows
print(Boston_from_R_to_Python.head(5))

# Find unique values of chas
print(Boston_from_R_to_Python['chas'].unique())

# Convert chas from int to categorical
Boston_from_R_to_Python['chas'] = pd.Categorical(Boston_from_R_to_Python.chas)

# Check data types after conversion
print(Boston_from_R_to_Python.info())
```

Output

```
       crim    zn  indus  chas    nox     rm   age     dis  rad
tax  ptratio  \
0  0.00632  18.0   2.31     0  0.538  6.575  65.2  4.0900    1
296     15.3
1  0.02731   0.0   7.07     0  0.469  6.421  78.9  4.9671    2
242     17.8
2  0.02729   0.0   7.07     0  0.469  7.185  61.1  4.9671    2
242     17.8
3  0.03237   0.0   2.18     0  0.458  6.998  45.8  6.0622    3
222     18.7
4  0.06905   0.0   2.18     0  0.458  7.147  54.2  6.0622    3
222     18.7

     black  lstat  medv
 0  396.90   4.98  24.0
 1  396.90   9.14  21.6
 2  392.83   4.03  34.7
 3  394.63   2.94  33.4
 4  396.90   5.33  36.2
 [0 1]
 <class 'pandas.core.frame.DataFrame'>
 RangeIndex: 506 entries, 0 to 505
 Data columns (total 14 columns):
  #   Column   Non-Null Count  Dtype
 ---  ------   --------------  -----
  0   crim     506 non-null    float64
  1   zn       506 non-null    float64
  2   indus    506 non-null    float64
  3   chas     506 non-null    category
  4   nox      506 non-null    float64
  5   rm       506 non-null    float64
  6   age      506 non-null    float64
  7   dis      506 non-null    float64
  8   rad      506 non-null    int64
  9   tax      506 non-null    int64
  10  ptratio  506 non-null    float64
  11  black    506 non-null    float64
  12  lstat    506 non-null    float64
  13  medv     506 non-null    float64
dtypes: category(1), float64(11), int64(2)
memory usage: 52.1 KB
None
```

Python code snippet

```
# Carry out some data exploration between the dependent variable and all independent variables

# Scatter plot between medv and crim
x1 = Boston_from_R_to_Python['medv']
y1 = Boston_from_R_to_Python['crim']
plot.scatter(x1, y1, alpha=0.5)
plot.title('Scatter plot')
plot.xlabel('House Price')
plot.ylabel('Crime Rate')
plot.show()
```

Output

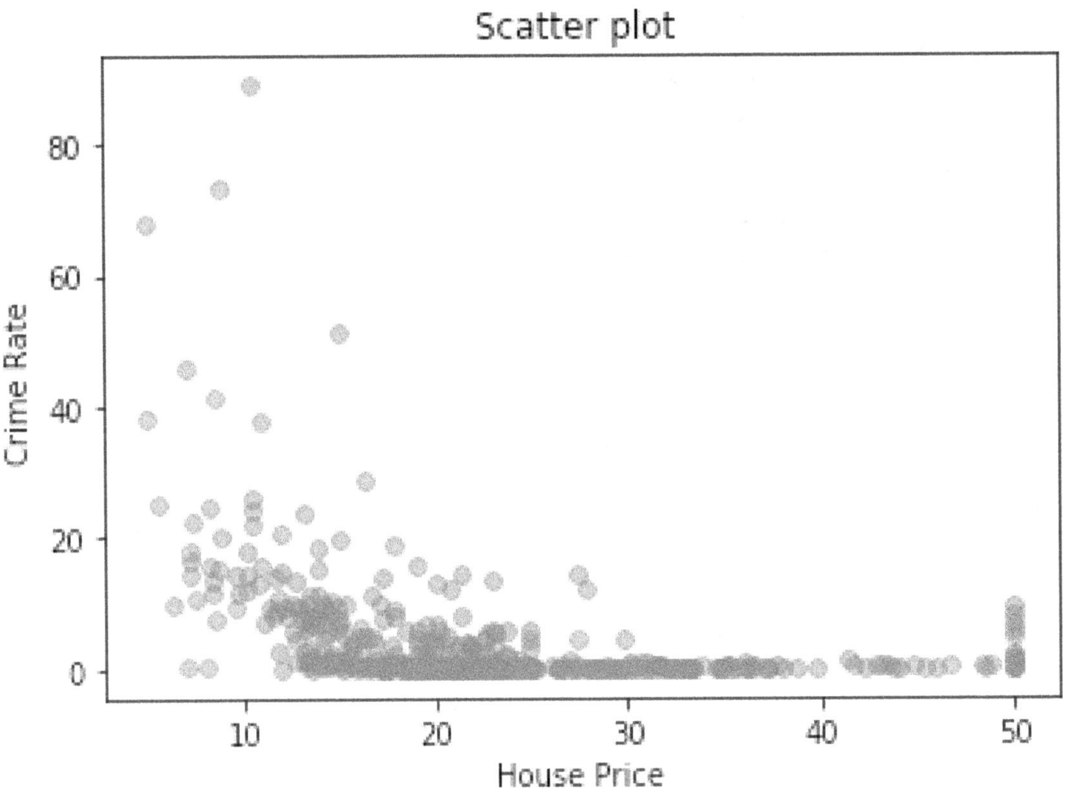

Python code snippet

```
# Scatter plot between medv and zn
x2 = Boston_from_R_to_Python['medv']
y2 = Boston_from_R_to_Python['zn']
plot.scatter(x2, y2, alpha=0.5)
plot.title('Scatter plot')
plot.xlabel('House Price')
plot.ylabel('zn')
plot.show()
```

Output

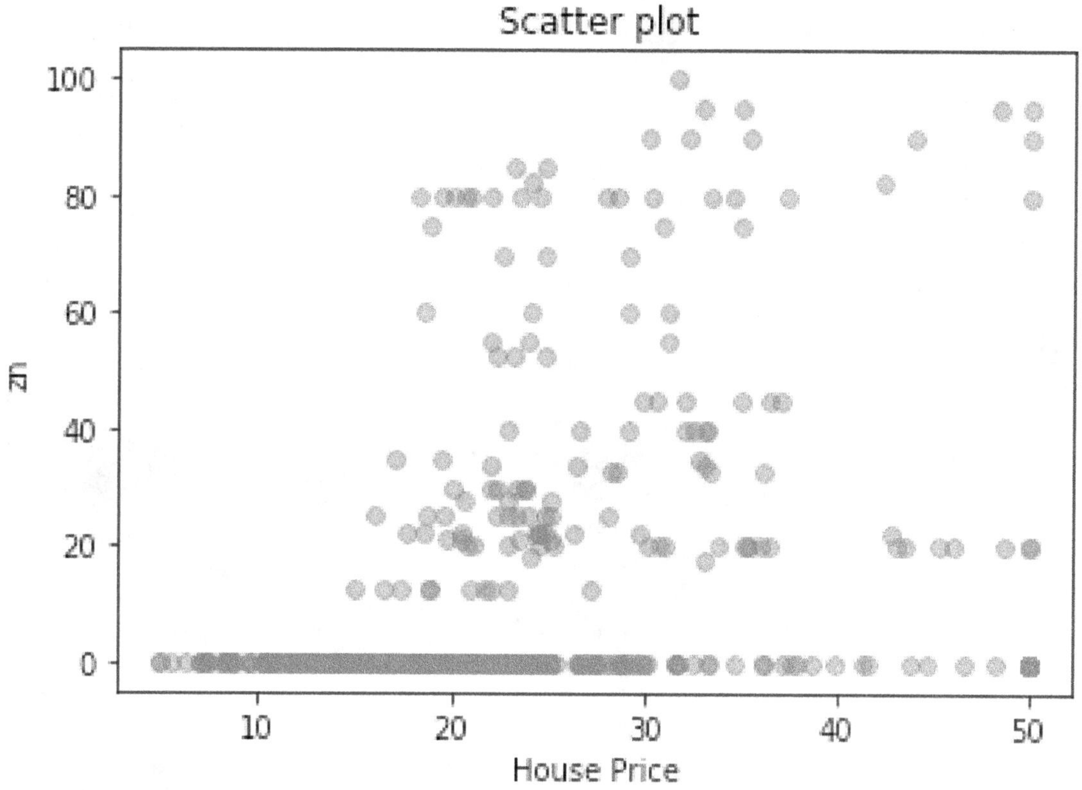

Python code snippet

```
# Scatter plot between medv and indus
x3 = Boston_from_R_to_Python['medv']
y3 = Boston_from_R_to_Python['indus']
plot.scatter(x3, y3, alpha=0.5)
plot.title('Scatter plot')
plot.xlabel('House Price')
plot.ylabel('indus')
plot.show()
```

Output

Python code snippet

```
# Scatter plot between medv and nox
x4 = Boston_from_R_to_Python['medv']
y4 = Boston_from_R_to_Python['nox']
plot.scatter(x4, y4, alpha=0.5)
plot.title('Scatter plot')
plot.xlabel('House Price')
plot.ylabel('nox')
plot.show()
```

Output

Python code snippet

```
# Scatter plot between medv and rm
x5 = Boston_from_R_to_Python['medv']
y5 = Boston_from_R_to_Python['rm']
plot.scatter(x5, y5, alpha=0.5)
plot.title('Scatter plot')
plot.xlabel('House Price')
plot.ylabel('rm')
plot.show()
```

Output

Python code snippet

```
# Scatter plot between medv and age
x6 = Boston_from_R_to_Python['medv']
y6 = Boston_from_R_to_Python['age']
plot.scatter(x6, y6, alpha=0.5)
plot.title('Scatter plot')
plot.xlabel('House Price')
plot.ylabel('age')
plot.show()
```

Output

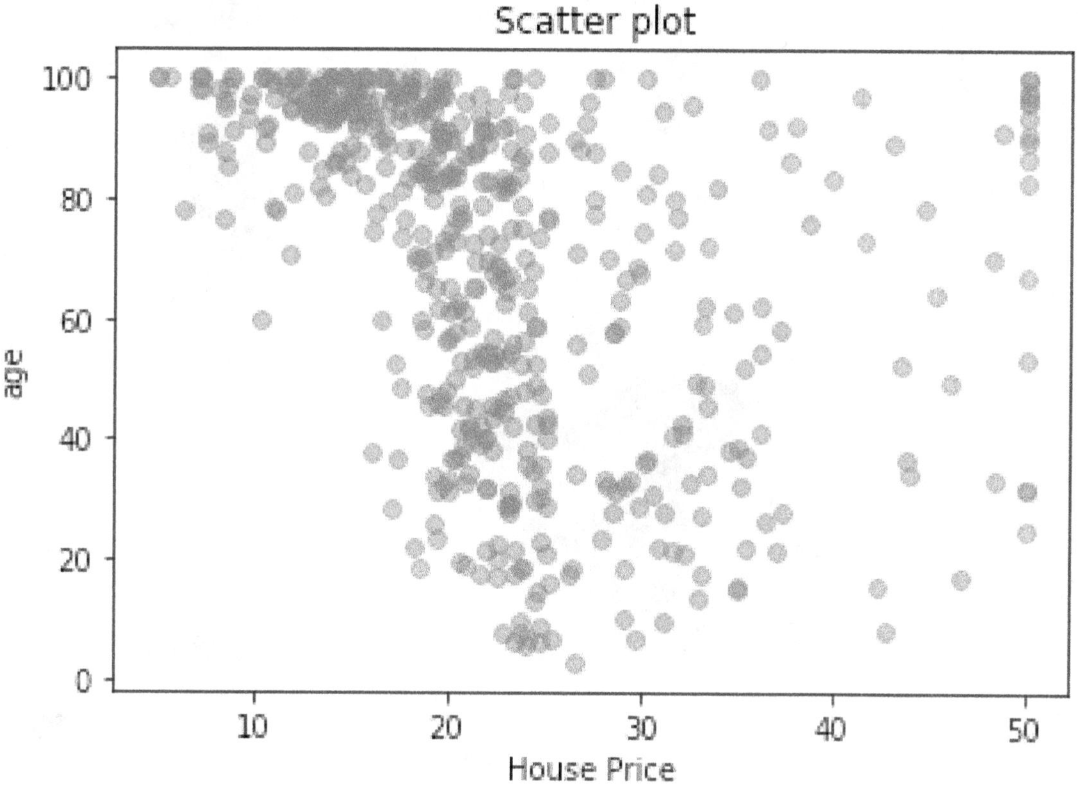

Python code snippet

```
# Scatter plot between medv and dis
x7 = Boston_from_R_to_Python['medv']
y7 = Boston_from_R_to_Python['dis']
plot.scatter(x7, y7, alpha=0.5)
plot.title('Scatter plot')
plot.xlabel('House Price')
plot.ylabel('dis')
plot.show()
```

Output

Python code snippet

```
# Scatter plot between medv and rad
x8 = Boston_from_R_to_Python['medv']
y8 = Boston_from_R_to_Python['rad']
plot.scatter(x8, y8, alpha=0.5)
plot.title('Scatter plot')
plot.xlabel('House Price')
plot.ylabel('rad')
plot.show()
```

Output

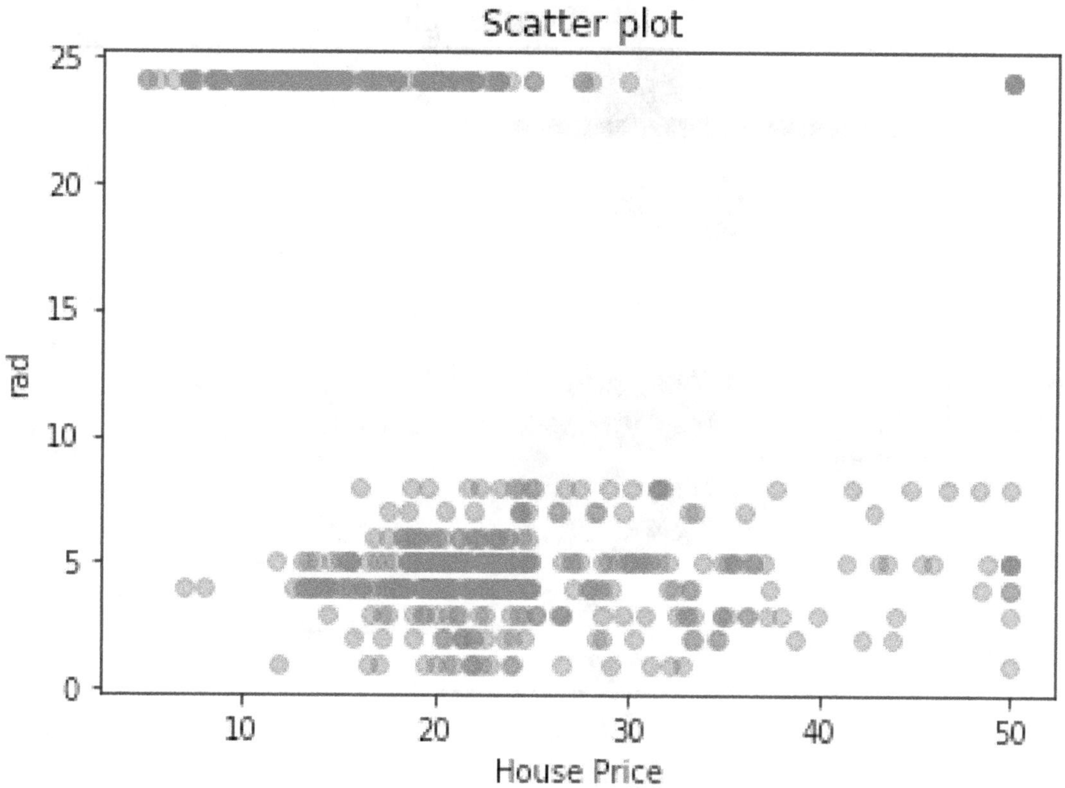

Python code snippet

```
# Scatter plot between medv and tax
x9 = Boston_from_R_to_Python['medv']
y9 = Boston_from_R_to_Python['tax']
plot.scatter(x9, y9, alpha=0.5)
plot.title('Scatter plot')
plot.xlabel('House Price')
plot.ylabel('tax')
plot.show()
```

Output

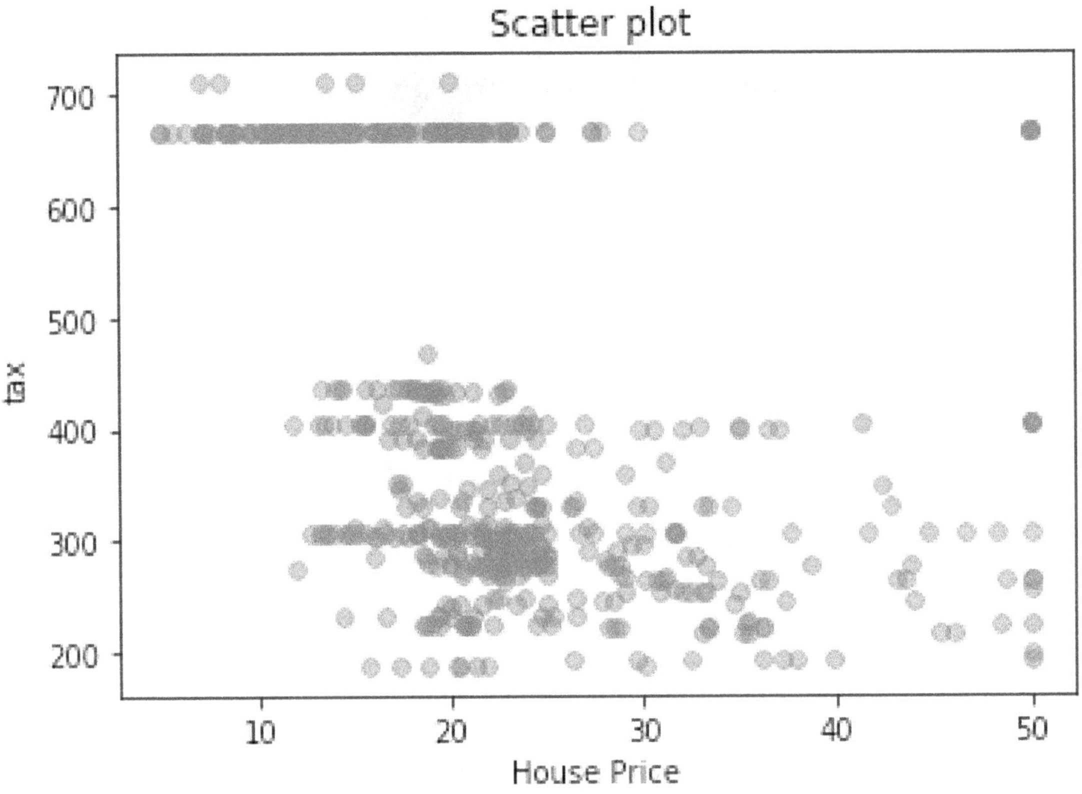

Python code snippet

```
# Scatter plot between medv and ptratio
x10 = Boston_from_R_to_Python['medv']
y10 = Boston_from_R_to_Python['ptratio']
plot.scatter(x10, y10, alpha=0.5)
plot.title('Scatter plot')
plot.xlabel('House Price')
plot.ylabel('ptratio')
plot.show()
```

Output

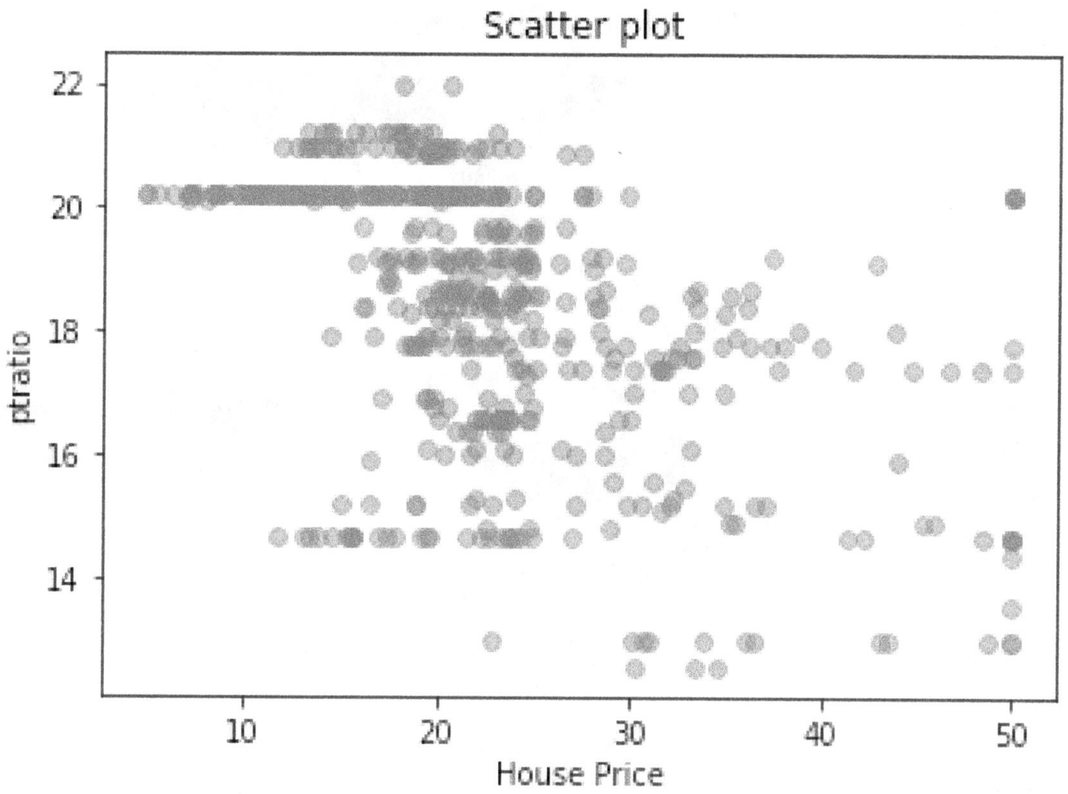

Python code snippet

```
# Scatter plot between medv and black
x11 = Boston_from_R_to_Python['medv']
y11 = Boston_from_R_to_Python['black']
plot.scatter(x11, y11, alpha=0.5)
plot.title('Scatter plot')
plot.xlabel('House Price')
plot.ylabel('black')
plot.show()
```

Output

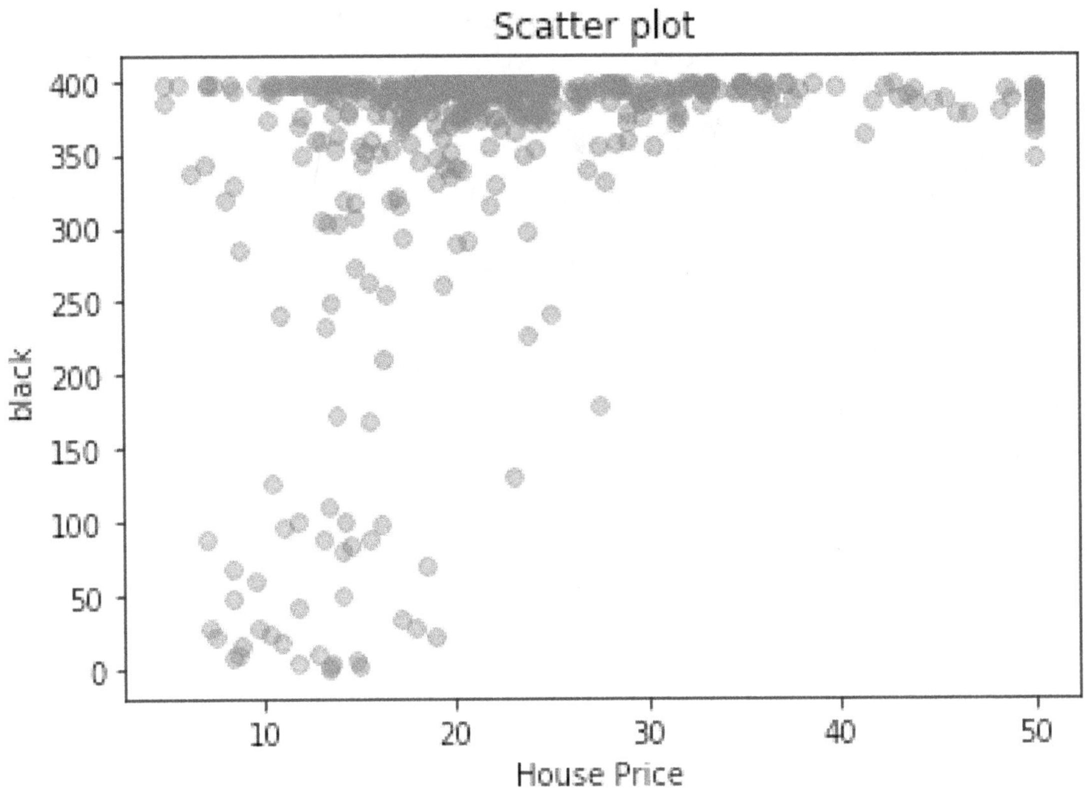

Python code snippet

```
# Scatter plot between medv and lstat
x12 = Boston_from_R_to_Python['medv']
y12 = Boston_from_R_to_Python['lstat']
plot.scatter(x12, y12, alpha=0.5)
plot.title('Scatter plot')
plot.xlabel('House Price')
plot.ylabel('lstat')
plot.show()
```

Output

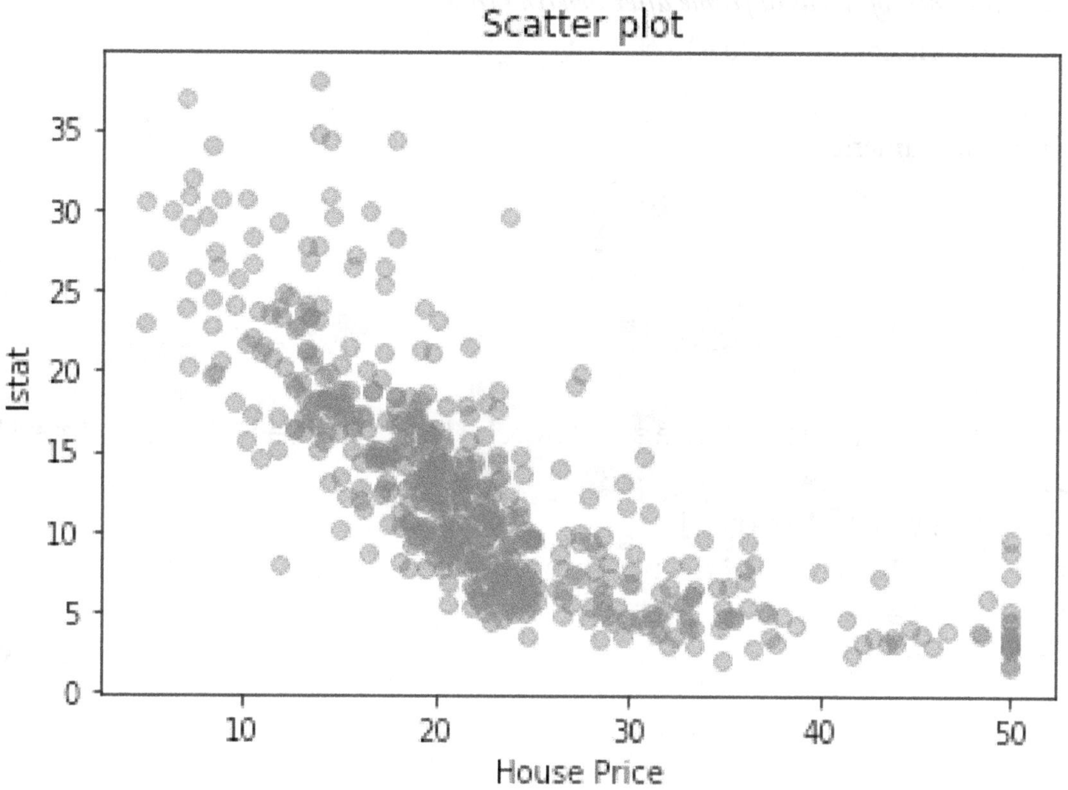

Python code snippet

```
# Pairwise scatter plot. It will be useful to plot a scatter plot matrix
import seaborn as sb

Boston_numeric = Boston_from_R_to_Python

# Display column names of the data frame before deleting name
print(Boston_numeric.columns.values)

# Drop categorical variables
Boston_numeric = Boston_numeric.drop('chas' , axis='columns')

# Display column names of the data frame after deleting chas
print(Boston_numeric.columns.values)

sb.pairplot(Boston_numeric)
plot.show()
```

Output

```
['crim' 'zn' 'indus' 'chas' 'nox' 'rm' 'age' 'dis' 'rad' 'tax'
'ptratio'
 'black' 'lstat' 'medv']
['crim' 'zn' 'indus' 'nox' 'rm' 'age' 'dis' 'rad' 'tax'
'ptratio' 'black'
 'lstat' 'medv']
```

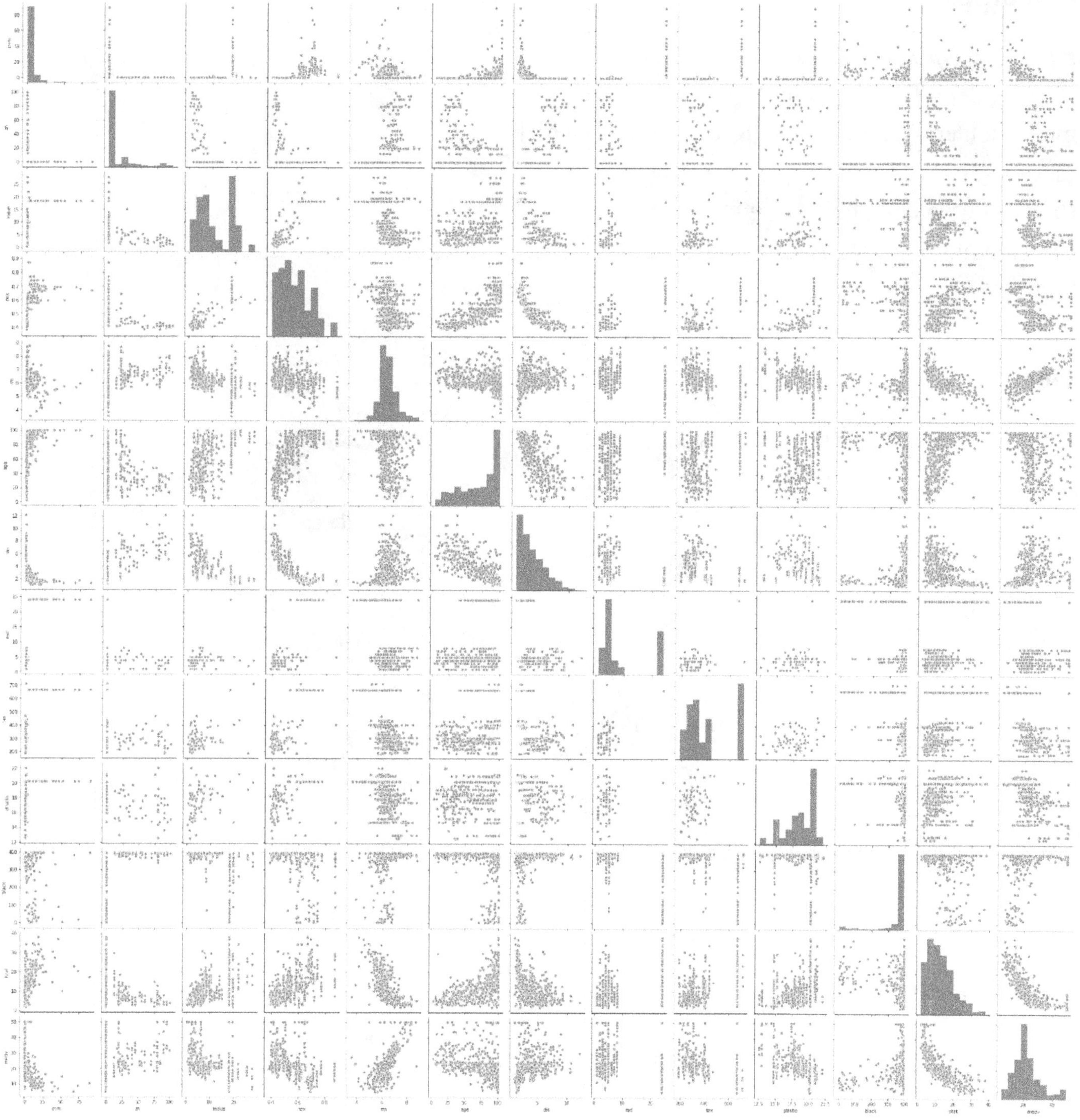

Python code snippet

```
# Relationship between chas and medv
chas_holder = Boston_from_R_to_Python['chas']
medv_holder = Boston_from_R_to_Python['medv']

sb.boxplot(x = chas_holder, y = medv_holder)
sb.swarmplot(x = chas_holder, y = medv_holder, color = '0.25')
plot.show()
```

Output

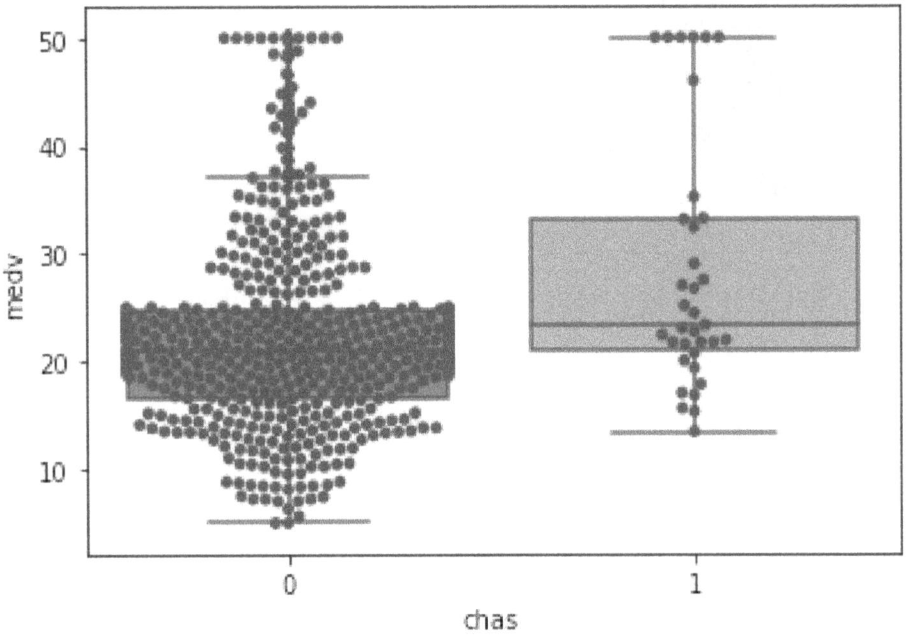

Python code snippet

```
boston_dataset = Boston_from_R_to_Python

print(type(Boston_from_R_to_Python))
print(type(boston_dataset))

print('Before deleting target ', boston_dataset.columns.values)

# Drop the target variable medv
boston_dataset = boston_dataset.drop('medv', axis='columns')

print('After deleting target ', boston_dataset.columns.values)
```

Output

```
<class 'pandas.core.frame.DataFrame'>
<class 'pandas.core.frame.DataFrame'>
Before deleting target  ['crim' 'zn' 'indus' 'chas' 'nox' 'rm'
'age' 'dis' 'rad' 'tax' 'ptratio'
 'black' 'lstat' 'medv']
After deleting target  ['crim' 'zn' 'indus' 'chas' 'nox' 'rm'
'age' 'dis' 'rad' 'tax' 'ptratio'
 'black' 'lstat']
```

Python code snippet

```
x = boston_dataset
print('Information about x is as follows: \n', x.head(3))
print('datatype of x is ', type(x))

print('Remark 100 is ', Boston_from_R_to_Python.columns.values)
```

Output

```
Information about x is as follows:
      crim    zn  indus chas    nox     rm   age     dis  rad
tax  ptratio  \
0  0.00632  18.0   2.31    0  0.538  6.575  65.2  4.0900    1
296      15.3
1  0.02731   0.0   7.07    0  0.469  6.421  78.9  4.9671    2
242      17.8
2  0.02729   0.0   7.07    0  0.469  7.185  61.1  4.9671    2
242      17.8

    black  lstat
0  396.90   4.98
1  396.90   9.14
2  392.83   4.03
datatype of x is  <class 'pandas.core.frame.DataFrame'>
Remark 100 is  ['crim' 'zn' 'indus' 'chas' 'nox' 'rm' 'age'
'dis' 'rad' 'tax' 'ptratio'
 'black' 'lstat' 'medv']
```

Python code snippet

```
# Find out if there is any missing value in the data frame
print('The following is missing value summary of the data frame column wise \n', x.isnull().sum())
```

Output

```
The following is missing value summary of the data frame
column wise
 crim        0
zn          0
indus       0
chas        0
nox         0
rm          0
age         0
dis         0
rad         0
tax         0
ptratio     0
black       0
lstat       0
dtype: int64
```

Python code snippet

```
y = Boston_from_R_to_Python['medv']

print('Information about y is as follows: \n', y.head(3))

# Replace chas 0, 1 with chas_yes, chas_no
x['chas'].replace(1, 'chas_yes',inplace=True)
x['chas'].replace(0, 'chas_no',inplace=True)

# Convert data type of target variable from series to data frame
print('datatype of y before conversion is ', type(y))
y = y.to_frame()
print('datatype of y after conversion is ', type(y))
```

Output

```
Information about y is as follows:
 0    24.0
1    21.6
2    34.7
Name: medv, dtype: float64
datatype of y before conversion is  <class
'pandas.core.series.Series'>
datatype of y after conversion is  <class
'pandas.core.frame.DataFrame'>
```

Python code snippet

```
# Carry out one hot encoding for categorical variables
for j in x.columns:

print('x[j].dtype is ', x[j].dtype)
if (x[j].dtype == object or str(x[j].dtype) == 'category'):
dummy_columns = pd.get_dummies(x[j])
x = x.join(dummy_columns)
print('I am deleting column', j, 'from the data set. ', 'Value of j is ', j)
del x[j]

x_train, x_test, y_train, y_test = train_test_split(x, y, test_size=0.30, random_state=200)

# Find out the dimensions of train and test sets
row_count_train, col_count_train = x_train.shape
print('Number of rows in train ', row_count_train)
print('Number of columns in train ', col_count_train)

row_count_test, col_count_test = x_test.shape
print('Number of rows in test ', row_count_test)
print('Number of columns in test ', col_count_test)

print('List of column names are: ', x_train.columns.values)
```

Output

```
x[j].dtype is  float64
x[j].dtype is  float64
x[j].dtype is  float64
x[j].dtype is  category
I am deleting column chas from the data set.  Value of j is
chas
x[j].dtype is  float64
x[j].dtype is  float64
x[j].dtype is  float64
x[j].dtype is  float64
x[j].dtype is  int64
x[j].dtype is  int64
x[j].dtype is  float64
x[j].dtype is  float64
x[j].dtype is  float64
Number of rows in train  354
Number of columns in train  14
Number of rows in test  152
Number of columns in test  14
List of column names are:  ['crim' 'zn' 'indus' 'nox' 'rm'
'age' 'dis' 'rad' 'tax' 'ptratio' 'black'
 'lstat' 'chas_no' 'chas_yes']
```

Python code snippet

```
print(x_train.head(10))
print(x_train.shape)
print(list(x_train.columns))
```

Output

```
          crim    zn  indus    nox     rm   age     dis  rad
tax  ptratio  \
4    0.06905   0.0   2.18  0.458  7.147   54.2  6.0622    3
222     18.7
393  8.64476   0.0  18.10  0.693  6.193   92.6  1.7912   24
666     20.2
387 22.59710   0.0  18.10  0.700  5.000   89.5  1.5184   24
666     20.2
452  5.09017   0.0  18.10  0.713  6.297   91.8  2.3682   24
666     20.2
343  0.02543  55.0   3.78  0.484  6.696   56.4  5.7321    5
370     17.6
68   0.13554  12.5   6.07  0.409  5.594   36.8  6.4980    4
345     18.9
341  0.01301  35.0   1.52  0.442  7.241   49.3  7.0379    1
284     15.5
442  5.66637   0.0  18.10  0.740  6.219  100.0  2.0048   24
666     20.2
34   1.61282   0.0   8.14  0.538  6.096   96.9  3.7598    4
307     21.0
62   0.11027  25.0   5.13  0.453  6.456   67.8  7.2255    8
284     19.7

      black  lstat  chas_no  chas_yes
4    396.90   5.33        1         0
393  396.90  15.17        1         0
387  396.90  31.99        1         0
452  385.09  17.27        1         0
343  396.90   7.18        1         0
68   396.90  13.09        1         0
341  394.74   5.49        1         0
442  395.69  16.59        1         0
34   248.31  20.34        1         0
62   396.90   6.73        1         0
(354, 14)
['crim', 'zn', 'indus', 'nox', 'rm', 'age', 'dis', 'rad',
'tax', 'ptratio', 'black', 'lstat', 'chas_no', 'chas_yes']
```

Python code snippet

```
from sklearn.tree import DecisionTreeRegressor
from sklearn import tree

model = DecisionTreeRegressor(random_state = 100, max_leaf_nodes = 7, min_samples_leaf = 5,
max_depth= 5)
model.fit(x_train, y_train)

from sklearn.tree import export_graphviz
import pydotplus
from IPython.display import Image

# Create DOT data
dot_data = tree.export_graphviz(model)

# Draw graph
graph = pydotplus.graph_from_dot_data(dot_data)

# Create PDF
graph.write_pdf("Boston_1.pdf")

# Create PNG
graph.write_png("Boston_1.png")
```

Output

```
True
```

Python code snippet

```
# User defined function for calculating MAPE
def mape(y_true, y_pred):

y_true, y_pred = np.array(y_true), np.array(y_pred)
return np.mean(np.abs((y_true - y_pred) / y_true)) * 100
```

```
# User defined function for calculating regression tree performance metrics
def regression_tree_performance_metrics(y_true, y_pred):

mean_absolute_percentage_error = mape(y_true, y_pred)
mean_squared_error = metrics.mean_squared_error(y_true, y_pred)

print('Mean Absolute Percentage Error: ', round(mean_absolute_percentage_error, 4))
print('Mean Squared Error: ', round(mean_squared_error, 4))

# Get the predicted values of y from train data
y_pred_train = model.predict(x_train)

# Get the train performance metrics
print('TRAIN PERFORMANCE')
regression_tree_performance_metrics(y_train, y_pred_train)
```

Output

```
TRAIN PERFORMANCE
Mean Absolute Percentage Error:  45.0189
Mean Squared Error:  15.6997
```

Python code snippet

```
# Get the predicted values of y from test data
y_pred_test = model.predict(x_test)

print('TEST PERFORMANCE')
# Get the test performance metrics
regression_tree_performance_metrics(y_test, y_pred_test)
```

Output

```
TEST PERFORMANCE
Mean Absolute Percentage Error:  54.4424
Mean Squared Error:  29.439
```

Python code snippet

```
# Random Forest Classifier
# Let's get back to the Titanic use case that we discussed while studying logistic regression modeling technique
# You can skip EDA. However, you have to do all data preprocessing steps before passing the data to model builder

# Read CSV file from working directory
Titanic_from_R_to_Python = pd.read_csv("Titanic_from_R_to_Python.csv")

# View the column names and their data types from a data frame
print(Titanic_from_R_to_Python.dtypes)
```

Output

```
PassengerId      int64
Survived         int64
Pclass           int64
Name            object
Sex             object
Age            float64
SibSp            int64
Parch            int64
Ticket          object
Fare           float64
Cabin           object
Embarked        object
dtype: object
```

Python code snippet

```
# Change PassengerId, Survived and Pclass to categorical variables
Titanic_from_R_to_Python['PassengerId'] = pd.Categorical(Titanic_from_R_to_Python.PassengerId)
Titanic_from_R_to_Python['Survived'] = pd.Categorical(Titanic_from_R_to_Python.Survived)
Titanic_from_R_to_Python['Pclass'] = pd.Categorical(Titanic_from_R_to_Python.Pclass)

# Check data types after conversion
print(Titanic_from_R_to_Python.dtypes)
```

Output

```
PassengerId    category
Survived       category
Pclass         category
Name             object
Sex              object
Age             float64
SibSp             int64
Parch             int64
Ticket           object
Fare            float64
Cabin            object
Embarked         object
dtype: object
```

Python code snippet

```
# You should carry out various data exploration exercises at this point of time

# Divide the data into train and test sets
from sklearn.model_selection import train_test_split

titanic_dataset = Titanic_from_R_to_Python

print(type(Titanic_from_R_to_Python))
print(type(titanic_dataset))

print('Before deleting target and variables is ' , titanic_dataset.columns.values)

# Drop target and other non relevant variables
titanic_dataset = titanic_dataset.drop('Survived' , axis='columns')
titanic_dataset = titanic_dataset.drop('PassengerId' , axis='columns')
titanic_dataset = titanic_dataset.drop('Name' , axis='columns')
titanic_dataset = titanic_dataset.drop('Ticket' , axis='columns')
titanic_dataset = titanic_dataset.drop('Cabin' , axis='columns')

print('After deleting target and variables ' , titanic_dataset.columns.values)
```

Output

```
<class 'pandas.core.frame.DataFrame'>
<class 'pandas.core.frame.DataFrame'>
Before deleting target and variables is  ['PassengerId'
'Survived' 'Pclass' 'Name' 'Sex' 'Age' 'SibSp' 'Parch'
 'Ticket' 'Fare' 'Cabin' 'Embarked']
After deleting target and variables  ['Pclass' 'Sex' 'Age'
'SibSp' 'Parch' 'Fare' 'Embarked']
```

Python code snippet

```
x = titanic_dataset

# Replace Pclass 1, 2, 3 with Pclass1, Pclass2 and Pclass3
x['Pclass'].replace(1, 'Pclass1',inplace=True)
x['Pclass'].replace(2, 'Pclass2',inplace=True)
x['Pclass'].replace(3, 'Pclass3',inplace=True)

# Find out if there is any missing value in the data frame
print('The following is missing value summary of the data frame column wise \n' , x.isnull().sum())

# Replace missing age values with mean age
x['Age'].fillna((x['Age'].mean()), inplace=True)

# Replace missing embarked values with the most frequent embarked value
x = x.apply(lambda x: x.fillna(x.value_counts().index[0]))

# Find out if there is any missing value in the data frame
print('Check the missing value summary now \n' , x.isnull().sum())
```

Output

```
The following is missing value summary of the data frame colum
n wise
 Pclass        0
Sex           0
Age         177
SibSp         0
Parch         0
Fare          0
Embarked      2
dtype: int64
Check the missing value summary now
 Pclass      0
Sex         0
Age         0
SibSp       0
Parch       0
Fare        0
Embarked    0
dtype: int64
```

Python code snippet

```
y = Titanic_from_R_to_Python['Survived']

# Convert data type of target variable from series to data frame
y = y.to_frame()

# Carry out one hot encoding for categorical variables
for j in x.columns:

print('x[j].dtype is ' , x[j].dtype)
if (x[j].dtype == object or str(x[j].dtype) == 'category'):
dummy_columns = pd.get_dummies(x[j])
x = x.join(dummy_columns)
print('I am deleting column' , j, 'from the data set. ' , 'Value of j is ' , j)
del x[j]
```

```
x_train, x_test, y_train, y_test = train_test_split(x, y, test_size=0.30, random_state = 200)

# Find out the dimensions of train and test sets
row_count_train, col_count_train = x_train.shape
print('Number of rows in train ', row_count_train)
print('Number of columns in train ', col_count_train)

row_count_test, col_count_test = x_test.shape
print('Number of rows in test ', row_count_test)
print('Number of columns in test ', col_count_test)

print('List of column names are: ', x_train.columns.values)
```

Output

```
x[j].dtype is  category
I am deleting column Pclass from the data set.  Value of j is
Pclass
x[j].dtype is  object
I am deleting column Sex from the data set.  Value of j is
Sex
x[j].dtype is  float64
x[j].dtype is  int64
x[j].dtype is  int64
x[j].dtype is  float64
x[j].dtype is  object
I am deleting column Embarked from the data set.  Value of j
is  Embarked
Number of rows in train  623
Number of columns in train  12
Number of rows in test  268
Number of columns in test  12
List of column names are:  ['Age' 'SibSp' 'Parch' 'Fare'
'Pclass1' 'Pclass2' 'Pclass3' 'female'
 'male' 'C' 'Q' 'S']
```

Python code snippet

```
print(x_train.shape)
print(list(x_train.columns))
print(y_train['Survived'].value_counts())
```

Output

```
(623, 12)
['Age', 'SibSp', 'Parch', 'Fare', 'Pclass1', 'Pclass2',
'Pclass3', 'female', 'male', 'C', 'Q', 'S']
0    384
1    239
Name: Survived, dtype: int64
```

Python code snippet

```
# Build the model
from sklearn.ensemble import RandomForestClassifier

# Create the model with 1000 trees
model = RandomForestClassifier(n_estimators=1000, bootstrap = True, max_features = 4)
# Fit on training data
model.fit(x_train, y_train)

# Predict using model and find out test performance measures
from sklearn import metrics

# Following are the performance measures on the test set
# Accuracy of test set
print(model.score(x_test, y_test))

# Get the confusion matrix
from sklearn.metrics import confusion_matrix

# Predict on the test data
y_pred_test = model.predict(x_test)
```

```
confusion_matrix_test = confusion_matrix(y_test, y_pred_test)
print('The confusion matrix is as follows \n' , confusion_matrix_test)

# Get the classification report
from sklearn.metrics import classification_report

print(classification_report(y_test, y_pred_test))
```

Output

```
C:\Users\Malaya\anaconda3\lib\site-
packages\ipykernel_launcher.py:7: DataConversionWarning: A
column-vector y was passed when a 1d array was expected.
Please change the shape of y to (n_samples,), for example
using ravel().
  import sys
0.7910447761194029
The confusion matrix is as follows
 [[143  22]
 [ 34  69]]
              precision    recall  f1-score   support

           0       0.81      0.87      0.84       165
           1       0.76      0.67      0.71       103

    accuracy                           0.79       268
   macro avg       0.78      0.77      0.77       268
weighted avg       0.79      0.79      0.79       268
```

Python code snippet

```
# Plot the ROC curve and get the AUC value
from sklearn.metrics import roc_auc_score
from sklearn.metrics import roc_curve
import matplotlib.pyplot as plot

roc_auc_test = roc_auc_score(y_test, model.predict(x_test))
fpr, tpr, thresholds = roc_curve(y_test, model.predict_proba(x_test)[:,1])
plot.figure()
```

```
plot.plot(fpr, tpr, label='Random Forest Classification (area = %0.2f)' % roc_auc_test)
plot.plot([0, 1], [0, 1],'r--')
plot.xlim([0.0, 1.0])
plot.ylim([0.0, 1.05])
plot.xlabel('FPR')
plot.ylabel('TPR')
plot.title('Test ROC')
plot.legend(loc="lower right")
plot.show()
```

Output

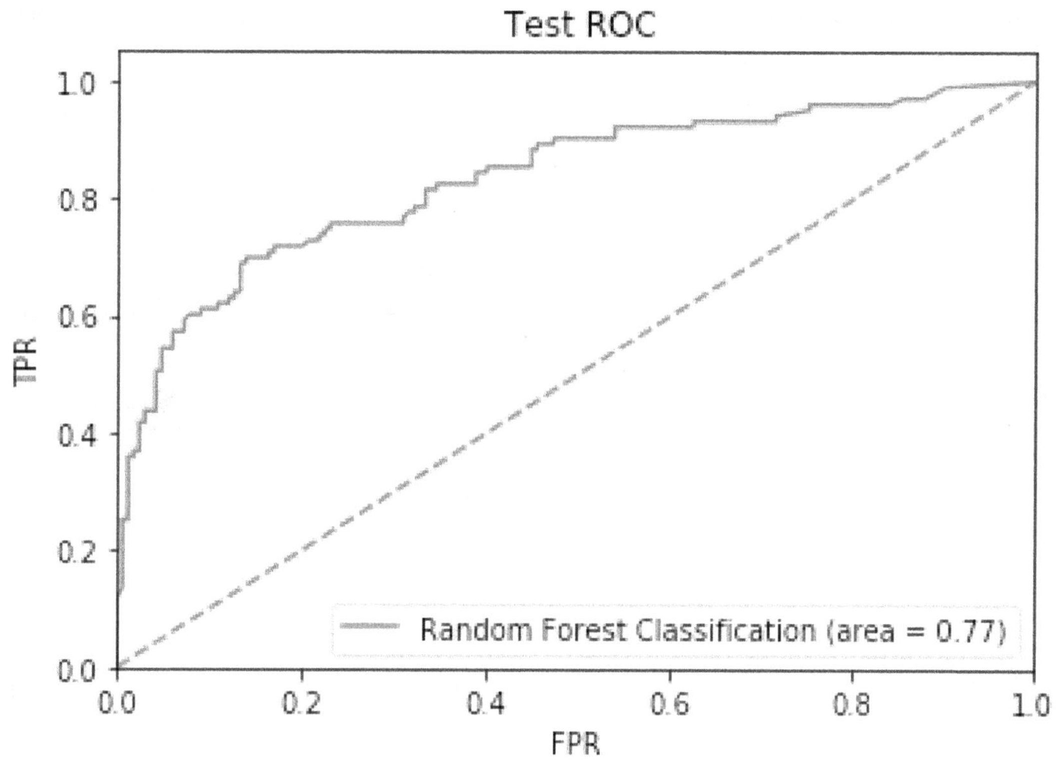

 # Now is the time you should compare the performance of random forest classifier with that of logistic regression
 # for the same Titanic use case

Clustering

Python code snippet

```
# Read CSV file from working directory
Iris_from_R_to_Python = pd.read_csv("Iris_from_R_to_Python.csv")

# Print the data frame
print(Iris_from_R_to_Python)

# Get the data type of Iris_from_R_to_Python
print(type(Iris_from_R_to_Python))

# View the column names and their data types from a data frame
print(Iris_from_R_to_Python.dtypes)
```

Output

```
     Sepal.Length  Sepal.Width  Petal.Length  Petal.Width    Species
0             5.1          3.5           1.4          0.2     setosa
1             4.9          3.0           1.4          0.2     setosa
2             4.7          3.2           1.3          0.2     setosa
3             4.6          3.1           1.5          0.2     setosa
4             5.0          3.6           1.4          0.2     setosa
..            ...          ...           ...          ...        ...
145           6.7          3.0           5.2          2.3  virginica
146           6.3          2.5           5.0          1.9  virginica
147           6.5          3.0           5.2          2.0  virginica
148           6.2          3.4           5.4          2.3  virginica
149           5.9          3.0           5.1          1.8  virginica

[150 rows x 5 columns]
<class 'pandas.core.frame.DataFrame'>
Sepal.Length    float64
Sepal.Width     float64
Petal.Length    float64
Petal.Width     float64
Species          object
dtype: object
```

Python code snippet

```
# Check information related to columns of the data frame
print(Iris_from_R_to_Python.info())

# Take only numeric attributes for K Means
# Drop Species
iris_dataset = Iris_from_R_to_Python
iris_dataset = iris_dataset.drop('Species', axis='columns')

# Verify that only numeric columns are present for K Means clustering
print(iris_dataset.dtypes)
```

Output

```
<class 'pandas.core.frame.DataFrame'>
RangeIndex: 150 entries, 0 to 149
Data columns (total 5 columns):
 #   Column        Non-Null Count  Dtype
---  ------        --------------  -----
 0   Sepal.Length  150 non-null    float64
 1   Sepal.Width   150 non-null    float64
 2   Petal.Length  150 non-null    float64
 3   Petal.Width   150 non-null    float64
 4   Species       150 non-null    object
dtypes: float64(4), object(1)
memory usage: 6.0+ KB
None
Sepal.Length    float64
Sepal.Width     float64
Petal.Length    float64
Petal.Width     float64
dtype: object
```

Python code snippet

```
# Understand the distribution of each variable - Univariate analysis

# Import
import seaborn as sb
import matplotlib.pyplot as plot

# Box plot of sepal length
sb.boxplot(data = Iris_from_R_to_Python['Sepal.Length'])
sb.swarmplot(data = Iris_from_R_to_Python['Sepal.Length'], color = '0.25')
plot.show()
```

Output

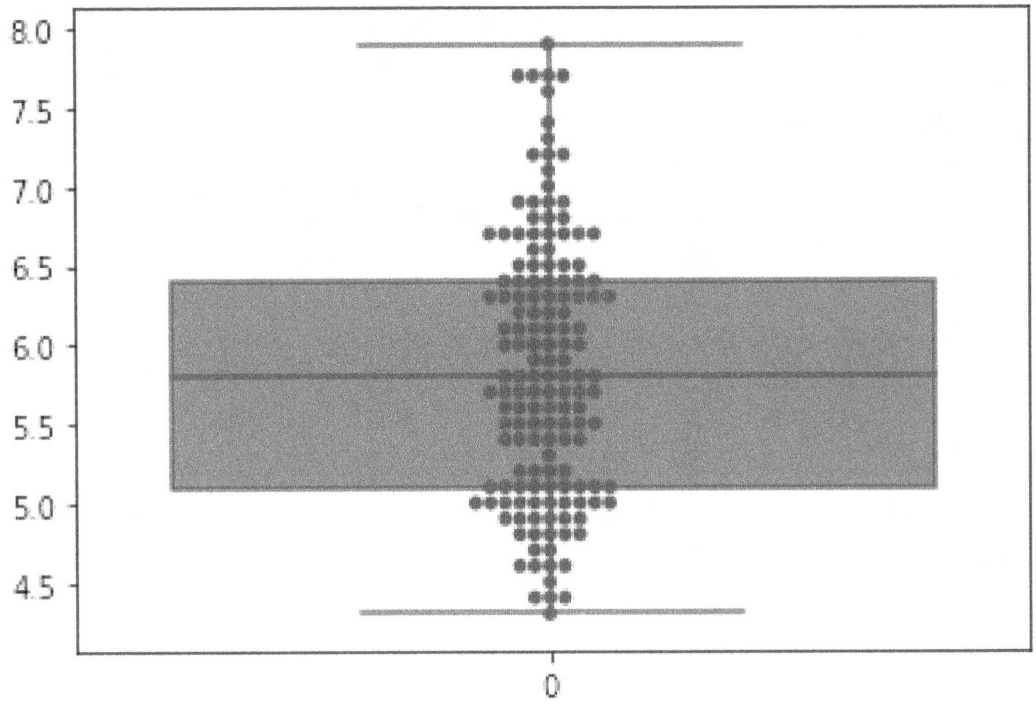

Python code snippet

```
# Box plot of sepal width
sb.boxplot(data = Iris_from_R_to_Python['Sepal.Width'])
sb.swarmplot(data = Iris_from_R_to_Python['Sepal.Width'], color = '0.25')
plot.show()
```

Output

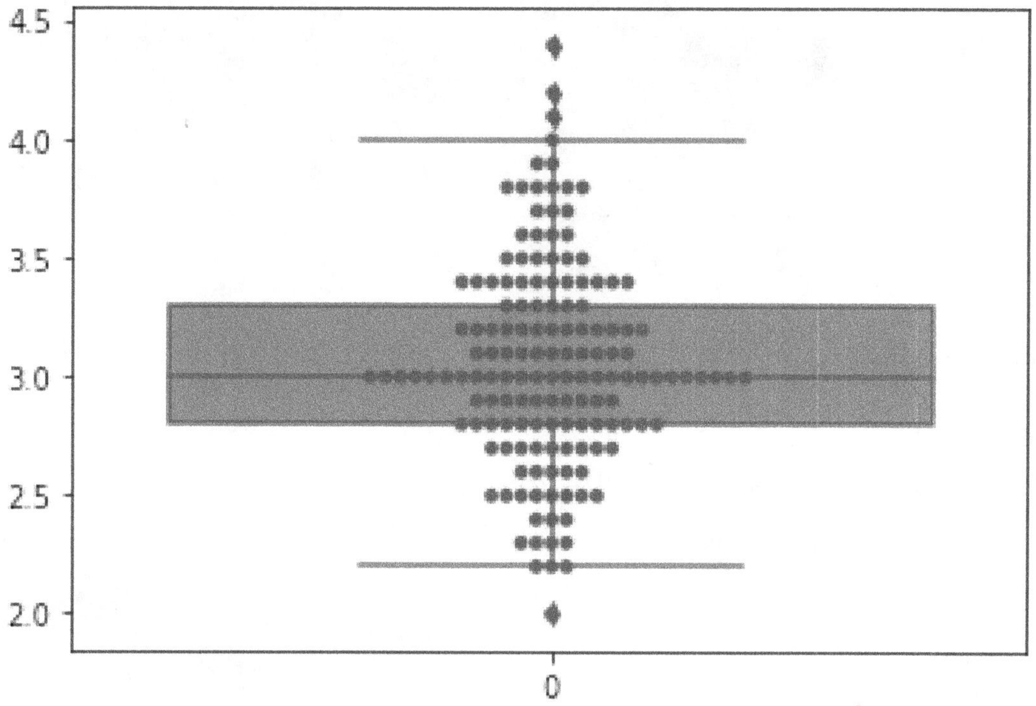

Python code snippet

```
# Box plot of petal length
sb.boxplot(data = Iris_from_R_to_Python['Petal.Length'])
sb.swarmplot(data = Iris_from_R_to_Python['Petal.Length'], color = '0.25')
plot.show()
```

Output

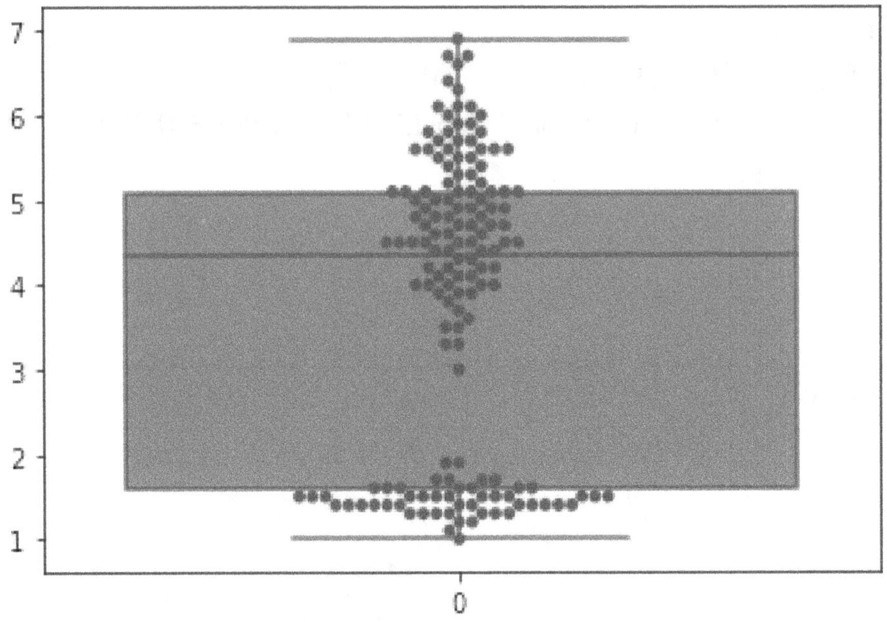

Python code snippet

```
# Box plot of petal width
sb.boxplot(data = Iris_from_R_to_Python['Petal.Width'])
sb.swarmplot(data = Iris_from_R_to_Python['Petal.Width'], color = '0.25')
plot.show()
```

Output

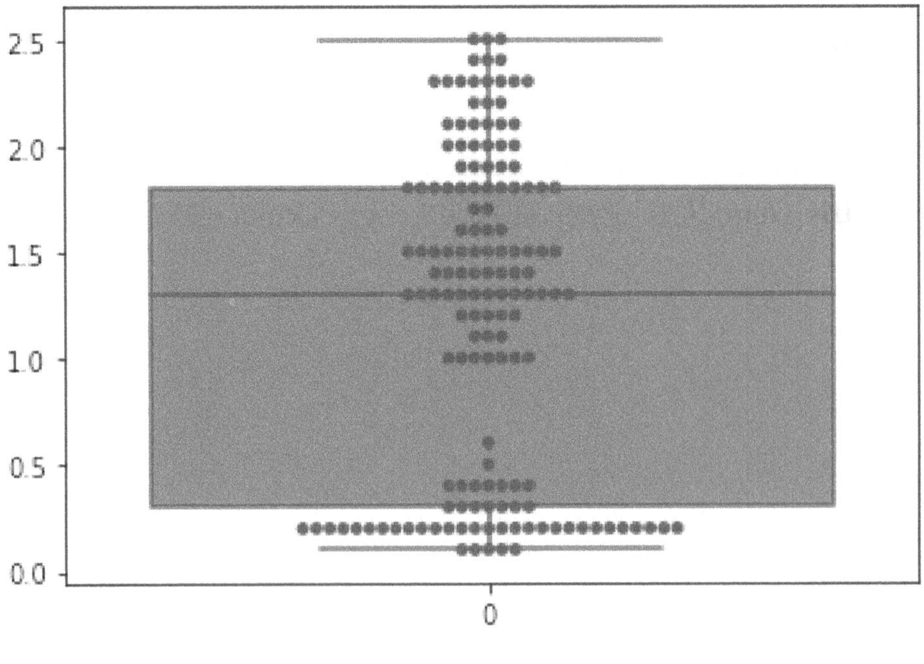

Python code snippet

```
# Import K Means
from sklearn.cluster import KMeans

model = KMeans(n_clusters = 4, random_state = 300)
model.fit(iris_dataset)

# Print cluster centers (centroids)
print('Cluster Centers as below \n' , model.cluster_centers_)
```

Output

```
Cluster Centers as below
 [[5.006      3.428      1.462      0.246     ]
 [6.2525     2.855      4.815      1.625     ]
 [6.9125     3.1        5.846875   2.13125   ]
 [5.53214286 2.63571429 3.96071429 1.22857143]]
```

Python code snippet

```
# Check how to access the cluster center elements
# Cluster 0
center_0_0 = round(model.cluster_centers_[0,0], 4)
center_0_1 = round(model.cluster_centers_[0,1], 4)
center_0_2 = round(model.cluster_centers_[0,2], 4)
center_0_3 = round(model.cluster_centers_[0,3], 4)

print('center_0_0 is \n' , center_0_0)
print('center_0_1 is \n' , center_0_1)
print('center_0_2 is \n' , center_0_2)
print('center_0_3 is \n' , center_0_3)
```

Output

```
center_0_0 is
 5.006
center_0_1 is
 3.428
center_0_2 is
 1.462
center_0_3 is
 0.246
```

Python code snippet

```
# Cluster 1
center_1_0 = round(model.cluster_centers_[1,0], 4)
center_1_1 = round(model.cluster_centers_[1,1], 4)
center_1_2 = round(model.cluster_centers_[1,2], 4)
center_1_3 = round(model.cluster_centers_[1,3], 4)

print('center_1_0 is \n' , center_1_0)
print('center_1_1 is \n' , center_1_1)
print('center_1_2 is \n' , center_1_2)
print('center_1_3 is \n' , center_1_3)
```

Output

```
center_1_0 is
 6.2525
center_1_1 is
 2.855
center_1_2 is
 4.815
center_1_3 is
 1.625
```

Python code snippet

```
# Cluster 2
center_2_0 = round(model.cluster_centers_[2,0], 4)
center_2_1 = round(model.cluster_centers_[2,1], 4)
center_2_2 = round(model.cluster_centers_[2,2], 4)
center_2_3 = round(model.cluster_centers_[2,3], 4)

print('center_2_0 is \n' , center_2_0)
print('center_2_1 is \n' , center_2_1)
print('center_2_2 is \n' , center_2_2)
print('center_2_3 is \n' , center_2_3)
```

Output

```
center_2_0 is
 6.9125
center_2_1 is
 3.1
center_2_2 is
 5.8469
center_2_3 is
 2.1312
```

Python code snippet

```
# Cluster 3
center_3_0 = round(model.cluster_centers_[3,0], 4)
center_3_1 = round(model.cluster_centers_[3,1], 4)
center_3_2 = round(model.cluster_centers_[3,2], 4)
center_3_3 = round(model.cluster_centers_[3,3], 4)

print('center_3_0 is \n' , center_3_0)
print('center_3_1 is \n' , center_3_1)
print('center_3_2 is \n' , center_3_2)
print('center_3_3 is \n' , center_3_3)
```

Output

```
center_3_0 is
 5.5321
center_3_1 is
 2.6357
center_3_2 is
 3.9607
center_3_3 is
 1.2286
```

Python code snippet

```
# New clusters
y_kmeans = model.fit_predict(iris_dataset)

# See what y_kmeans contains
print('y_kmeans as below \n' , y_kmeans)

# Check the data type of y_kmeans
print('Data type of y_kmeans is ' , type(y_kmeans))

print('Variable data types before adding the new column for cluster number \n' , iris_dataset.dtypes)
```

Output

```
y_kmeans as below
 [0 0 0 0 0 0 0 0 0 0 0 0 0 0 0 0 0 0 0 0 0 0 0 0 0 0 0 0 0 0 0 0 0 0 0 0 0
 0 0 0 0 0 0 0 0 0 0 0 0 0 1 1 1 3 1 3 1 3 1 3 3 3 3 1 3 1 3 3 1 3 1 3 1 1
 1 1 1 1 1 3 3 3 3 1 3 1 1 1 3 3 3 1 3 3 3 3 3 1 3 3 2 1 2 2 2 3 2 2 2 1
 1 2 1 1 2 2 2 2 1 2 1 2 1 2 2 1 1 2 2 2 2 2 1 1 2 2 2 1 2 2 2 1 2 2 2 1 1
 2 1]
Data type of y_kmeans is  <class 'numpy.ndarray'>
Variable data types before adding the new column for cluster
number

 Sepal.Length    float64
Sepal.Width     float64
Petal.Length    float64
Petal.Width     float64
dtype: object
```

Python code snippet

```
# Tie back cluster numbers to each row
iris_dataset['Cluster_Number'] = y_kmeans

print('Variable data types after adding the new column for cluster number \n' , iris_dataset.dtypes)

print('Data types as below \n' , iris_dataset.dtypes)
print('Sample rows as below \n' , iris_dataset.head())
```

Output

```
Variable data types after adding the new column for cluster
number
 Sepal.Length      float64
Sepal.Width       float64
Petal.Length      float64
Petal.Width       float64
Cluster_Number      int32
dtype: object
Data types as below
 Sepal.Length      float64
Sepal.Width       float64
Petal.Length      float64
Petal.Width       float64
Cluster_Number      int32
dtype: object
Sample rows as below
    Sepal.Length  Sepal.Width  Petal.Length  Petal.Width
Cluster_Number
0            5.1          3.5           1.4          0.2
0
1            4.9          3.0           1.4          0.2
0
2            4.7          3.2           1.3          0.2
0
3            4.6          3.1           1.5          0.2
0
4            5.0          3.6           1.4          0.2
0
```

Python code snippet

```
#Check unique values of cluster number
print('Unique cluster numbers \n' , iris_dataset['Cluster_Number']. unique())

# Convert cluster number to categorical variable
iris_dataset['Cluster_Number'] = pd.Categorical(iris_dataset.Cluster_Number)
```

Output

```
Unique cluster numbers
 [0 1 3 2]
```

Python code snippet

```
sb.pairplot(iris_dataset, hue = 'Cluster_Number')
plot.show()
```

Output

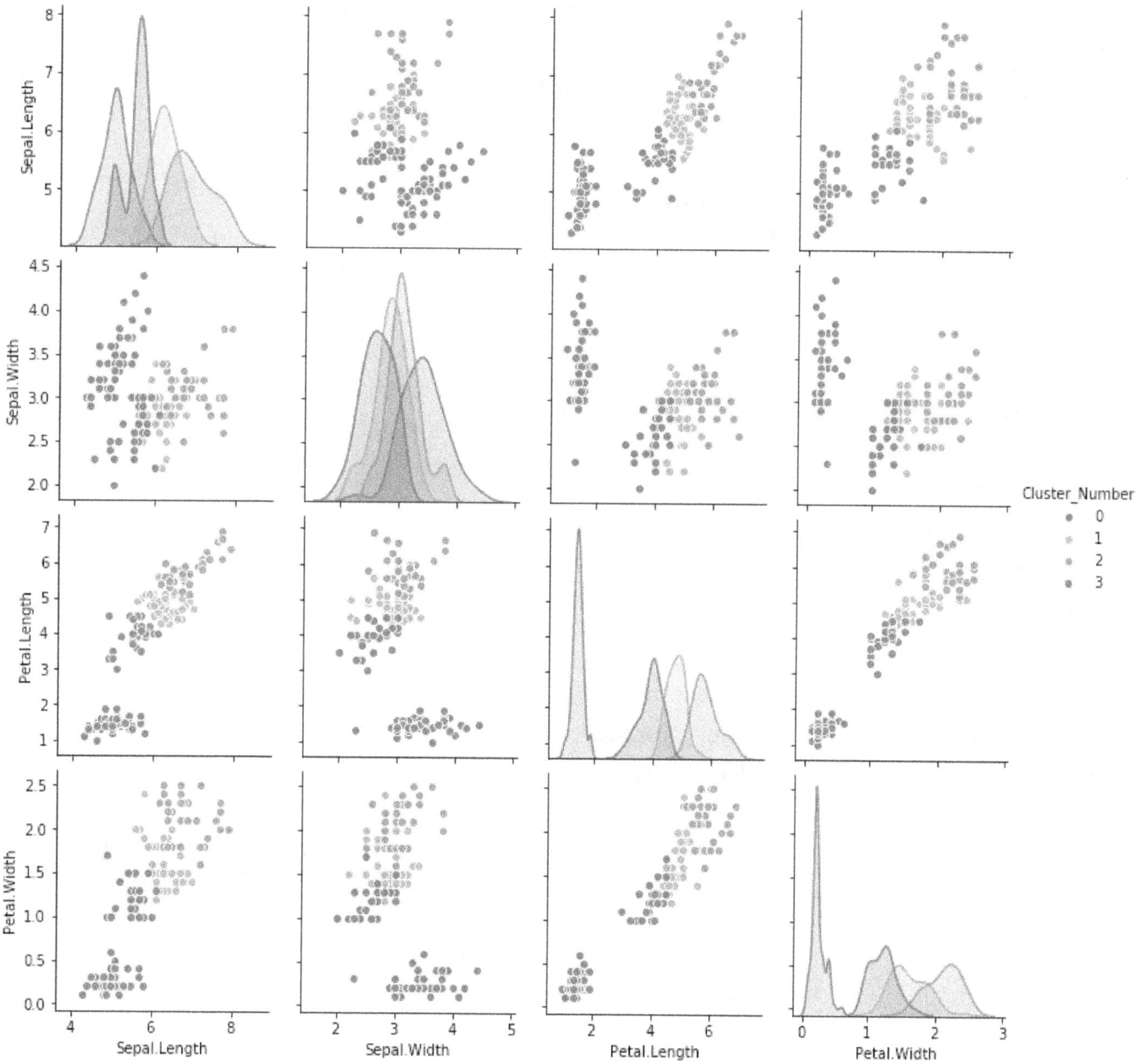

Python code snippet

```
# The elbow curve
# The function returns WSS score for each k
def calculate_WSS(data, kmax):
  sse = []
    for k in range(1, kmax + 1):
      kmeans = KMeans(n_clusters=k).fit(data)
      centroids = kmeans.cluster_centers_
      pred_clusters = kmeans.predict(data)
      curr_sse = 0

      list_of_distances = []
      # calculate square of Euclidean distance of each point from its cluster center and add to current WSS
    for i in range(len(data)):

      curr_center = centroids[pred_clusters[i]]
      curr_sse += (data.iloc[i, 0] - curr_center[0]) ** 2 + (data.iloc[i, 1] - curr_center[1]) ** 2 + (data.
      iloc[i, 2] - curr_center[2]) ** 2 + (data.iloc[i, 3] - curr_center[3]) ** 2
      list_of_distances.append(curr_sse)
    sse.append(curr_sse)
    plot.hist(list_of_distances, density = False, bins = 10)
    plot.ylabel('Frequency')
    plot.xlabel('Distance')
    plot.title('Distribution of WSS for each Cluster')
    plot.show()
return sse

print('iris data set dtypes \n' , iris_dataset.dtypes)
iris_dataset = iris_dataset.drop('Cluster_Number', axis='columns')
print('iris data set dtypes \n' , iris_dataset.dtypes)
```

Output

```
iris data set dtypes
 Sepal.Length       float64
Sepal.Width        float64
Petal.Length       float64
Petal.Width        float64
Cluster_Number    category
dtype: object
iris data set dtypes
 Sepal.Length    float64
Sepal.Width     float64
Petal.Length    float64
Petal.Width     float64
dtype: object
```

```
WSS_iris = calculate_WSS(iris_dataset, 10)

print('Within Sum Square \n' , WSS_iris)
print('WSS data type ' , type(WSS_iris))
x_index = list(range(len(WSS_iris)))

print('x_index is \n' , x_index)

plot.plot(x_index, WSS_iris, marker='o', linestyle='--', color='r')

plot.ylabel('WSS')
plot.show()
```

Output

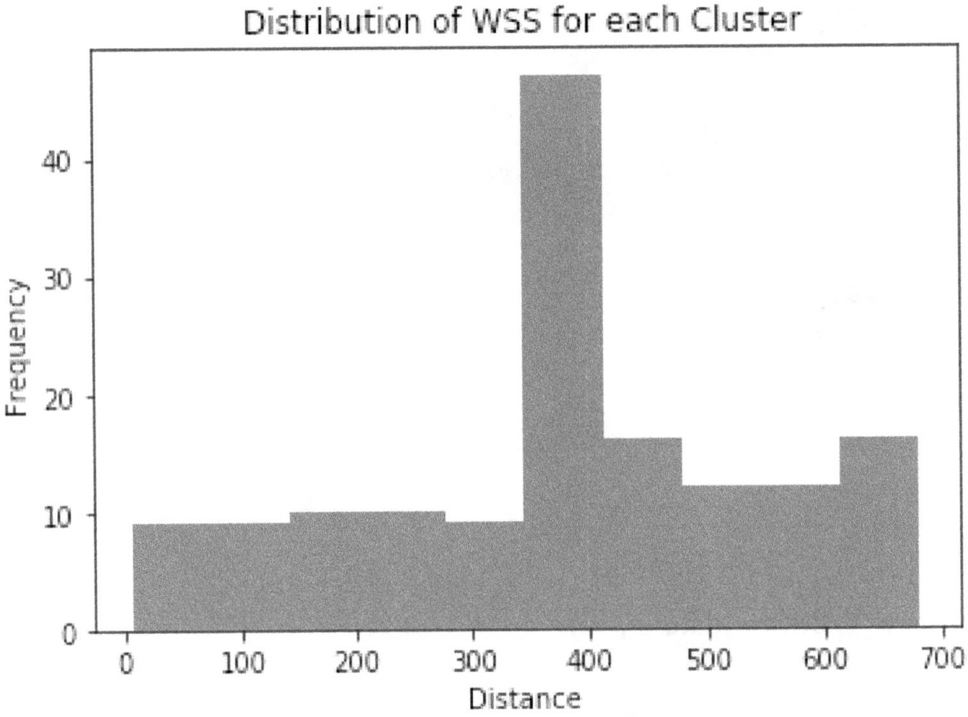
Distribution of WSS for each Cluster
Frequency
Distance
0
10
20
30
40
0
100
200
300
400
500
600
700

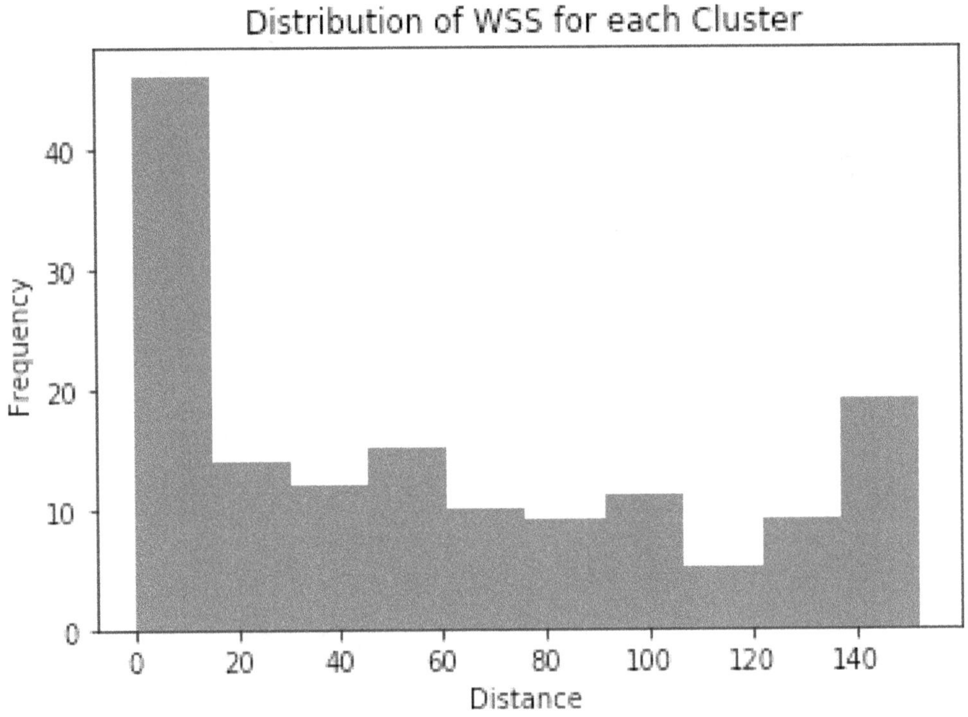
Distribution of WSS for each Cluster
Frequency
Distance
0
10
20
30
40
0
20
40
60
80
100
120
140

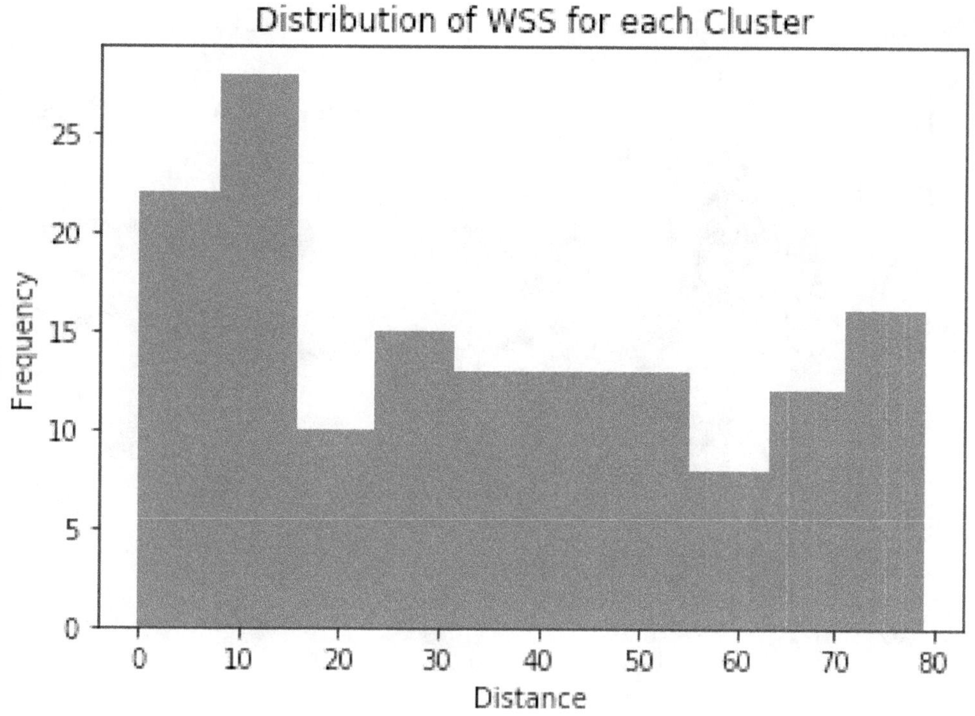
Distribution of WSS for each Cluster
Frequency
Distance
0
5
10
15
20
25
0
10
20
30
40
50
60
70
80

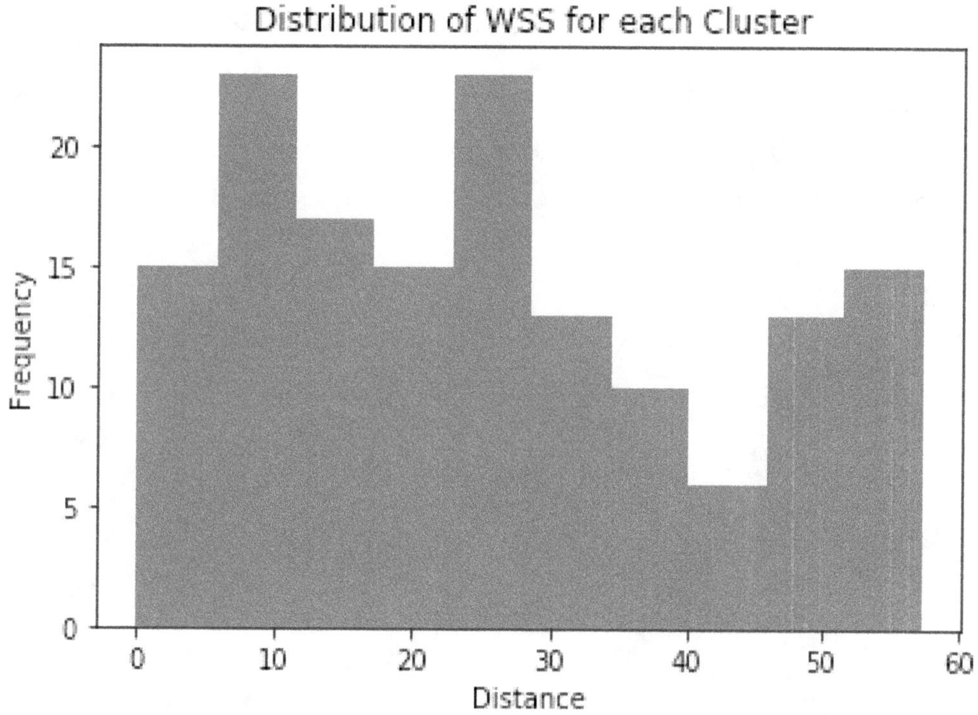
Distribution of WSS for each Cluster
Frequency
Distance
0
5
10
15
20
0
10
20
30
40
50
60

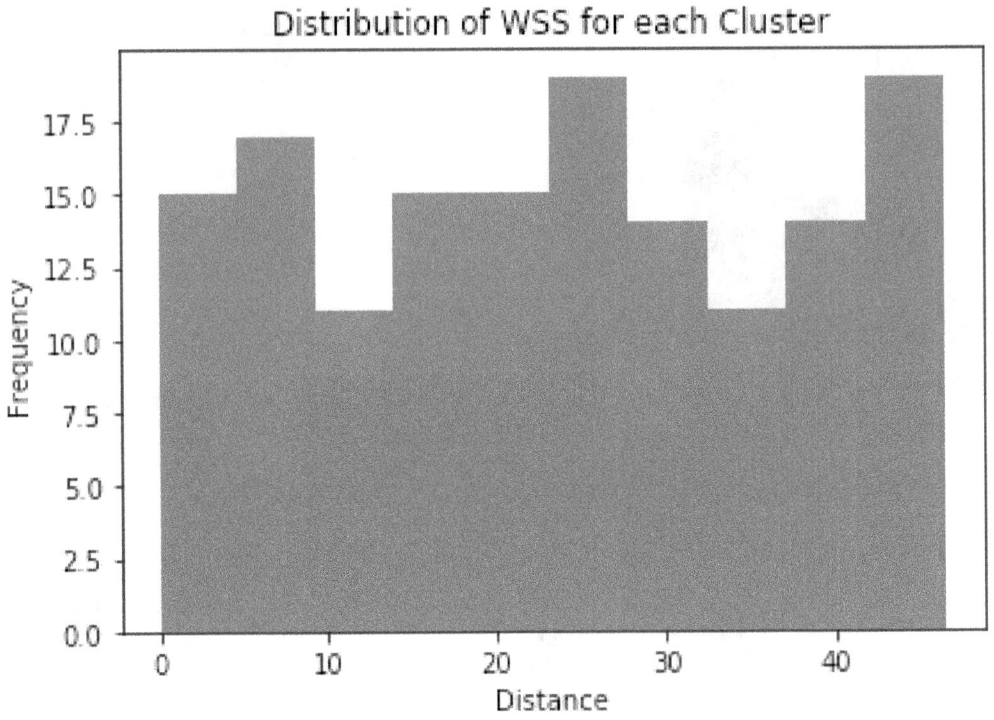
Distribution of WSS for each Cluster
Frequency
Distance
0.0
2.5
5.0
7.5
10.0
12.5
15.0
17.5
0
10
20
30
40

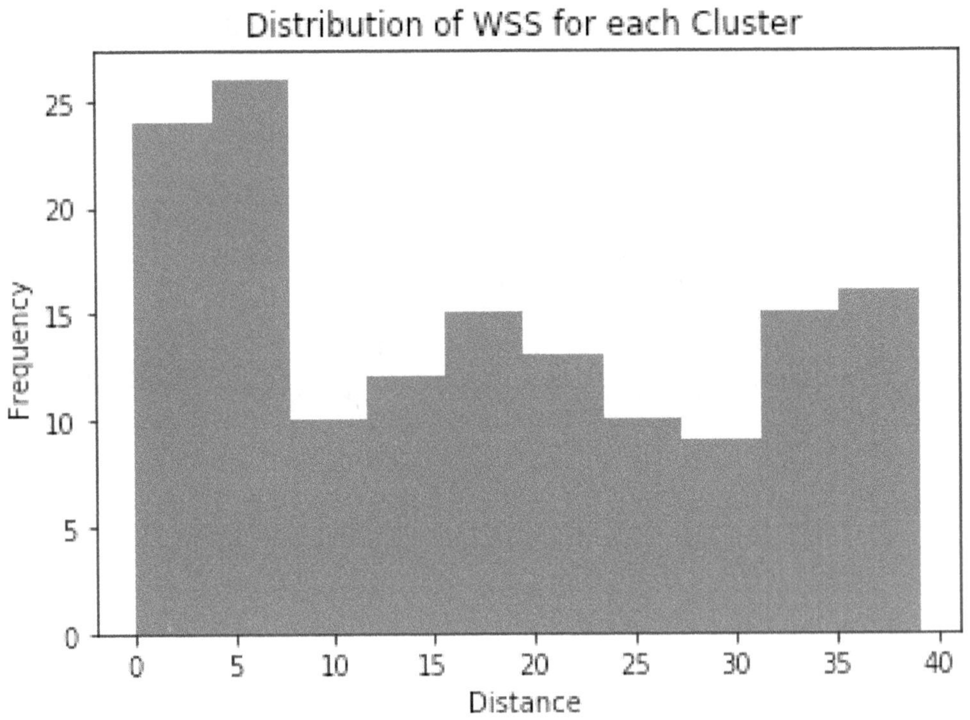
Distribution of WSS for each Cluster
Frequency
Distance
0
5
10
15
20
25
0
5
10
15
20
25
30
35
40

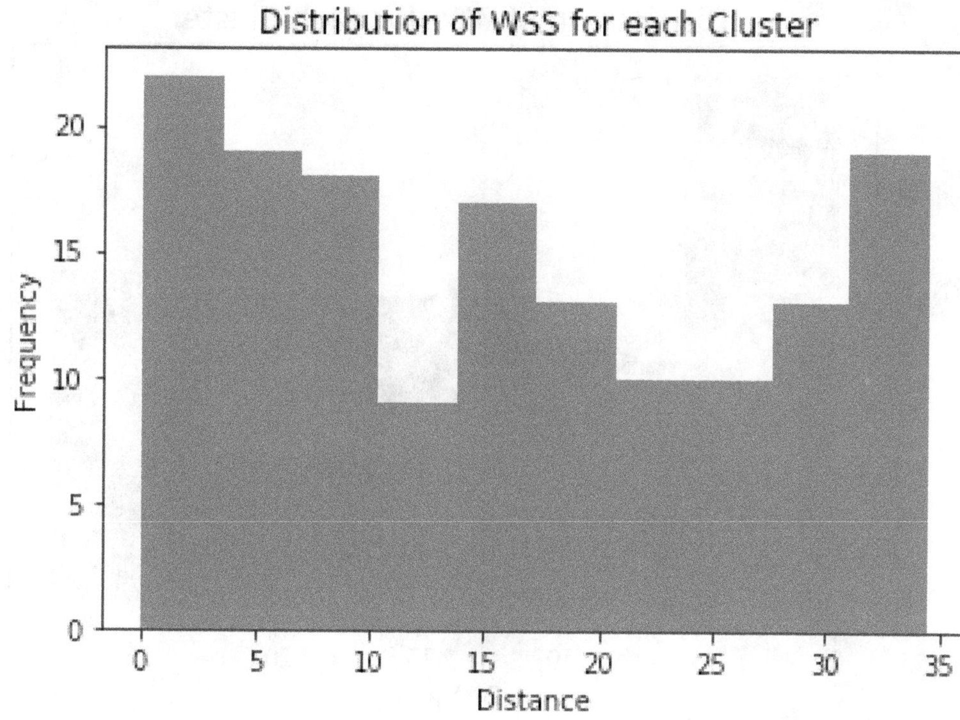
Distribution of WSS for each Cluster
Frequency
Distance
0
5
10
15
20
25
30
35

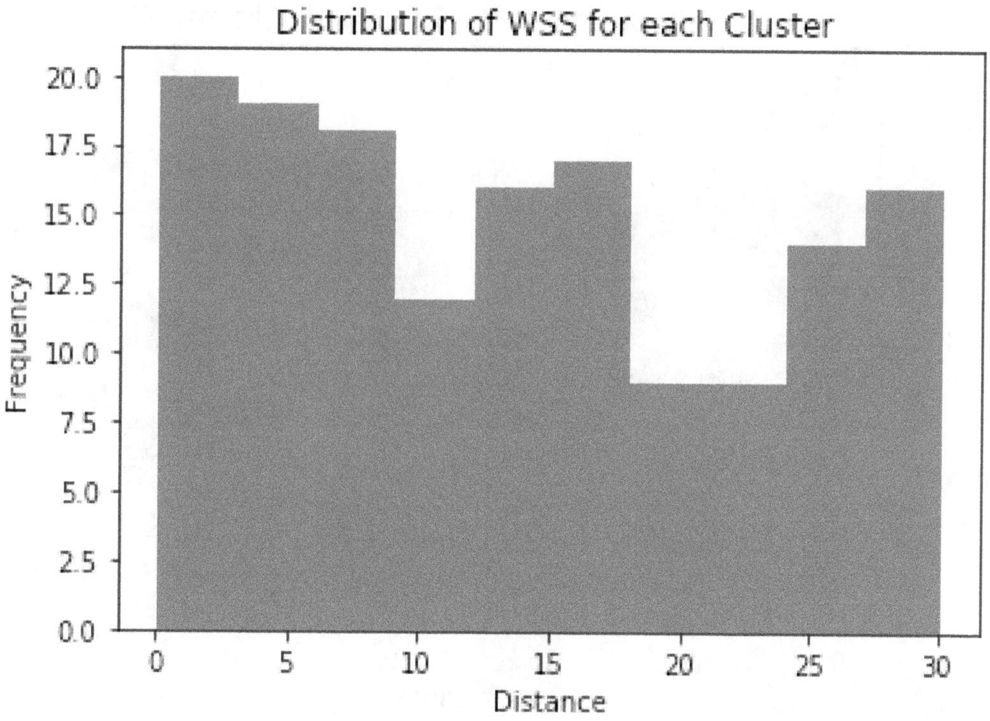
Distribution of WSS for each Cluster
Frequency
Distance
0.0
2.5
5.0
7.5
10.0
12.5
15.0
17.5
20.0
0
5
10
15
20
25
30

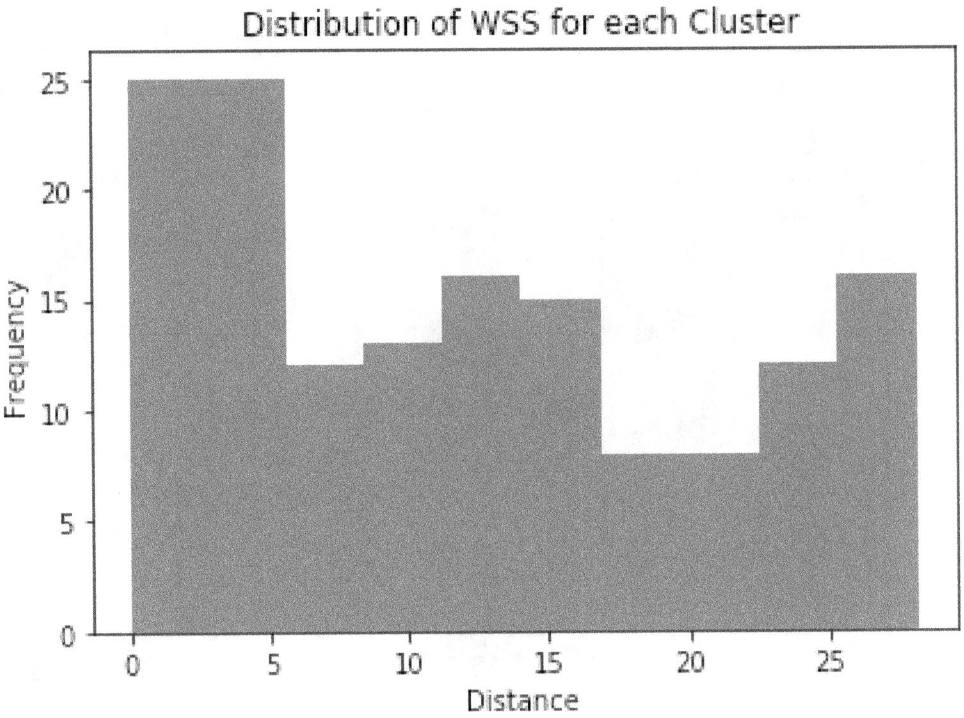
Distribution of WSS for each Cluster
Frequency
Distance
0
5
10
15
20
25
0
5
10
15
20
25

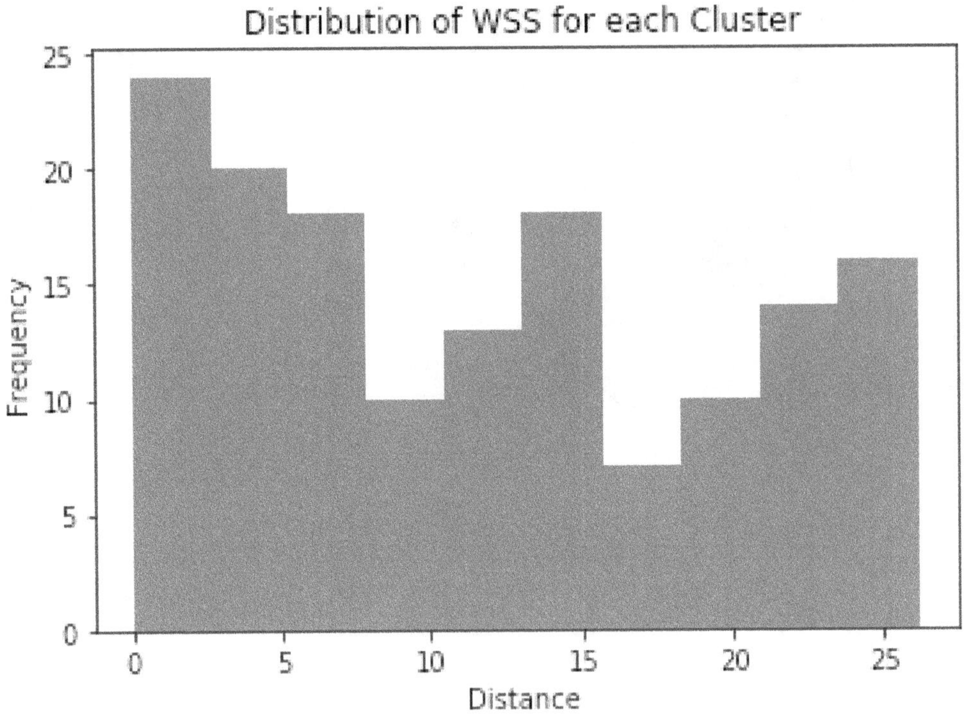
Distribution of WSS for each Cluster
Frequency
Distance
0
5
10
15
20
25
0
5
10
15
20
25

Within Sum Square
[681.3705999999995, 152.34795176035797, 78.85144142614601, 57.256009315718146, 46.44618205128204, 39.05845904095905, 34.421674242424245, 30.132440554614476, 28.1241292610898, 26.12940504670769]
WSS data type <class 'list'>
x_index is
[0, 1, 2, 3, 4, 5, 6, 7, 8, 9]

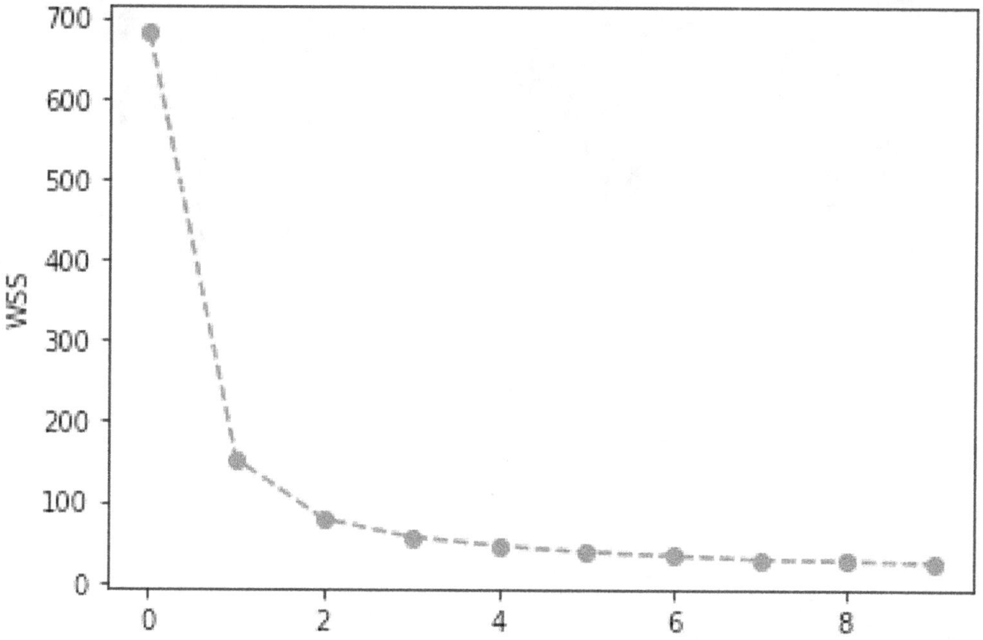

Testimonial

This is a perfect handbook for budding data scientists to get a quick dose of foundational analytics concepts. It is absolutely crucial to understand the basics and this book provides that in clear language.

– Muthusriram Rengaswamy,
Leading data analytics and
infrastructure of Verizon business Group

This book uncovers the way of working in statistical projects unorthodoxically. This is more than a book. It's a handbook or guide for all budding data scientists to have it handy during their project development. This handbook will miraculously guide you to understand the algorithmic outputs and hone your statistical knowledge.

– Sudeesh Sankaravel,
Senior Manager – Data Analytics,
Verizon India

This book is a humble attempt at paving the analytics path for budding data scientists. This is how analytics in practice looks like.

– Anandavel Kanagavel
Founder and CEO, PG Analytics

www.ingramcontent.com/pod-product-compliance
Lightning Source LLC
Chambersburg PA
CBHW060537060326
40690CB00017B/3514
9781648929243